STUDIES IN METHODOLOGY
IN TEXTUAL CRITICISM
OF THE NEW TESTAMENT

NEW TESTAMENT TOOLS AND STUDIES

EDITED BY

BRUCE M. METZGER, Ph.D., D.D., L.H.D.

Professor of New Testament Language and Literature
Princeton Theological Seminary

VOLUME IX

LEIDEN
E. J. BRILL
1969

STUDIES IN METHODOLOGY
IN TEXTUAL CRITICISM
OF THE NEW TESTAMENT

BY

ERNEST C. COLWELL
Ph.D., Litt.D., LL.D., S.T.D., L.H.D.
President Emeritus, School of Theology at Claremont

LEIDEN
E. J. BRILL
1969

CONTENTS

PREFACE

For more than thirty years I have been studying the textual criticism of the New Testament. Through those years the study of method has interested me. Occasionally a specific manuscript has invited me into an investigation that was not primarily one of method. Yet the study of method has been the dominant element in most of my writing.

From that writing I have selected the eleven essays included here. They are for the most part concerned with external evidence, with the appraisal of manuscripts as manuscripts. Two of them are concerned with problems of dating manuscripts, but the rest focus on the significance of groups of manuscripts and the means of grouping them. Two of them, Chapters IV and VII, are the result of collaboration with Ernest W. Tune, now Director of the Library of the School of Theology at Claremont.

In this republication the essays have been modified slightly for the sake of cross-reference and by the addition of some bibliographical reference to later studies. I hope that in this new form they may contribute to the advancement of our knowledge of the manuscript tradition of the Greek New Testament.

Claremont, California
May 22, 1967

ERNEST CADMAN COLWELL

CHAPTER ONE

METHOD IN GROUPING NEW TESTAMENT MANUSCRIPTS [1]

New Testament manuscripts have been grouped by scholars into "Texts," like Hort's Neutral, Western, Alexandrian, and Syrian. They have been grouped in "Families," like Family ı and Family II, and into "Text-types" and subgroups of types—as in the work of von Soden. The question of the significance of these groupings of New Testament manuscripts can be answered by taking either of two sharply opposed positions. The first regards these groupings as of paramount importance; the second sees no importance in them. Each of these positions has been taken by a number of scholars in modern study of New Testament manuscripts. A third mediating position is possible, and it is the purpose of this chapter to urge that it be adopted and to point out its implications for specific procedures in future study of New Testament manuscripts.

The first position champions one group of manuscripts, a Text or Text-type, as the original, and attempts to reconstruct it. In some degree, the champions of the Textus Receptus took this position. At least some defenders of this Alpha Text-type [2] preferred this form to rival forms because of the nature of its attestation and of the role it played in their reconstruction of the manuscript history of the New Testament.

Hort's epoch-making work explicitly championed one group of manuscripts: the Beta Text-type. His convincing arguments for

---

[1] Originally published in *New Testament Studies*, IV (1958), 73-92, under the title, "The Significance of Grouping of New Testament Manuscripts."

[2] This paper uses Kenyon's labels for the major Text-types. His terminology has two virtues: first, it claims nothing; second, it is memorable. Kenyon's Alpha equals Hort's Syrian, von Soden's Kappa, Lagrange's *A*; and it is the Text-type to which codex A, Alexandrinus, is most closely related. Kenyon's Beta equals Hort's Neutral plus Alexandrian, von Soden's Eta, Lagrange's *B*; and it is the Text-type to which codex B, Vaticanus, is most closely related. Kenyon's Delta equals part of Hort's Western, part of von Soden's Iota, and Lagrange's *D*; and it is the Text-type to which codex D, Bezae, is most closely related. Gamma equals Lake and Streeter's Caesarean, von Soden's Iota-alpha-eta-iota, and Lagrange's *C* for Caesarean; and it is the Text-type to which the codex Θ is most closely related.

genealogical method suggested a reliance upon objective use of groupings of manuscripts as the basic element in his method, and his reconstruction of the Neutral Text as the original text was hailed as a triumph for external evidence. But that he used genealogical method very little and that the basic element in his method was judgment of readings is now widely recognized.[1] Yet the influence of what he claimed to be his objective method (supported by the undoubted excellence of the text he produced) was great enough to give that method a vogue even among his hostile critics.

Several champions of the Delta Text-type were in basic agreement with Hort's statements on method but chose the Delta rather than the Beta Text-type as the best. Hort argued the virtues of an unedited Text; they pointed out the unedited nature of the Delta Text-type. Hort argued the chronological priority of Beta to Alpha; they argued the chronological priority of Delta to Beta. In the United States this position was taken by Henry A. Sanders;[2] in England and on the Continent by other distinguished scholars.[3] Hort himself admitted the facts concerning the Delta Text-type on which its champions based their claim for its superiority. In fact, his statement as to the early date and wide usage of the Delta Text-type has not been surpassed in strength. Yet he rejected that Text-type.

He rejected it because in many readings the Beta Text-type showed a better quality than the Delta Text-type. He did not claim that he could demonstrate this superiority in quality in all the readings of the Beta Text-type. Yet he claimed this superiority in general for the Beta Text-type. He based his claim on the argument that what has been shown to be superior in part may be assumed to be superior in the whole. Since, for him, the Beta Text-type rapidly narrowed down to Vaticanus and its most intimate kin, he was in effect arguing that since some of the readings of manuscript B were superior, all were superior. This basic assumption of the homogeneity of a Text-type is no longer tenable.

But it was held by von Soden. Von Soden agreed with Hort on

---

[1] See Chapter V (pp. 63-83 below).

[2] Henry A. Sanders, "The Egyptian Text of the Four Gospels and Acts," *Harvard Theological Review*, XXVI (1933), 77-98.

[3] For a recent review of the literature on this topic, see A. F. J. Klijn, *A Survey of the Researches into the Western Text of the Gospels and Acts* (Utrecht, [1949]).

method but, like the champions of the Delta Text-type, disagreed with him on its application to the reconstruction of the history. Like Hort, he began his study of Text-types with a study of the late text, the Alpha Text-type. To read his discussion of any one of the Text-types is to gain the impression that he was strongly influenced by the nineteenth century's emphasis on stemmata and genealogical method. Thus he began at the latest period and worked his way back toward earlier periods, exactly as Hort did.

In his study of the Beta Text-type (his Eta Type), he argued that one could begin either with Eta or with Kappa, but that it was better to begin with Kappa since its readings are usually more certain than those of Eta.[1] He pleaded for the prior establishment of the history of the Kappa Type so that the place of the individual Eta sources might be accurately determined.

The essential thing here is not the truth or falsity of his main conclusions resulting from the application of his methods in dealing with groupings of manuscripts, but rather the recognition of his basic agreement with Hort in the methods used in dealing with groups. As you read von Soden's discussion of Types, you are struck by the similarity in assumptions, concepts, and procedures with those used by Hort. The original of a Text-type can be reconstructed; *the* reading of a Text-type can be ascertained;[2] harmonization is the dominant corruption; the Alpha Text-type has corrupted almost all witnesses of the other Text-types; Alpha is so much more secondary than the others that the major value of its study is to eliminate it from the supporters of the other Text-types. With all of this Hort would have agreed.

A distinguished follower of Hort, Sir Frederic Kenyon, is, in fact, agreeing with von Soden's method in the following comment on his work:

> This analysis of the great mass of K MSS., the result of a vast amount of detailed labour, is a contribution to the history of the

---

[1] "Daraus ergiebt sich als methodisch richtig, zuerst den *K*-Typ zu fixieren und dann die Aufmerksamkeit den Stellen zuzuwenden, an welchen *H* sicher oder möglicherweise von *K* abweicht," H. von Soden, *Die Schriften des Neuen Testaments*, I. Teil: *Untersuchungen*, ii. Abteilung: *Die Textformen* (Berlin, 1907), p. 711.

[2] This is continually assumed in the major part of his work even though he occasionally admits that it is not universally possible; e.g., in his lists of "divided" Eta-readings he includes as a category "readings in which the reading of Eta cannot be definitely determined" (*ibid.*, pp. 1004 ff.).

New Testament text in the Middle Ages, but in view of the relative
lateness of the K text as a whole, and its entirely secondary
character, it has little bearing on the recovery of the primitive text,
which is the prime object of textual criticism.[1]

Note the complete repudiation of the Alpha Text-type in the phrase,
"its entirely secondary character."

Several studies in our generation have carried on this assumption
of the paramount importance or complete unimportance of some
Text-type. The agreement upon the unimportance of the Textus
Receptus has led to a concentration upon variants from this form
of the Alpha Text-type as the basis for all grouping of manuscripts.
This was done in some of the early studies of the Caesarean Text; [2]
and although the practice is now generally discouraged, it is still
used.[3] The inadequacy of this method was recognized and plainly
stated by Harold Murphy several years ago.[4]

Nowhere was this method followed more disastrously than in
Streeter's elaboration of Lake's work on the Caesarean Text.
Streeter shared von Soden's optimistic conviction that Text-types
can be reconstructed. He believed with Hort that genealogical

---

[1] Frederic G. Kenyon, *The Text of the Greek Bible*, 2nd ed. (London, 1949),
p. 180.

[2] Lake, Blake, and New, "The Caesarean Text of the Gospel of Mark,"
Harvard Theological Review, XXI (1928), 207-404.

[3] See, for example, M. J. Suggs, "The Eusebian Text of Matthew,"
Novum Testamentum, I (1956), 233-45. Suggs presents in Tables I and II
agreements of individual manuscripts and groups of manuscripts with
Eusebius against the Textus Receptus. Agreements with the Textus Receptus
are unsatisfactorily dealt with in the following paragraph:
"One other line of evidence must be introduced. There is a marked
tendency in Eusebius to reject the 'eccentricities' of each of the 'Great
Texts'. This became apparent in an analysis of Eusebius' agreements *with*
TR which showed him in frequent disagreement with the special readings of
Aleph, D, OL, and 'Caesarean' authorities. Lest this should be misinterpreted
as suggesting that Eusebius' text was really Byzantine, two further facts
may be mentioned. First, most of Eusebius' agreements with TR also are
found in the Nestle text. Second, in those infrequent cases where Eusebius'
agreement with TR means disagreement with Nestle, his readings are almost
without exception found in pre-Byzantine witnesses and have some claim
to be primitive."
Note that Suggs does not mention codex B in this paragraph, nor does he
give us data to support or overthrow our suspicion that Eusebius' agreements
with the TR are as significant for his relation to other sources as his disagreements. He leaves us with such questions as, "What would the agreements with TR and Nestle do to the position of Vaticanus in Table I?"

[4] "Eusebius' New Testament Text in the *Demonstratio Evangelica*,"
Journal of Biblical Literature, LXXIII (1954), 167-8.

method can be applied to groups of manuscripts. And by extending Lake's use of agreement in variants from the Textus Receptus, he made large additions to the list of "Caesarean witnesses." [1] In fact, he included most of von Soden's Iota Text-type in the Caesarean group.

The method used by Streeter can easily be reduced to an absurdity. At one time I did some work on a collation of the Terrell Gospels Manuscript [2] with the Textus Receptus. This manuscript's variants from the Textus Receptus are supported by one or more Caesarean manuscripts, but the variants are few in number, the support is varied, and the manuscript has been shown to be a leading member of von Soden's K^r group. Limitation of attention to variants from the Textus Receptus obscures the kinship of manuscripts.

At the same time that many scholars were championing the importance of some Text-type, others were vigorously repudiating it in favor of the internal evidence of readings. This trend has been summarized elsewhere, and yet some examples may be of value here. Tischendorf himself never yielded to the current reverence for groups of manuscripts. [3] In only one of Tischendorf's Rules for Establishing the Text does he mention groups of manuscripts and in that one he mentions the group only to disclaim its significance in certain circumstances. [4] He had no confidence in the accuracy of groupings, and he relied on the internal evidence of readings for the reconstruction of his text.

I have commented elsewhere on the brilliant work of Bédier, Collomp, and Lagrange, who attacked the use of stemmata, advocated the use of internal evidence and of *la critique rationnelle*. [5] But as Collomp pointed out, the enemies of external evidence, or

---

[1] B. H. Streeter, *The Four Gospels: A Study of Origins* (London, 1924). Brief summaries of major criticisms of this work are given by B. M. Metzger, *Annotated Bibliography of the Textual Criticism of the New Testament, 1914-1939* ("Studies and Documents," XVI [Copenhagen, 1955]), pp. 82 ff.

[2] Gregory's 2322, in the library of the University of Texas.

[3] "Haec vero omnia ita comparata sunt ut textus historiam ex ingenio potius quam ex documentis conficere videantur," Klijn, *A Survey of the Researches. . .*, p. 10, and n. 35.

[4] "Pro suspectis habenda sunt cum quae uni vel alteri horum testium prorsus peculiaria sunt, tum quae classium quae videntur esse certam indolem ab homine docto profectam redolent," C. Tischendorf, *Novum Testamentum Graece*, 8th ed.; vol. III, C. R. Gregory, *Prolegomena*, pars prior (Leipzig, 1884), p. 53. Cf. a similar negative appraisal, *ibid.*, p. 196.

[5] See Chapter V (pp. 63-83 below).

recensions and Text-types, often end with championing a "best manuscript," or even a "best Text-type." This was true of Lagrange himself. He summarized his position clearly: textual criticism today confirms the existence of three recensions—headed respectively by manuscripts D, B, and A—of which the type *B* has generally escaped the faults of the others. However, these recensions can only be reconstructed in general. In many details it is impossible to determine the reading of the recension. It will, therefore, always be necessary to come back to the manuscripts themselves, which are not artificial quantities but real entities. Thus we turn to the study of the great manuscripts which are in a way the starting-points for the principal recensions.[1]

The recognition of B as the starting point for the Neutral or Beta Text-type was not made with reference to the Beta Text-type *as such*. It was made with reference to the Beta Text-type *as the original text of the New Testament*. If a central or "lead" manuscript were to be selected for the Beta Text-type as a group of manuscripts, some other manuscript would probably be chosen.

The confusion (to which Klijn so cogently objected) between appraisal of readings (*a*) with reference to groupings of manuscripts, and (*b*) with reference to the establishment of the original text, has misled Lagrange. In brief, Lagrange, the champion of "rational criticism" versus the external evidence of manuscripts, comes round the circle to the championing of the "best manuscript" of one Text-type. In almost Hortian terms he pleads for following codex Vaticanus even where the evidence is not clear—on the grounds of its general excellence.

Another instance of opposition to Text-types is found in the work of H. J. Vogels. In 1923 he surveyed critically previous efforts to write the history of the New Testament in terms of Text-types. He concluded that little had been accomplished and that we need more rigorous historical reconstruction as well as new methods of procedure. His new method is "an entirely different way from the search for Types." He urges that the effort begin with the study of the versions, not with the Greek witnesses, and specifically with the Old Latin and the Old Syriac.[2]

---

[1] M.-J. Lagrange, *Critique textuelle*, II, *La Critique rationnelle* (Paris, 1935), p. 41.

[2] H. J. Vogels, *Handbuch der neutestamentlichen Textkritik* (Münster, 1923), pp. 228 f.

The reasons for this preference for the ancient versions have been stated in many of the manuals. The first reason and the one most commonly urged is that these versions reach back deep into the second century; that is, to a time that is claimed to be at least two hundred years earlier than our oldest Greek manuscripts.[1]

This argument is unsound. It can be formally presented as follows:

Latin	Greek
Origin of the Version, II A.D.	Earliest manuscripts, IV A.D.

But the origin of a version is not comparable to existing copies. The comparison to be valid should read as follows:

Latin	Greek
Origin of the Version, II A.D.	Origin, I A.D.
Earliest manuscripts, IV-V A.D.	Earliest manuscripts, IV A.D.

If early origin demands priority, the Greek tradition's roots go back deep into the first century, and the Latin with all other versions loses any claim to priority.

Kenyon said of the early translations, *"If* we can determine their text with certainty, we shall have evidence earlier by some generations than the earliest extant manuscripts in the original Greek."* [2] It is then silently assumed that we *can* determine their text *and* it is silently assumed that we cannot determine the Greek text. In the present state of our knowledge both these assumptions are invalid. Look at Jülicher's edition of the *Itala*; it is not a text but an apparatus of readings. Look again at the variations between the Sinaitic and Curetonian Syriac. And note the prudent warning of Souter, who had done extensive work on the versions, and the even more negative judgment of Klijn.[3]

---

[1] *Ibid.*, pp. 231 f., "Reichen doch jedenfalls die lateinische und die syrische Übersetzung mit ihren Wurzeln bis tief in das 2. Jahrh. hinab, also in eine Zeit, die wohl wenigstens 200 Jahre vor unseren ältesten griechischen Handschriften liegt."

[2] Kenyon, *op. cit.*, p. 111 (italics mine).

[3] Alexander Souter, *The Text and Canon of the New Testament* (London, 1913), p. 14. A. F. J. Klijn, "Welke waarde hebben de vertalingen voor de textkritiek van het Nieuwe Testament?" *Nederlandsch theologisch tijdschrift*, VII (1953-54), pp. 165-8; English translation by Harold H. Oliver, "The Value of the Versions for the Textual Criticism of the New Testament," *The Bible Translator*, VIII (1957), 127-30. See also Wikgren's discussion of the difficulties of using versional evidence and the need for careful discrimination in his chapter, "The Citation of Versional Evidence in an Apparatus Criticus,"

The argument has lost weight as the result of the finding of Greek manuscripts of extensive content from the second and third centuries. The alleged greater antiquity of the Latin fades before the actual antiquity of Greek papyri of the New Testament, which now number more than 76, with 6 of these coming from the second century, and 30 from the third.[1]

The other argument used by Vogels is that the Greek tradition is colorless while the Latin is colorful. Stripped of its metaphor, the argument claims that the greater variety in wording within the Latin tradition makes the writing of its history easier than the writing of the history of the Greek tradition. But at the end of the Latin road the translation back into the Greek exemplar remains an almost insurmountable obstacle—due to this very freedom, the colorfulness of this tradition.[2]

The major task of historical reconstruction is the replacing of the multitude of sources into their original groupings or Text-types. Then locating these types in time and place as accurately as possible builds the framework upon which the history depends.

This is as true of a version as of an individual Greek manuscript. For example, since the work of Blake on the Old Georgian, and of Lyonnet on the Armenian, these versions (in the Gospels) have been recognized as being closely akin to the Gamma Text-type. The division of the Gamma witnesses into two groups, or even into a process, and their possibly non-Caesarean origin, does not alienate these two versions. They are two witnesses to that Gamma sub-Text-type which is found in Θ, 700, 565, and their patristic supporters. To study these versions apart from the Gamma sub-Text-type Theta may illuminate the internal history of these versions, but the major task is the location of these versions in

---

New Testament Manuscript Studies: The Materials and the Making of a Critical Apparatus, ed. by Merrill M. Parvis and Allen P. Wikgren (Chicago, 1950), pp. 99-106.

[1] See Kurt Aland, *Kurzgefasste Liste der griechischen Handschriften des Neuen Testaments,* I (Berlin, 1963); Aland, "Das Johannesevangelium auf Papyrus," *Forschungen und Fortschritte,* XXXI (February, 1957), 50; Georg Maldfeld and B. M. Metzger, "Detailed List of the Greek Papyri of the New Testament," *Journal of Biblical Literature,* LXVIII (1949), 359-70; G. Maldfeld, "Der Beitrag ägyptischer Papyruszeugen für den frühen griechischen Bibeltext," in *Mitteilungen aus der Papyrussammlung der österreichischen Nationalbibliothek,* N.S., V. Folge, ed. H. Gerstinger (Vienna, 1956), pp. 79-84.

[2] See the same warning forcibly presented by Vogels, *op. cit.,* p. 232.

the history of the Greek New Testament, and that requires constant reference to the history of the Gamma Text-type.

In the cases referred to above, the preference for "readings" over Text-types is a preference for "original readings." But "non-original readings" have had their champions too—at least, in my native land. Certain scholars, interested in history, have argued convincingly that the variant readings in any particular manuscript have something to tell us about the history of the Church. The historical data contained in these variant readings may be of value for the understanding of contemporary culture or theological fashion. This type of study has no interest in groups of manuscripts; all it needs to know is the approximate date and place of the individual codex.[1]

Thus in various ways scholars have championed a Text-type or attacked a Text-type. In equally various ways scholars have repudiated all efforts at grouping manuscripts into Text-types. A third, mediating position is made possible by a more careful and controlled use of manuscript groupings. To achieve such a use, the following procedures are suggested. They are given here, not as the Law from Sinai, but as a possible working basis, to be revised and improved by scholarly criticism. Nor are they presented as a New Law, because for the most part they are a summary of the work of many scholars over the past fifty years. For the convenience of the critic, they are presented as a series of numbered imperatives.

I. Carefully distinguish different kinds of groups. The largest group is what has been called a Text, as in the phrase, "the Neutral Text." The wide range of meanings given the word "Text" even within textual criticism demands a more precise term, and the term "Text-type" is suggested.

A Text-type is the largest group of sources which can be objectively identified. This objective identification centers upon external evidence—upon a study of manuscripts. This definition is a definition of a Text-type as a group of manuscripts, not a definition of a Text-type as a list of readings. The definition must be based here (or begin here) if it is to make any contribution to our understanding of the history of the manuscript tradition. Without a

[1] Donald W. Riddle, "Textual Criticism as a Historical Discipline," *Anglican Theological Review*, XVIII (1936), 220-33; M. M. Parvis, "The Nature and Tasks of New Testament Textual Criticism: An Appraisal." *Journal of Religion*, XXXII (1952), 165-74.

beginning at this point we run the risk of slipping prematurely into subjective judgment. With this beginning we can establish a list of readings as the readings of a Text-type and be referring to some objective reality, for the statements about the readings can always contain the qualifying clause "readings found in the members of the Text-type." On the other hand, if the definition begins with readings, we are prone to identify a reading as the reading of a Text-type solely by some generalization; such as, "it is a full reading." Our definition does not deny the obvious truth that the kinship of manuscripts is established by a study of readings. It grants that and requires the sharpening of procedures in that study. But once the kinship of the witnesses to a Text-type has been established, it is the presence of a reading in some of these witnesses that justifies reference to it in terms of the Text-type, and the total content of the Text-type's witnesses can be legitimately involved in an explication of the Text-type, and must be involved in the writing of its history. The content of the Text-type is studied to illuminate the history of the group, for (as we shall say more than once) the Text-type finds its significance in the history of the manuscript tradition.

The objective identification of membership in a Text-type rests upon agreements by a group of manuscripts against other groups. Some of these agreements must be singular, unique; that is, peculiar to the group. The members of the group must share some readings that do not appear outside the group. This is one of two essential criteria for the demonstration of the existence of a group. This list need not be large, for the general habits of editors and scribes would tend to reduce it in the process of transmission. For the same reason, one cannot expect all the witnesses to a Text-type to have all the readings in the list. But the list must exist if the existence of a Text-type is to be demonstrated.

The following readings are samples of Singular Readings of the Beta Text-type in the Gospel of John. (I have drawn these readings from the Fourth Gospel since I hope to write a comprehensive study of the manuscript tradition of that Gospel).

SOME DISTINCTIVE READINGS OF THE BETA TEXT-TYPE IN JOHN

1:18 υιος] θεος: $\mathfrak{P}^{66}$ $\mathfrak{P}^{75}$ ℵ B C* L W* (?) syr[p, h, pal] cop[bo] eth[ro]

3:13 omit ο ων εν τω ουρανω: $\mathfrak{P}^{66}$ $\mathfrak{P}^{75}$ ℵ B L W 083 33 cop[bo(ms)] eth

4:21 πιστευε μοι γυναι: $\mathfrak{P}^{66}$ $\mathfrak{P}^{75}$ ℵ B C* L W cop[sa]

7:20 απεκριθη ο οχλος: $\mathfrak{P}^{66}$ $\mathfrak{P}^{75}$ ℵ B L T X W 33 cop[sa, bo]

7:46 omit ως ουτος λαλει ο ανθρωπος: 𝔓⁶⁶ corr 𝔓⁷⁵ ℵ B L T W 225 229* cop^bo
7:49 επικαταρατοι] επαρατοι: 𝔓⁶⁶ (𝔓⁷⁵ απαρατοι) ℵ B T W 1 33

The second objective criterion for the existence of a Text-type is the agreement of a group of manuscripts in a large majority of the total readings where the manuscript evidence is divided. Some hard facts underlie the current opinion that all texts are mixed texts. The insistence upon agreement in a large majority of all readings rests on these facts. A particular manuscript should be placed in that group in which the manuscript's dominant element is central. Anything less than this will lead to such absurdities as grouping the Terrell Gospels (a member of von Soden's K^r Group) with the Gamma Text-type.[1]

In many of the cases that come under this second criterion, one Text-type will be joined by a second Text-type in agreement against a third Text-type. In such cases, it is confusing to call a reading by the name of one or the other group. In a certain sense it is part of the content of each separate group, but if any label is used for such readings, it should be a compound referring to both groups. Thus, if a reading is supported by a majority of the members of the Beta Text-type and by a majority of the members of the Delta Text-type, it should be characterized as a Beta-plus-Delta reading. There are large numbers of variant readings shared thus by two Text-types.

To avoid confusion, the Text-type must be carefully distinguished from three other groups of lesser size.

The Family stands at the opposite extreme from the Text-type. It is the smallest identifiable group. It can be defined as that group of sources whose genealogy can be clearly established so that its text may be reconstructed solely with reference to the external evidence of documents. In the family there is seldom any gap in the generations, and its members come from a narrow span of time and a limited geographical region.[2] Members of a Family usually contain the same pattern of mixture. In the Text-type, on the other hand, members may contain diverse patterns of mixture.

---

[1] Cf. Lagrange's sound indictment of Sanders' grouping of Manuscript W in Luke 1:1-8:12 and John 5:12 ff. on the basis of minority agreements (*op. cit.*, p. 148).

[2] "In a 'family' the manuscripts are so closely related to each other that their common archetype can be reconstructed with a very slight margin of error," Silva Lake, *Family* Π *and the Codex Alexandrinus* ("Studies and Documents," V [London, 1937]), p. 5, n. 12.

Nearly a score of these Families have been identified. The best known in the Gospels is Lake's Family 1.[1] Several other Families (in the terms of our definition) have been identified. One of these exists within the Ferrar Group.[2] Silva Lake identified a Family on Patmos.[3] The study of the Four Gospels of Karahissar identified Families, some of which had been identified by von Soden.[4] Much of von Soden's grouping has been substantially confirmed, and some of his Kappa and Iota Text-type subdivisions may actually be Families which trail off into weaker and weaker members. The Claremont Profile Method of establishing and evaluating groups, a method developed by Paul McReynolds and Fred Wisse,[5] suggests that this is true for several of von Soden's groups. The work of Dr. Voss on K^r indicates that there is a close relationship between the leading witnesses.[6] I am not aware that a successful effort has been made to create a stemma for this group. But the facts reported by Voss suggest that it could be done.[7] The complete reconstruction

---

[1] Kirsopp Lake, *Codex 1 of the Gospels and its Allies* ("Texts and Studies," VII, No. 3 [Cambridge, 1902]).

[2] Kirsopp and Silva Lake, *Family 13 (The Ferrar Group). The Text According to Mark with a Collation of Codex 28 of the Gospels* ("Studies and Documents," XI [London, 1941]). See also Jacob Geerlings, *Family 13—The Ferrar Group: The Text According to Matthew, Luke, and John* ("Studies and Documents," XIX-XXI [Salt Lake City, 1961-62]).

[3] Silva New, "A Patmos Family of Gospel Manuscripts," *Harvard Theological Review*, XXV (1932), 85-92. This Family contains manuscripts 1169, 1173, 1204, and 1385.

[4] E. C. Colwell, *The Four Gospels of Karahissar*, I, *History and Text* (Chicago, 1936), pp. 170-222. These Families are: Family 574—containing 574, 330, 1815; Family 2327—containing 2327, 1186, 111, 2144, 1148, 1604; Family 179—containing 2327, 1186, 111, 2144, 1148, 1604; Family 179—in von Soden's *I*φ b group; and von Soden's *I*β type—containing in Mark 61, 1216, 1243, 16, 119, 120.

[5] These two graduate students presented their method to the American Textual Criticism Seminar of the Society of Biblical Literature and Exegesis in December, 1967.

[6] Of the ten K^r manuscripts available to him, every one read at least 80% of a list of 180 variants from Stephanus in Mark; and seven of the ten read over 90%. Only four of the ten manuscripts had more than fifteen variants in addition to those in the list. And Voss was able to identify ten readings in Mark peculiar to K^r; see D. O. Voss, "K Variants in Mark," in *Studies and Documents*, V (London, 1937) pp. 155-8; cf. also the same author's article, "Is von Soden's K^r a Distinct Type of Text?" *Journal of Biblical Literature*, LVII (1938), 311-18.

[7] In the eleventh chapter of Mark, seven of Voss's manuscripts (see article cited in preceding footnote) read a total of nine variations from the Textus Receptus; each of these variants has the support of a majority of the K^r witnesses; and no one of these seven manuscripts reads any other

of the K^r Text-type seems feasible, and it is either a rigidly controlled edition (a sub-Text-type of Alpha) as McReynolds and Wisse believe, or an enormous family.

Is Family Π (von Soden's K^a sub-Text-type) a Family or a subdivision of a Text-type? Silva Lake was able to establish a stemma for twenty-one members of this group.[1]

Her choice of the word *Family* in the title of her study was deliberate. She says:

> With five manuscripts attesting more than ninety-five per cent of the readings and eleven more than ninety per cent, it is obvious that this is a family of manuscripts, rather than a loosely related group, and that a practically perfect Family text can be reconstructed from the evidence of the three best witnesses. If all those just mentioned are included the theoretical margin of error in the reconstructed text is reduced almost to the vanishing point, and the collation of further weaker members of the group is useless from the point of view of the Family text, however interesting it may be to determine their relation to it.[2]

The argument for calling this a Family is strengthened by the small amount of non-Family readings in its leaders. Manuscript 1219, for example, has only nineteen variants from the reconstructed Family text, nine of them spellings. It differs from manuscript Π about twenty-five times in the entire Gospel of Mark. Compare this with the amount of difference found within a late Byzantine Family—Family 2327. Manuscripts 574 and 2327 disagree with each other only thirty-four times in Mark 9: 4b-16: 20, and only twenty-six times in Luke 8: 16-16: 23. Contrast these with the differences between Vaticanus and Sinaiticus. They differ from each other

---

variant in this chapter. Six other K^r manuscripts read only one non-K^r variant.

[1] Silva Lake, *Family* Π *and the Codex Alexandrinus* ("Studies and Documents," V [London, 1936]), 29. It is true that in that stemma no one of the twenty-one is the father of another one; it is true also that there is enough variation between fidelity to the family text and position in the family tree to require a large number of corrupting intermediaries—for example, the manuscript closest to the archetype in the stemma (manuscript 114) is ninth in fidelity to the family text, while the least faithful in content (manuscript 116) has eight manuscripts below it in the tree. Mrs. Lake calls attention to this fact with reference to manuscripts 178 and 116 (*op. cit.*, p. 28). Jacob Geerlings, *Family* Π *in John* ("Studies and Documents," XVIII [Salt Lake City, 1959]); *Family* Π *in Luke* ("Studies and Documents, "XXII [Salt Lake City, 1962]). Here, as in Family 13, Geerlings is in general agreement with Silva Lake.

[2] Silva Lake, *op. cit.*, p. 15.

about 550 times in the Gospel of Mark. If Vaticanus and Sinaiticus are related to each other as members of a Text-type, 1219 and Π, and 574 and 2327, must be given a different and closer kind of relationship.

It is unfortunate that the word "family" was applied to the so-called Caesarean Text. Family Theta was never a family in the sense in which we are using the term. A real family, Family 1, is a part of a part of the Caesarean Group, but that group is something much more complex and loosely related than a family. Nor should the term "family" be applied to the Ferrar Group, often called Family 13. The Lakes' studies show (what von Soden earlier indicated) that this group contains families but itself belongs to the next larger order or group—a Tribe within a Text-type. The Ferrar Group as a whole is now seen to belong with a pre-Caesarean Group, a sub-Text-type, including $\mathfrak{P}^{45}$, W, Family 1, and 28.[1]

In the Lakes' publication of the Ferrar Group in Mark,[2] this variation in the nature of groups was clearly recognized. They identified their Group *a* as a Family of five manuscripts (13, 346, 543, 826, and 828), whose family tree they reconstructed, and whose family text is almost identical with that of manuscript 826. Their Group *c* was quite distinct, although unfortunately controllable in only one manuscript—983. Their Group *b* consisted of three manuscripts (69, 124, 788) more loosely related to each other than the members of Group *a* are. Moreover, the reconstruction of the text of Group *b* is in many cases problematic. When they come to the text of *x*, the archetype of the Ferrar Group as a whole, they are frankly unsure of the text in many passages, but rely on the publication of a full apparatus of variants read in the manuscripts of *a*, *b*, and *c* as a corrective to the inevitable error in the reconstruction of *x*.

The Lakes pointed out that the distinction between a Family and a Text-type is real, but—in their words—is "progressive." The Family (e.g., Family Π or Family *a* of the Ferrar Group) and the Text-types (e.g., the Beta or Gamma Text-type) are the extremes of a continuum. Intermediate stopping points occur, such as

---

[1] This grouping, argued by T. Ayuso in an article in *Biblica*, XVI (1935), 369-415, was accepted by the Lakes (*Studies and Documents*, V [1937], p. 4, n. 5; and *Revue Biblique*, XLVIII [1939], 497-505), and this revision of Caesarean grouping is reviewed by B. M. Metzger in *Journal of Biblical Literature*, LXIV (1945), 457-89; LXVI (1947), 406-7.

[2] Kirsopp and Silva Lake, *op. cit.*, pp. ix-x.

Group *b* of the Ferrars, or *x*—the Ferrar archetype. Neither of these is a Family.

This clearly indicates the need for labels for four groups of manuscripts that are quantitatively distinct. (1) Group *a* of the Ferrar Group is a Family. (2) The Ferrar Group as a whole is larger and more loosely related. (3) Beyond its confines, it is closely related to that large sub-division of the "Caesarean Text" which centers on $\mathfrak{P}^{45}$. (4) As part of that sub-division it is related to the total Caesarean group. In the following table, if Group (1) is called a Family, (2) can be called a Tribe, (3) a sub-Text-type, and (4) a Text-type:

(1)   13 346 543 826 828
(2)   13 346 543 826 828 + 69 124 788 983
(3)   13 346 543 826 828 + 69 124 788 983 + $\mathfrak{P}^{45}$ W Fam1 28 Or
(4)   13 346 543 826 828 + 69 124 788 983 + $\mathfrak{P}^{45}$ W Fam1 28 Or + Θ 565 700 arm

II. The second suggestion is, "Abandon the effort to restore *the* text of a Text-type." In 1933 Burkitt wrote, "It is easier, from some points of view, to reconstruct the original than some half-way house like the 'neutral' or the 'Caesarean' text, that contains some corruptions but not all." [1] Other scholars have come to this position; for example, Silva Lake. "The known representatives of a 'text,' on the other hand (as contrasted with a 'family'), show such similarities that they may once have had a common archetype, but each of them has been so considerably modified by successive copying, or even revision, that this archetype can be only approximately reconstructed, with due allowance for alternative possibilities in almost every reading." [2]

III. Closely related to the second suggestion is the third: "Recognize fully the existence of process within a Text-type." The paradox is that all Text-types are later than previously thought, but the process started earlier than was previously thought.

The "Texts" which have been the subject of discussion for the past generation are not single, not homogeneous, not the work of one hand. They are now seen to be a process, gradual in achieving a high degree of distinctiveness and uniformity. This was claimed

---

[1] F. C. Burkitt, "The Chester Beatty Papyri," *Journal of Theological Studies*, XXXIV (1933), 367.

[2] Silva Lake, *Family* II. . ., p. 5, n. 12.

by Baikie for the Caesarean Text in 1936 and by Pasquali in his *Storia della tradizione e critica del testo* (Firenze, 1934).[1] Theretore, no single year or editor will suffice to explain them. Therefore, the earliest witness will not be closest to the center of the Text-type, but will be a forerunner, a proto-member of the group. The member of the group that will be closest to the center will come at a second or third stage, for the Text-type grows out of a continuing editorial process.

This seems to be true also of study of the manuscripts of the Septuagint. Würthwein quotes Kahle as follows: "The manuscripts handed down in the church lead us at best to a standard text used in the church, which had, however, only gradually established itself and does not mark the beginning of the development." [2]

The recent studies of early papyri have identified some of them as forerunners of texts whose leading members are later manuscripts. Thus Ayuso located $\mathfrak{P}^{45}$ with Origen and some others as pre- or proto-Caesarean; while the full flower of the Caesarean Text-type appears in later witnesses: in Θ, 565, 700, Old Georgian, and Armenian. Zuntz in his study of the Pauline Epistles gives a similar location to $\mathfrak{P}^{46}$ with reference to the Beta Text-type. He describes the group $\mathfrak{P}^{46}$, B, 1739, sah, boh, Clem, Orig, as proto-Alexandrian.[3] The evidence overwhelmingly supports his emphasis upon process and upon continuous editing: ". . .the distinction between an older and more recent section of the 'Alexandrian' family" is, as he says, "a fact";—a fact also in the manuscript tradition of the Gospels; and there, also, "the demarcation of the two groups is not rigid." [4] A careful appraisal of $\mathfrak{P}^{66}$ requires more extended study than can be given in this chapter, but tentative samplings indicate that it, too, will merit a "proto-" label.

[1] James E. McA. Baikie, "The Caesarean Text *inter pares*." This Cambridge thesis is summarized by Metzger in *Journal of Biblical Literature*, LXIV (1945), 475-6. Pasquali's "conclusions" include as number 10 a clear recognition of process, which is freely summarized as follows: "The Greek papyri, the quotations of the Latin tradition, show that in antiquity for popular authors every copy represents, in some way, a particular edition that is a mixture, graduated variously from preexisting variations, genuine or spurious. The process of contamination, of equalization, had begun in antiquity among the different traditions which culminate in the form of the 'Vulgate.' Such conditions explain how papyri that restore, in one point, a genuine reading, contain also particular corruptions."

[2] Ernst Würthwein, *The Text of the Old Testament* (Oxford, 1957), p. 45.

[3] G. Zuntz, *The Text of the Epistles* (London, 1953), p. 156.

[4] *Ibid.*, pp. 63-5.

Zuntz was able to quote the approval of K. Lake for a date for the "Ecclesiastical Text" later than the accepted one.[1] Actually, the recognition of process in Text-types, while not explicitly stated, was implicit in much earlier work. Hort himself posited at least two stages in the development of the Syrian Text-type.[2] And von Soden's sound identification of Kappa sub-types was, of course, a recognition of continuing editorial work within the Byzantine framework. Many earlier judgments of the so-called Western Text-type are recognitions of process, of its involvement in the life of the churches. Hort himself can be quoted on "progressive change" in the Western Text:

> To what extent the earliest MSS of the distinctively Western ancestry already contained distinctive Western readings, cannot now be known. However they may have differed from the apostolic autographs, there was at all events no little subsequent and homogeneously progressive change. It is not uncommon to find one, two, or three of the most independent and most authentically Western documents in agreement with the best representatives of Non-Western Pre-Syrian texts against the bulk of Western authorities under circumstances which render it highly difficult to account for the concurrence by mixture: and in such cases these detached documents must attest a state of the Western text when some of its characteristic corruptions had not yet arisen, and others had.[3]

Nestle's abandonment of a single symbol for the "Western Text" recognizes the underlying fact. This rejection is justified in the twenty-second edition as follows:

> Von Soden's sign for his third main group, J = Jerusalem type of text, has, as a unity, not been used, because this group really contains too many diverse elements; also I was not inclined to use a common sign for the so-called "Western" text, because its representatives differ too much among themselves, and are, therefore, better mentioned individually, as D, it, sy[sc].[4]

Vaganay's reluctance to give it a label comparable to the other two types is due to the fact that he saw the variation within the Western area with greater clarity than he saw it in the Alpha and Beta Text-types.[5]

---

[1] *Ibid.*, p. 151, n. 1.

[2] B. F. Westcott and F. J. A. Hort, *The New Testament in the Original Greek: Introduction*, 2nd ed. (London, 1896), p. 145.

[3] *Ibid.*, p. 122.

[4] Nestle, *Novum Testamentum Graece*, 22nd ed. (Stuttgart, [1956]), pp. 68 f.

[5] "Apart from the three great recensions there are *a large number of early and dissimilar variants* that, having been first noticed in the Old Latin texts,

I believe that we should accept explicitly what is implicit in the general conclusions reached by Zuntz; i.e., that the Beta Text-type *par excellence* is the type found in the later rather than the earlier witnesses; that the Alpha Text-type is found in von Soden's K^x or K^r rather than in K^a (Family Π) or K^1 or Alexandrinus or Chrysostom. The work of Silva Lake on Family Π sets Alexandrinus off from that Family (and from any other Alpha Text-type group) in a fashion somewhat analogous to the relation of the early papyri to other Text-types.[1]

Support for the assumption that Chrysostom's text is proto-Syrian rather than Syrian is found in the study of Chrysostom's text of Mark by Jacob Geerlings and Silva Lake [2] which claims that no extant manuscript closely resembles the text of Chrysostom. Zuntz says that occasional tests of the text of Chrysostom in the homilies on Matthew have led him to the same conclusion.[3]

The identification of antiquity with purity must be abandoned in this area of textual criticism as well as elsewhere.

If a Text-type is progressive in nature, then we should aim at establishing a list of the readings of the Text-type rather than a Text. This list will frequently contain variations within the Text-type for the same passage. Some years ago Dr. Merrill Parvis and I spent considerable time in an attempt to reconstruct the Beta Text-type of the Gospel of Mark. Our conclusion was that we should aim at the establishment of a list of Beta readings rather than of a text.

After a careful study of all alleged Beta Text-type witnesses in the first chapter of Mark, six Greek manuscripts emerged as primary witnesses: ℵ B L 33 892 2427. Therefore, the weaker Beta manuscripts C Δ 157 517 579 1241 and 1342 were set aside. Then on the basis of the six primary witnesses an "average" or mean text was reconstructed, including all the readings supported by the majority of the primary witnesses. Even on this restricted basis

---

are grouped together under the name of Western" (Leo Vaganay, *Introduction to the Textual Criticism of the New Testament* [London, 1937], p. 116); the italics are mine.

[1] *Op. cit.*, p. 69, "By far the most probable hypothesis, therefore, is that both A and Π were stages in the early development of the Ecclesiastical text, more similar to it than ℵ, B, D or Θ and less similar than E F G H or Ω." See also *ibid.*, pp. ix and 68.

[2] *Harvard Theological Review*, XXIV (1931), 142.

[3] *Journal of Theological Studies*, XLIII (1942), 184, n. 4.

the amount of variation recorded in the apparatus was dismaying. In this first chapter, each of the six witnesses differed from the "average" Beta Text-type as follows: L, nineteen times (Westcott and Hort, twenty-one times); ℵ, twenty-six times; 2427, thirty-two times; 33, thirty-three times; B, thirty-four times; and 892, forty-one times. These results show convincingly that any attempt to reconstruct an archetype of the Beta Text-type on a quantitative basis is doomed to failure. The text thus reconstructed is not reconstructed but constructed; it is an artificial entity that never existed. Time and space will be saved if the readings of the Beta Text-type are presented in significant lists or in an apparatus.

An instance of the variation within a Text-type is found in von Soden's citation of his Eta Text-type (our Beta) in the first chapter of John. He prints the bold-faced type H as equal to the Eta Text-type twenty-one times in this chapter. But eight out of the twenty-one times (37 per cent of the instances), the Eta Text-type is the reading of a minority of the Eta witnesses.[1] This large minority of disagreements does not invalidate his claim that in the majority of passages the large number of Eta witnesses agree. But he notes that the composition of the majority group changes in kaleidoscopic fashion.[2]

These facts forced von Soden to elaborate six criteria for the selection of an Eta reading where the Eta witnesses differed.[3] These criteria indicate clearly his basic concept of Text-type. Some of von Soden's assumptions clearly are (1) that a Text-type can be reconstructed by determining in specific passages *the* reading of the Text-type; (2) that the Eta Text-type was made at a definite time in a definite single form; (3) that it was corrupted by two forces: conformity to a parallel reading and the Kappa Text-type; (4) that older manuscripts are purer than later manuscripts; (5) that probability increases enormously when the number of witnesses increases from two to three or more. Assumptions (1), (2) and (4) are certainly false; while (3) and (5) are so over-emphasized by von

---

[1] The total number of H manuscripts listed by von Soden is eleven. He prints H with the exception of 3 members 2 times; with the exception of 4 members 7 times; with the exception of 5 members 1 time; with the exception of 6 members 3 times; with the exception of 7 members 1 time.

When he cites H positively, he does it with 5 members 1 time; with 6 members 1 time; with 7 members 1 time; with 8 members 2 times.

[2] Von Soden, *op. cit.*, I. Teil: ii. Abteilung: A. *Die Evangelien*, p. 1000.

[3] *Ibid.*, pp. 1001-2.

Soden as to distort the validity they contain. The recognition of process within a Text-type in all its implications requires the rewriting of such assumptions.

IV. The fourth suggestion is, "Study simultaneously both variants and Text-types." It is often asserted that the study of Text-types (i.e., of groupings of manuscripts) should precede the study of individual readings. "We must reconstruct the history of the text before we turn our attention to the individual reading." Hort with a practicality that disregarded logic went "'round and 'round" the circle from readings to groups of manuscripts. If the next generation is to advance our knowledge in this field then it must work at both tasks: the appraisal of readings and the grouping of manuscripts in the history of the church.

V. The fifth suggestion is implied in the fourth: "Explore carefully the nature of the tension between value judgment (clearly appropriate for readings) and identification of a manuscript as part of a group." This distinction has been strongly and ably argued by Klijn.[1]

In what concerns Text-types, we deal with externals capable of quantitative statement. A manuscript, we can show, agrees with a fairly stable group of other manuscripts a certain number of times when there is no (or very little) support from outside the group; and in a large majority of all cases where variation occurs, it agrees often in a pattern of mixture that can be quantitatively defined. None of this is concerned with quality. So long as we avoid the temptation to reconstruct the Text-type, we have no use here for "good" or "bad," "original" or "corrupt."

But once the grouping has thus been established externally, the question of its quality is relevant in two ways—both of them rest upon an analysis of the quality of its readings. Here quantity means nothing, as no one has said better than two classical scholars.[2]

(1) A knowledge of the quality of an individual reading contributes to our confidence in grouping manuscripts. It is here that the old rule, "agreement in error shows a common ancestry," has its application to the study of Text-types. The relevance of this rule for the study of Family relationships has never been challenged. But in Text-types, we are dealing not with ordinary trees but with

---

[1] Klijn, *op. cit.*, pp. 167-71.
[2] Most recently Zuntz has equalled the force and irony of Housman in indictment of those who would stop with quantities (*op. cit.*, pp. 59-60).

a thicket or jungle composed of banyans and mangroves, trees growing upside down, dropping roots from branches. In this jungle Hort silently eliminated the criterion of agreement in error by urging the significance of agreement in readings—whether or not the readings were errors. Klijn is in agreement with this rule of Hort when he urges an exclusive attention to quantity. But this throws away a valuable tool that need not be discarded. A variation from the original reading is an error, and its presence in a group of manuscripts is more significant for their relationship than their agreement in a reading judged to be original.[1] All our manuscripts are descended somehow or other from the original. Where the original reading can be determined (and I agree with Zuntz that pessimism here is unwarranted), agreement in variation from that original is important evidence for membership in a Text-type.

The one exception to this is the agreement of one group, one small group, in a reading judged to be original against the vast mass of manuscripts. For example, von Soden claims that Vaticanus probably has the original reading in Mark in three passages[2] in which it is not supported by the rest of its Text-type although it is, once, supported by codex Bezae. Since ms. 2427 reads all three of these, the argument for its kinship to codex Vaticanus is exceedingly strong.

(2) A knowledge of the quality of the readings of a Text-type cannot but help us in the ultimate reconstruction of the history of the text. The probability of our decision as to the location of a Text-type within a particular section of the life of the church at a particular period will be increased by our knowledge of the quality of the Text-type.

VI. The sixth suggestion is, "Study Text-types in the New Testament book by book or section by section." Our canonical New Testament does not enjoy a single manuscript history. The manuscript history of the gospels is distinct from that of other parts of the canon—Pauline Epistles, Acts, and Apocalypse. Whether subdivision of the Pauline corpus is necessary or not for this kind of study I do not know; but the gospels must be studied one by one. Enough single-gospel papyri are available now to demonstrate that

---

[1] This has been cogently argued and effectively used by Zuntz in locating $\mathfrak{P}^{46}$ in the manuscript tradition (*op. cit.*, pp. 64-66, 95-96).

[2] Mark 1:32; 1:40 (von Soden erroneously 1:46); and 12:36 (von Soden, *op. cit.*, p. 910).

the gospels existed as single books for some time. The nature of the
mixture of Text-types in the Freer Gospels (W) demonstrates the
existence of separate strands for separate books and parts of books
into the early Byzantine period. Its text is a mixed text, not only
in the sense that one Text-type has been blended with another,
but also because Text-types are different in one gospel from what
they are in another, or even in various parts of a single gospel.[1]

The recurrence of this block-type of mixture in the thirteenth
century is evident in the Four Gospels of Karahissar.[2] In this
manuscript (Gregory's 574), types of text change eight times.
Matthew is a single block of text; Mark and Luke each have three
blocks; John has two blocks of text.[3]

Many other manuscripts have the same kind of mixture. It
occurs in ms. 700; in five Beta Text-type mss.—Ψ, L, Δ, 579,
1241; in 2400, 61, 485 and 59; and in ms. 1204.[4] Those are certainly

---

[1] Thus the text of W in Matthew is usually classified as Alpha Text-type;
in John 1:1-5:11, Sanders says it is unclassifiable—Kenyon says it is
Alpha—Lagrange suggests it is Delta (equals Latin); in John 5:12 to end,
it is Beta Text-type; in Luke 1:1-8:12 it is Beta; in Luke 8:13 to end it is
Alpha; in Mark 1:1-5:30 it is Delta (equals Latin); in Mark 5:31 to end it
belongs to the $\mathfrak{P}^{45}$ sub-Text-type of the Caesarean Text-type.

[2] See my article, "The Complex Character of the Late Byzantine Text of
the Gospels," *Journal of Biblical Literature*, LIV (1935), 211-21; and *The
Four Gospels of Karahissar*, I, *History and Text* (Chicago, 1936).

[3] Matthew: (1) One type throughout gospel, a mixture of a Chrysostom
text, plus Family 2327, plus 330-1815 of von Soden's I$^{\beta b}$. (This type occurs
in ms. 2400 in Matt. 2:1-8:25).

Mark: (2) 1:1-6:15 Family 574 (574, 330, 1815), a mixture of Family 2327,
and von Soden's I$^{\beta}$.

(3) 6:16-9:4a ms. 574 is a mixture of von Soden's I$^{\varphi b}$ (as in ms. 179), by
correction to von Soden's K^1 (as in ms. V).

(4) 9:4b-16:20 Family 574 is an indirect ancestor of Family 2327, an
identifiable group within von Soden's K^x.

Luke: (5) 1:1-8:15 ms. 574 predominantly K with some early non-
neutral survival.

(6) 8:16-16:23 ms. 574 is again part of Family 2327.

(7) 16:24 ff. ms. 574 equals type (5) above.

John: (8) 1:1-18:26 ms. 574 equals type (5) above but with more correction
to a Stephanus type of text.

(9) 18:27-21:25 ms. 574 is a mixture of a "Caesarean" type as in ms. 544,
by correction to a K^a type as in mss. 2400 and 482.

[4] Ms. 700 Matt. 1:1—Luke 10 is Gamma Text-type; Luke 11—John 21 is
Alpha. Ms. Ψ Mark is B; Luke-John is A. Ms. L Matt. 1-17 is A, the rest B.
Ms. Δ Mark 3-12 is B, the rest is A. Ms. 579 Matt. is A, the rest B. Ms. 1241
Matt.—Mark is A, the rest B. Ms. 2400 Matt. 2:1-8:25 is Family 2327 (or
Family 2327 + 330); in Rom. 10:19 ff. joins ms. 330. Ms. 61 Matt. 9:15—
Mark 16 is I$^{\beta}$. Ms. 485 Mark 1:1-8:14 is Family 2327; Mark 8:14-Luke 24

only a fraction of the total instances. But they indicate the importance of studying group relationships book by book or section by section, and they show clearly the dangers involved in spot samplings or in uncharacterized totals of agreement and disagreement.

VII. The seventh suggestion is, "In the study of Text-types, priority should be given to the gospels that are frequently quoted." Thus Matthew, Luke, and John should be preferred to Mark. The last generation's preference for Mark rested on the importance given to variations from the Textus Receptus. This importance has been diminished both by discovery and by study. Since groupings of manuscripts are important for the reconstruction of the history of the text, we should concentrate our attention upon those books or parts of books that are frequently quoted. Patristic evidence (for all its limitations) gives us our clearest indications of place and of time; and indications of place and time are essential to the writing of history. In this respect Mark is the least valuable of the gospels.

Matthew might win the palm over Luke and John were it not for one fact. Correctors did their most intensive work at the beginning of a manuscript. Vogels warns us of this habit, and gives us interesting examples of the gradual diminution in the corrector's work from the first folio of a codex to the last. His instances, drawn from the Latin versions of the New Testament, are numerous and strikingly significant in the variation concerning the amount of correction.[1] Note also in the block-mixture of Beta Text-type manuscripts listed above the number of instances in which the correction to the Alpha Text-type began in Matthew but did not continue throughout the gospels. In ms. L only the first seventeen chapters of Matthew were affected; in ms. 579 only the Gospel of Matthew; in ms. 1241 only Matthew and Mark. On general grounds, one would expect this to be much more true in cases of mixture by blending. Therefore, it is probable that we shall gain more from our study of groupings of manuscripts in the gospels if we turn to the study of Luke and John.

VIII. The eighth suggestion is, "Begin at the beginning."

---

joins mss. 251 ff. Ms. 59 Luke 11:32 ff. is Family 2327. For ms. 1204, see Silva New, *Harvard Theological Review*, XXV (1932), pp. 90-91.

[1] They involve the Latin mss. *l, c, e, g, a, b, ff², ff¹, g¹*. He seriously urges beginning the study of a mixed text at the end of a book or the codex.

The nineteenth century's battle with the Textus Receptus fastened attention upon that text, and the study of variation from it was a natural development. The wide acceptance of the theory of genealogical method after A.D. 1880 supported this trend; as good genealogists always do, textual critics started with the lowest, the most recent generations, and worked back. But current theory and currently available sources from the early centuries demand a reversal. We should start with the earliest sources and work our way down to the late medieval copies, refashioning our concepts as we go. There is something upside down in our applying the term "mixed text" to $\mathfrak{P}^{66}$, as Aland, for example, does.[1] If the history were written from the beginning instead of from the end, more appropriate terms would suggest themselves to us. As a result we would work with more clarity in the reconstruction of the history of the text.

IX. The ninth suggestion is, "Recognize different values in the different kinds of groupings." Fundamentally all groups are valuable as they contribute to our understanding of the history of the text. But a group that is a Family has a usefulness unknown to the Text-type. Once the archetype of a Family has been reconstructed, additional members can be ignored. In the case of Family Π, for example, it is inconceivable that the discovery of new members would contribute new readings to the Family Text. Thus the knowledge of this group makes it possible to save time and effort by ignoring all further members of the group as soon as their membership has been established.

The same thing cannot be said of the Text-type. Here the evidence from one additional member may be invaluable, and must be recorded and preserved. As to Tribes and sub-Text-types the case is obscure. I would argue that sub-Text-types should be treated as analogous to Text-types, and that Tribes are in this matter closer to Text-types than to Families. Thus it would be safe in a critical apparatus to quote a bona fide Family by a single symbol, but not a Tribe nor a Text-type. A further implication of this appraisal is that graduate students' theses and monographs of the future should not be devoted to exhaustive studies of new members of known Families, but rather to the placing of witnesses within the larger groupings of Tribe, and Text-type.

---

[1] K. Aland, op. cit., pp. 52-3. He applies this label to all early texts: "Der Mischtext charakterisiert die Frühzeit."

The Beta Text-type in Mark 1: 1-6

This is an average or "mean" text which is determined by the agreement of the readings of the majority of the primary witnesses (א B L 33 892 2427) to the Beta Text-type. It is in no way an attempt to reconstruct an archetype or original text. The readings of Westcott and Hort are cited in the apparatus.

The following statistics show the number of times the primary witnesses and WH^txt differ from the "mean" Beta text in significant readings in the first chapter of Mark: L, nineteen times; WH, twenty-one times; א, twenty-six times; 2427, thirty-two times; 33, thirty-three times; B, thirty-four times; 892, forty-one times.

Mark 1

1. Αρχη του ευαγγελιου Ιησου Χριστου υιου Θεου. 2. Καθως γε-γραπται εν τω Ησαια τω προφητη Ιδου εγω αποστελλω τον αγγελον μου προ προσωπου σου ος κατασκευασει την οδον σου· 3. φωνη βοωντος εν τη ερημω Ετοιμασατε την οδον Κυριου ευθειας ποιειτε τας τριβους αυτου· 4. εγενετο Ιωαννης ο βαπτιζων εν τη ερημω κηρυσσων βαπτισμα μετανοιας εις αφεσιν αμαρτιων. 5. και εξεπορευετο προς αυτον πασα η Ιουδαια χωρα και οι Ιεροσολυμιται παντες και εβαπτιζοντο υπ αυτου εν τω Ιορδανη ποταμω εξομολογουμενοι τας αμαρτιας αυτων. 6. και ην ο Ιωαννης ενδεδυμενος τριχας καμηλου.

1. υιου θεου א^c B L 2427 WH^mg: omit א* WH^txt; υιου του θεου 33 892
2. εγω א L 33 892: omit B 2427 WH
   αποστελλω B L 33 892 2427 WH: αποστελω, א
   την οδον σου alone א B L 2427 WH: add εμπροσθεν σου 33 892
3. Ετοιμασατε την οδον Κυριου א B L 33 892 WH: omit 2427
4. εγενετο alone א^c B L 33 892 2427 WH: και εγενετο א*
   Ιωαννης א L 33 892 2427: Ιωανης B WH
   ο βαπτιζων א B L 33 892* 2427 WH: omit ο 892^c
   κηρυσσων alone B 33 892 2427 WH: και κηρυσσων א L
5. εξεπορευετο א B 33 892 2427 WH: εξεπορευοντο L
   η Ιουδαια א B L 33 892 WH: omit η 2427
   και (3) א^c B L 33 892 2427 WH: omit א*
6. ο א B L 892 2427 WH: omit 33
   Ιωαννης א L 33 892 2427: Ιωανης B WH

CHAPTER TWO

METHOD IN LOCATING A NEWLY-DISCOVERED MANUSCRIPT [1]

Discoveries of manuscripts of the New Testament follow one another in rapid succession. Scholars are confronted with the necessity of determining the date and place and exact content of the new find. They are confronted also with the more complex task of locating the "new" manuscript within the manuscript tradition. The same task remains to be done for many sources not newly-discovered but previously unstudied; as, for example, for many of the church fathers. In the doing of this task we have committed many errors and have wasted much time through lack of care in the choice of method.

If our newly-found manuscript is to be compared with previously known manuscripts, it should, ideally, be compared completely with all other manuscripts. How, otherwise, can complete accuracy be obtained? Partial comparisons—between two individuals or two groups—are often misleading; and ignoring large numbers of individuals reduces the probability that our conclusions are accurate. If we compare only a part of our manuscript's content with a part of the content of other manuscripts, we increase the chance of error. If we compare all of our manuscript's content with all the content of only one hundred others, how can we assume that the nine thousand nine hundred manuscripts we have ignored would not upset our conclusions?

More than ten thousand manuscript copies of the New Testament have been catalogued, but their evidence is not available to us for the complete comparison that rigorous method demands. We need a compass, a pathfinder, to guide us through the forests to the particular clump of trees to which our manuscript is closely related. Without such a pathfinder, our efforts too often will result in error or in nothing but exhaustion and frustration. This pathfinder must

---

[1] Originally published as "Method in Locating a Newly-Discovered Manuscript within the Manuscript Tradition of the Greek New Testament," *Texte und Untersuchungen zur Geschichte der altchristlichen Literatur*, LXXIII (1959), 757-77.

be partial but dependable as a guide. Initial guidance can be secured through looking for agreement in those readings where all sources are split into three or more groups. Such readings are a small percentage of the total number of variant readings—an essential element in our pathfinder. Moreover, in selecting these readings we have eliminated the very large number of readings in which two or three groups of manuscripts agree against two or three other groups. Readings with overlapping agreements do not yield easily their evidence for the location of a manuscript.

As long ago as 1911, E. A. Hutton urged the use of what he called "Triple Readings." [1] He published a list of readings in which the "Alexandrian," "Western," and "Syrian" authorities divide. This list is supported by Tables which show which manuscripts support each reading. Hutton's work is far from perfect. He fails to state the criteria which determine the classification of his "readings," although they could be painfully worked out from the Tables. His limitation to triple division is undesirable in the light of our present need to know more about half-a-dozen or more Text-types and sub-Text-types. He uses this method as the sole criterion for relationship. And, finally, the listing of Multiple Readings should begin with all cases where the evidence splits three or more ways rather than with an *a priori* determination of the number of texts and their grouping of witnesses.[2] Yet Hutton's work is valuable in suggesting an objective method of quickly if tentatively determining the Text-type to which a newly-found source belongs.

Some years ago in the study of the Beta Text-type in Mark, Dr. M. M. Parvis and I tried to add precision and greater objectivity to the use of Hutton's "Triple Readings." We changed the term from Triple to Multiple. We defined a Multiple Reading as one in

---

[1] Edward Ardron Hutton, *An Atlas of Textual Criticism: Being an Attempt to Show the Mutual Relationship of the Authorities for the Text of the New Testament up to about 1000 A.D.*, (Cambridge, 1911).

[2] Modern obsession with three text-types is derived from the oft-quoted passage in Jerome's preface to Chronicles, rather than from a study of manuscript groupings. This threefold grouping, which began in Septuagint studies, is being abandoned there. Würthwein points out that Lagarde's program has failed of completion because the Hesychian recension is not recoverable and because the surviving material is much more varied than Lagarde supposed. Cf. Ernst Würthwein, *The Text of the Old Testament* (Oxford, 1957), pp. 42-3. Thus in the New Testament the Western Text (e.g.) is not recoverable, and the manuscript material is much too varied to fit into only three text-types.

which the minimum support for each of at least three variant forms
of the text is either one of the major strands of the tradition, or the
support of a previously established group (such as Family 1,
Family Π, the Ferrar Group, K¹, Kⁱ, Kʳ), or the support of some one
of the ancient versions (such as af, it, syˢ, syᶜ, bo, or sa), or the
support of some single manuscript of an admittedly distinctive
character (such as D).

Moreover, if Multiple Readings are to be used effectively, the
evidence of a representative group of witnesses should be cited in
support of each reading. For this purpose (in the study referred to)
we used the following sources: א A B C D L W Δ Θ Ψ 28, 33,
565, 700, 892, 2427, Fam 1, Fam 13, Fam Π, K¹ (S V Ω) Kⁱ (E F G H)
Kʳ bo sa af it syˢ syᶜ. We selected these on the assumption that
they are a good sampling of the majority of manuscript groupings
known today.

Bruce Metzger's identification of my method for determining the
relationship of manuscripts is misleading. He says it is called
"the method of Multiple Readings." [1] I have never intentionally
called the method of locating a newly-found manuscript "the method
of Multiple Readings." I have urged the use of multiple readings
as one of three steps in locating a manuscript. I have tried to make
clear that it is a preliminary step and less important than the
two following steps: (1) the determination of agreement in a list
of distinctive readings, (2) the determination of agreement in a high
percentage of the total quantity of readings derived from a representative sample of all text groups in a specific block of text.

As a brief sample of a list of multiple readings, the first four
from the beginning of the Gospel of Mark are given with the support
from the twenty-eight "representative witnesses." See List I
(pp. 39-40). In making this list we were trying to locate ms. 2427, a
manuscript full of problems. [2] In each of the multiple readings it
supported a majority of the sources usually identified as Beta
Text-type witnesses. As a further sample, List II (pp. 40-43)
contains Multiple Readings in John, IIA in 7:18-8:12; and IIB
in John 1:1-4:40. Passages from John were selected because of the
relatively small amount of variation in that Gospel. The test of

---

[1] Bruce M. Metzger, *The Text of the New Testament* (New York and London,
1964), pp. 180-181.
[2] See Ernest C. Colwell, "An Ancient Text of the Gospel of Mark," *The
Emory University Quarterly*, I (1945), 65-75.

Hutton's method is thus a rigorous one. The specific passages were chosen at random. The manuscript evidence was drawn from Tischendorf's eighth edition with the addition of mss. W, $\mathfrak{P}^{75}$, and $\mathfrak{P}^{66}$.[1] This list is imperfect compared with List I. Here the consistent complete citation of supporting evidence from an extensive representative list of witnesses is lacking. The evidence (with three exceptions noted) is no more than can be found in Tischendorf. The addition of representative supporting evidence would probably remove some readings from the list and add others to it. It would certainly increase the number of variations in a specific passage. But Tischendorf's general availability for checking makes this list valuable as a preliminary indication of the value of lists of Multiple Readings.

In List IIA, eight Multiple Readings occur.

With reference to Hutton's list, it is noteworthy that it includes but two Triple Readings in this area. He explains the shortness of the list as due to his concern not to overstate the case. But since we do not begin with labels, but with multiple variation itself, the only caution that is appropriate is concerned with the actual existence in each passage of multiple variation. Of Hutton's two Triple Readings, one was rejected from our list. In John 7:40 he lists

εκ του οχλου ουν	A (lexandrian)
εκ του οχλου δε	W (estern)
πολοι ουν εκ του οχλου	S (yrian)

The support for the Western reading given in his Tables is c e ff² cop sah arm. The general ambiguity of versional evidence on conjunctions raises a question concerning this variant.

In our list, more than one grouping of manuscripts is clearly indicated; for example, the Beta Text-type emerges as a definite group with mss. B L T X 33 in its membership. In this area previous study has identified ms. W as a member of the Beta Text-type. Here W agrees seven out of eight times with the leaders of the Beta Text-type.

Ms. $\mathfrak{P}^{66}$ is as yet an unknown. List IIA establishes two relationships for it. The first is a relationship with Sinaiticus plus Bezae (א D); the second is with the Beta Text-type. But the shortness

---

[1] The patristic evidence in Tischendorf has been ignored. The evidence of W was taken from H. A. Sanders' facsimile edition; the evidence of $\mathfrak{P}^{66}$ from the facsimile published by V. Martin and J. W. B. Barns, *Papyrus Bodmer II, Supplément* (Geneva, 1962); the evidence of $\mathfrak{P}^{75}$ from the facsimile published by Victor Martin and Rodolphe Kasser, *Papyrus Bodmer XV* (Geneva, 1961).

of the selection and the internal incompleteness of the evidence
leave questions as to the exact nature of these relationships. No
such uncertainty exists for $\mathfrak{P}^{75}$. The list indicates a clear relationship
to the Beta Text-type.

In List IIB, twenty-two Multiple Readings occur. Hutton lists
only nine Triple Readings here: 1:19, 26, 27, 32, 39, 43, 50; 2:6, 17;
and he cites evidence for only two: 1:27 and 2:17. 1:32 cannot be
established as a multiple reading on the basis of the evidence in
Tischendorf (which is not determinative since it needs supplement-
ing throughout), but all the rest of Hutton's readings appear in
our list. Again the Beta Text-type emerges as a distinct group,
this time including ms. Sinaiticus (א). There are two contrasts
with List IIA: (1) The Washington ms. (W) frequently leaves the
Beta group for other company; (2) $\mathfrak{P}^{66}$ seems measurably closer to
the Beta Text-type.[1] $\mathfrak{P}^{75}$ seems in this area to be about as close to
the Beta Text-type as $\mathfrak{P}^{66}$ is. Using mss. W, $\mathfrak{P}^{66}$, and $\mathfrak{P}^{75}$ as stalking
horses, we turn first to an investigation of their relationship to
the Beta Text-type.

Practical considerations, ordinary common sense, urge that
groups already established be used in the process of location.
The most meaningful locations are within the largest groups:
the "texts" or Text-types. But a group is not a group unless it
has unique elements. Separate existence can be claimed only for
groups with some readings "of their own." The newly-found
manuscript cannot be related to a group without being related to
the singular readings of the group. Our second rule must be,
"Demonstrate the relationship of the new manuscript to existing
groups through a study of the singular readings of groups."

In this case through the study of Multiple Readings we have
identified one particular large group—the Beta Text-type—as
possible kin to mss. W, $\mathfrak{P}^{66}$, and $\mathfrak{P}^{75}$. List III exhibits distinctive

---

[1] Since we have noted the agreements of $\mathfrak{P}^{66}$ with the Beta Text-type in
our list of multiple readings, it may be worthwhile to measure this new
codex against Hutton's list of Triple Readings throughout John. $\mathfrak{P}^{66}$ has
Hutton's A(lexandrian) reading in 1:27; 2:17; 6:40; 6:45; 6:70; 6:71;
7:40; 9:6; 9:8; 9:11; 9:17; 9:20; 9:25; 9:26; 10:4a; 10:4b; 10:38; 12:47;
and 13:6. In 6:70 $\mathfrak{P}^{66}$ is not identical with his A reading but is much closer
to it than to either of the other two. In 7:40 and 10:4, the first reading in
$\mathfrak{P}^{66}$ would be labelled P (for peculiar) by Hutton, but in each case it has been
corrected to read with A. $\mathfrak{P}^{66}$ has Hutton's S(yrian) reading in 5:37; 10:31;
and 13:26. It has his W(estern) reading in 6:10 and 13:12. It has a gap at

readings of this Text-type in the two sections of John already studied. This list was compiled from Tischendorf's apparatus; it does not claim completeness—either in the number of singular readings, or in the citation of manuscript evidence.

But the List does tell us something about the relationship of mss. W, $\mathfrak{P}^{66}$, and $\mathfrak{P}^{75}$ to the Beta Text-type. In List III there are 28 Beta readings in John 1:1-4:40. Ms. W reads only 11 of these; $\mathfrak{P}^{66}$ reads 23; $\mathfrak{P}^{75}$ reads 25. Compare this with the range of well-known Beta mss., from 27 readings for B to 17 for L. In John 7:18-8:12 Ms. W has changed its character;[1] here it agrees with the Beta singular readings 8 times out of 11 readings. $\mathfrak{P}^{66}$ seems to have moved slightly in the other direction—it agrees with Beta 8 times, and 2 of these are corrections. But $\mathfrak{P}^{75}$ reads all eleven! Here the range of the Beta manuscripts runs from 11 for ms. T to 6 for mss. $\aleph$ and $\aleph^c$.

If Step One is to find related groups through the use of Multiple Readings, and Step Two is to demonstrate the relationship through the use of Distinctive Group Readings, Step Three is to confirm the relationship through the determination of the quantity of agreement. Members of a group must agree with one another in a large majority of the total amount of existing variant readings.[2]

Two other studies can be cited in support of this claim. Silva Lake discarded from significant membership in Family Π those manuscripts which read with the Family's five leading witnesses less than forty per cent of the time in variations from the Textus Receptus. Of the manuscripts she cited, the range of agreement was from 98 per cent to 45 per cent, and only two of 21 manuscripts read below fifty per cent.[3]

The second study was the study of the Beta Text-type in Mark which has been referred to above. In the course of that study Dr.

6:35. Thus of his 25 Triple Readings in the portion of John extant in $\mathfrak{P}^{66}$, 19 are A, 3 are S, 2 are W, one is missing. His test would mean that $\mathfrak{P}^{66}$ is predominantly a Beta Text-type with some Syrian and Western elements.

[1] This change is well-known and coincides with a change of scribes.

[2] It is assumed that the list of variants has been pruned of the vast mass of errors in which scribes agree by coincidence; e.g., misspellings, and the use of nu movable. That the pruning should go beyond this to eliminate agreement in small variations which are possibly due to chance coincidence has been argued by B. M. Metzger, "The Caesarean Text," *Journal of Biblical Literature*, LXIV (1945), 489.

[3] Silva Lake, *Family Π and the Codex Alexandrinus* ("Studies and Documents," V [London, 1936]), p. 8; cf. p. 15.

Parvis attempted to refine the meaning of the term, "variant reading." He attempted the identification of "unit readings" which included the smallest variations within themselves, and were large enough to contain all the elements involved in any single variation.[1] After establishing 148 of these Unit Readings in Mark, he added the attestation of 33 representative witnesses. Then, starting with a single manuscript, he tabulated the number of agreements with each of the other 32 witnesses in the 148 units of variation. The results were somewhat startling.

When agreements with B, the famous Codex Vaticanus, were tabulated, the Textus Receptus was in the group that agreed a majority of 148 times. Close to the Textus Receptus were Family Π, A, K^r, K^i and K^1. Also agreeing in a majority of the readings were all members of the Beta Text-type; ℵ B C L Δ 33 892 1342 and 2427. The only witnesses clearly below a majority agreement were D and W, with D only nine readings below a majority.[2]

This clearly indicates that the quantitative test that is needed for membership in a group cannot be merely agreement in a majority of the readings where variation occurs. The amount of agreement must be much more than a bare majority if it is to have a confirmative value (and this is obviously the only value such a statistic can have). Let's look again at the lists for Vaticanus and Θ. In the case of manuscript B, the Beta Text-type mss. 2427 ℵ L 33 892 and 579 preempt the top of the list and range from 125 agreements to 86. Then Family 1 (with 85), 28 (with 83), and Θ (with 82) intervene before C Δ and 1342 come in with 81 agreements. On the other hand, the Alpha Text-type manuscripts start at the 75 agreement-line with K^1 and range up only to 78 with the Textus Receptus. The Beta Text-type manuscripts (excluding C, Δ, and 1342) range from 84 per cent down to 58 per cent, while the Alpha Text-type ranges from 51 per cent to 52 per cent.

The situation is much more confused in the case of ms. Θ. The closest witness is C (93 times). The Caesareans cluster between 92 with Family 1 and 89 with 700—although 28 drops to 86. Meanwhile, 33 and G read 91 agreements, and the Textus Receptus K^1 and K^r

---

[1] On the need for considering related variants together, see H. J. Vogels, *Handbuch der neutestamentlichen Textkritik* (Münster, 1923), pp. 204-19.

[2] I regret very much that our notes do not include the ranking of these witnesses with Codex Bezae (D) as the starting point.

read 88 agreements. But most of the Beta Text-type manuscripts fall below 85 agreements.

The most that can be safely said is that in the total comparison of a single witness with others, agreements of less than 60 to 65 per cent are of no significance for primary relationships. In badly-mixed Text-types or sub-Text-types the non-primary relationships may read from 60 to 65 per cent agreement, while the primary group will be very little higher. For example, in the figures given for Θ, no confirmation of relationships exists. We shall return to the problem of mixture later.

There is another important lesson to be learned from Dr. Parvis's work. Since all that these lists deal with is uncharacterized quantities, small differences have no significance whatever in comparisons with individual manuscripts. What significance can there be in the fact that Θ agrees with B 82 times and 565 agrees with B 80 times, when C, Δ, and 1342 agree 81 times? Weak members of a Text-type may contain no more of the total content of a Text-type than strong members of some other Text-type contain. The comparison in totals of agreement of one manuscript with another manuscript has little significance beyond that of confirmation, and then only if the amount of agreement is large enough to be distinctive.

A particular warning must be given against the comparison of one manuscript with another in only a portion of its content. If totals of agreement with individual manuscripts are to be used to locate a new manuscript in the tradition, then it is necessary to make this type of comparison with all known manuscripts. But this is an impossibly laborious process, whose cost in time and effort is out of all proportion to the significance of the result. For practical reasons we have to replace "all known manuscripts" with a carefully selected list of representative witnesses. The evidence of such a list can be drawn from a critical apparatus. But for the type of comparison we have in mind this apparatus must give the complete evidence of each manuscript in the list. Unfortunately, no apparatus today meets this requirement, although the one being produced for the International Greek New Testament Project will meet it. With or without the help of a critical apparatus, we are forced to take samples of short sections of text. This is dangerous, because within a single manuscript different types of text alternate in large blocks. Today at least twenty manuscripts are known to have such mixture due to alternate use of exemplars.

The famous Washington Gospels (W) is a case in point. We have found similar changes in type from section to section in C and Δ and 574. Yet the use of a number of short passages is reasonable protection against error.

Statistics of agreement in variants from the Textus Receptus, for example, are not a safe guide to group relationships. "For obviously it is of slight value in determining family relationship to know only that in a certain area a given manuscript agrees with, say, B and ℵ ten times in differing from the Textus Receptus. If B and ℵ should in addition differ from the Textus Receptus in ninety instances, the Neutral element in the given manuscript would be slight indeed." [1] This danger has been pointed out elsewhere in connection with the Terrell Gospels ms., Gregory's 2322. This manuscript has nineteen variants from the Textus Receptus in Chapter 6 of Mark's Gospel. Five variants are meaningless misspellings and the like. Of the fourteen variants remaining, thirteen have Caesarean support: eleven from more than one Caesarean witness; two from a single Caesarean witness. This sounds like a demonstration of the Caesarean nature of this codex.

But it is not. Two things keep it from belonging to any Caesarean group. First, it agrees with the Textus Receptus against the leading Caesarean witnesses more than one hundred times in this chapter. The Caesarean element in it is much too small to merit a Caesarean title. Second, it is an orthodox member of the Byzantine group labelled K^r by von Soden.[2]

Harold Murphy after completing a study of Eusebius's *Demonstratio* in which he used variations from the Textus Receptus as the data turned to a convincing indictment of this method. "A complete description of the NT text of the *Demonstratio* must present not only the variants of Eusebius' NT text in the *Demonstratio* from the TR, but also those passages that agree with the TR." [3] He

---

[1] Metzger, *op. cit.*, p. 488.

[2] This was ably demonstrated by D. O. Voss, "K Variants in Mark," which appears as Appendix D in Silva Lake's *Family* II. . . ("Studies and Documents," V), pp. 155-8. In the whole Gospel of Mark, the Terrell Gospels ms. disagrees with nine other K^r mss., less than half the number of times it disagrees with Θ in Chapter 6. It reads 8 out of 10 readings in Mark which appear only in K^r mss. Thus it is a witness to the K^r text-type, and not to the Caesarean text-type.

[3] Harold S. Murphy, "Eusebius' NT Text in the *Demonstratio Evangelica*," *Journal of Biblical Literature*, LXXIII (1954), 167.

points out that ms. D (highest in agreement with Eusebius in
variants from the Textus Receptus) with 30 per cent of agreement
and with frequent variation from Textus Receptus not shared by
Eusebius cannot be claimed as the "type" to which the *Demonstratio*
belongs.

The error that lies in partial comparison is not limited to comparisons with the Textus Receptus. In the preparation of the present
chapter I noted frequent agreements between D (Codex Bezae)
and ℵ (Sinaiticus) in the Gospel of John. From 1:1-16 and 3:26-4:24
I collected fifteen agreements between these two manuscripts
with little support from others. When I turned to a more intensive
study of John 7:18-8:12, I found ℵ and D agreeing in eleven
variants from Tischendorf's text (8th edition). And although ℵ
has 47 variants from that text in that area (many of them singular
readings), it is supported in these readings only half-a-dozen
times by B (Vaticanus). Thus I concluded (prematurely) that D's
eleven agreements compared to B's six indicated a closer relationship to D than to B. But when I turned to agreements with
Tischendorf's text, I found 29 for ℵ *plus* B, and 23 for ℵ *plus* D.
In terms of quantities this brought the two pairs about on a par.

If statistical comparisons are to be made on the basis of raw
totals, all the data must be included. This requires a collation of
one manuscript with another one. When in John 7:18-8:12 ℵ is
collated with D, a list of about 80 variations is produced. When ℵ is
collated with B, about sixty-four variations appear. So far as gross
statistics are concerned ℵ is closer to B than to D.

Von Soden had made a detailed study of the peculiarities of ℵ,
and after running through eleven kinds of peculiarity he added
as a twelfth: agreements of ℵ with D.[1] He begins by carefully
discarding insignificant agreements, i.e., agreements in parallel
passages, agreements in readings derived from the Iota Text-type,
agreements shared with the Sahidic version. Of what remains, he
says, there is little of any significance in Matthew, Mark, and
Luke. But the case is different in John. Here he prints a list of
56 agreements between these two manuscripts.

This is an illustration of the difficulties created for the student
of New Testament manuscripts by the presence of mixture. It is an
illustration of a difficulty more easily overcome than others caused

---

[1] H. von Soden, *Die Schriften des Neuen Testaments*, I. Teil: *Untersuchungen*
(Berlin, 1911), p. 935.

by mixture of a different type. Where the mixture results from partial correction to a new standard, the location of the mixed text within the tradition is very difficult indeed.

The confusions existing today in the study of Caesarean manuscripts and versions, of most of von Soden's Iota witnesses, and of the Ecclesiastical Text in the Byzantine period are due to mixture of this sort. The clarification of these matters will result from working from known and definable Families, Tribes, and Text-types through these mixed areas. This means ultimately the clear identification of common components. But this will be achieved only by the most careful and precise work, which must begin with objectively verifiable comparisons.

Membership in a text-type has sometimes been established on grounds quite different from those that have been urged here. The label "Western" for one of the Text-types is misleading even in the very establishment of the group. Thus Zuntz has argued that only geographically Western sources can be included legitimately in this group.[1] But membership in a Text-type must be established on grounds other than the place of origin of a manuscript. While manuscripts have no legs and are not automotive, they are portable and were frequently carried to new homes before they lost their reproductive power.

Again, membership in the Caesarean Text-type has been held to depend on the presence of "a pattern"—sometimes described as "midway between mss. B and D." Thus B. H. Streeter places the Caesarean Text almost equidistant from both the Neutral and the Western Texts.[2] Later works identify individual sources as members of the Caesarean Text because they lie midway between the Neutral and the Western.

What are the possible meanings of "midway between Neutral and Western," or "midway between D and B"? Does it mean that the source in question in its variations from the Textus Receptus has support from Neutral manuscripts in one half the variants and support from Western manuscripts in the other half? This seems to

---

[1] E.g., in the Schweich Lectures for 1946, G. Zuntz, *The Text of the Epistles* (London, 1953).

[2] B. H. Streeter, *The Four Gospels, A Study of Origins* (London, 1924). Note Hollis Huston's reference to this as "the Caesarean pattern" in his article, "Mark 6 and 11 in 𝔓⁴⁵ and in the Caesarean Text," *Journal of Biblical Literature*, LXXIV (1955), 269.

be the meaning of the phrase in the actual practice of those who use it. But this is meaningless for the locating of a manuscript, for two reasons. In the first place, it eliminates from consideration that large block of the manuscript's text in which it agrees with the Textus Receptus. The pattern of this agreement in relationship to mss. B and D (or in relationship to any other witness) is an important element for the determination of a manuscript's place within the manuscript tradition.[1] In the second place, most Greek manuscripts of the New Testament are midway between D and B—provided "midway" is used as loosely as it has been in studies of the Caesarean Text-type. Two dozen manuscripts (at the most) veer off to the side of B; another dozen will veer off toward D, closer to D than to B. The mass of late minuscules will in their few variants from the Textus Receptus support now the one, now the other of these famous uncial codices. But these are weasel words, too slippery, too vague and ambiguous to be used for the location of manuscripts.

The confusion caused by this locating-definition of the Text-type can be seen clearly in Streeter's rebuttal of Burkitt's attack on the Caesarean Text. Streeter had abandoned the "midway" criterion when he explained that by the word "Text" in the phrase, "the Caesarean Text," he meant the majority of readings peculiar to the particular group of witnesses which he called Caesarean, plus those readings with slight support outside this group.[2] The primary part of this definition is surely the words "readings peculiar to." But how can the Caesarean Text (or any other) so defined be located midway between any other known witnesses? If a Text is the body of readings supported only by an identifiable group of manuscripts, a Text cannot be related to other Texts by such phrases as "midway between the Alexandrian and the Western."

If the definition of Text as a process rather than a homogeneous unit is sound (as current study claims), then the midway location is shifting at both ends. It would take an accordion-pleated source to hold a position midway between the whole range of Proto-Neutral to Late Neutral and that miscellaneous group of dissimilar readings which is called Western. The midway phrase has earned its right to oblivion.

---

[1] See the discussion of this point earlier in the chapter (pp. 34f.).

[2] B. H. Streeter and F. C. Burkitt, "The Caesarean Text of the Gospels," *Journal of Theological Studies*, XXVI (1924-25), 373-380.

In the location of a manuscript with reference to groups, the wealth of early sources strongly suggests beginning the story as close to the beginning as possible and working down toward the present. The papyri in addition to our earliest parchment manuscripts provide enough material for a new effort of this sort. In a study of the groupings of New Testament manuscripts,[1] I have tried to suggest some of the relevant procedures.

In the present chapter I have been concerned primarily with "objective" procedures, but I cannot close without admitting the value of "rational" criticism here as everywhere. With Zuntz, I believe that the identification of the original reading is of value in grouping witnesses, since the corrupt reading is the "error" which is significant for lineage. In further agreement with the same scholar, I believe that all the work of the student of manuscripts must be related to the history of the church, a very lively community, not easily described in formulas. Without this constant reference, error easily overcomes us.

We sometimes conjecture technical reasons for variations that are better explained by vital interests in the church. For example, Klijn describes as "most important" a conclusion of Plooij.[2] This conclusion was that the reading in the Dura fragment of Tatian —"the wives of those traveling with him" in place of "the women who were traveling with him"—is due to the omission of a letter in a Syriac original. (The Old Latin ms. *e* has the same reading). But in a study of apologetic interest in the Fourth Gospel I noted that John constantly omits details in the first three Gospels which had become or later became the basis of slanderous attacks.[3] The statement concerning women who traveled with Jesus was omitted by John, and it is not at all improbable that Tatian recognized the presence of these women as a liability to the Christian movement. In the second century, pagan attacks on the role of women in

---

[1] See Chapter I (pp. 1-25 above).

[2] A. F. J. Klijn, *A Survey of the Researches into the Western Text of the Gospels and Acts* (Utrecht, [1949]), p. 101.

[3] ". . . No rich man is rejected in John, nor is riches anywhere attacked. There is no declaration on the virtue of poverty and the vice of wealth. There is in John no importunate beggar, no leper, no lunatic, no epileptic, no demoniac of any kind, no pauper and no mention of prostitutes. There is no defense of the discipleship of children; nor any insistence on the virtue of being like children. There is no mention of the poverty of Jesus or his disciples. The crowd of ministering women who accompanied him on his travels have vanished" (E. C. Colwell, *John Defends the Gospel* [Chicago, 1936], p. 58).

Christianity were widespread and intense. Tatian devoted a chapter (xxxiii) of his *Address to the Greeks* to the vindication of Christian women. I am convinced that the variant in the Dura fragment is an evidence of apologetic interest either on the part of Tatian or on the part of the scribe who wrote this copy. Lagrange took a similar position and argued convincingly that Tatian made the alteration in order to remove all trace of suspicion of immorality from the account. The only change involved in the Greek text is the substitution of the genitive case for the nominative case of the participle.[1]

In conclusion I suggest that the location of a manuscript within the tradition should use Multiple Readings to find the related group, Distinctive Readings to demonstrate the kinship, and total comparison to confirm the relationship.[2] These steps begin with objectivity of a high degree; they progress to an increasingly careful appraisal of the significance of individual readings. By this method relationships can be established which will endure the criticism of later generations.

List I

MULTIPLE READINGS IN MARK 1

1:5 παντες και εβαπτιζοντο: B D L Δ 28 33 579 892 1241 1342 2427 bo it
παντες εβαπτιζοντο: א
και εβαπτιζοντο παντες: A W 157 517 700 Fam. 1 Fam. Π K¹ Kⁱ Kʳ ς
και παντες εβαπτιζοντο: 565 Fam. 13
και εβαπτιζοντο: Θ sa
Hiatus: C Ψ af syᶜ syˢ
1:5 υπ αυτου εν τω ιορδανη ποταμω: א B L 33 892 1241 2427 bo sa

---

[1] The Synoptic passages are Mark 15:40-41; Matt. 27:55-56; Luke 23:49. The new page of the Diatessaron was published by Professor C. H. Kraeling, *A Greek Fragment of Tatian's Diatessaron from Dura* (London, 1935). For Lagrange's convincing suggestion see M.-J. Lagrange, "Deux nouveaux textes relatifs à l'Évangile," *Revue Biblique*, XLIV (1935), 325; or *Critique textuelle*, II: *La Critique rationnelle* (Paris, 1935), p. 631.

[2] As soon as the International Greek New Testament Project has published Luke, a list of Multiple Readings for that Gospel with representative attestation could be produced without much effort. Such a list should be published as an official or standard sampler for hitherto unclassified manuscripts. The "total comparison" called for here must wait for such an apparatus as that of the International Greek New Testament Project. In the meantime the Claremont Profile Method developed by Fred Wisse and Paul McReynolds may be relied on for the Gospel of Luke, and, progressively, for other books. See Ernest Cadman Colwell, with Irving Alan Sparks, Frederik Wisse, Paul McReynolds, "The International Greek New Testament Project: A Status Report," *Journal of Biblical Literature*, LXXXVII (1968), pp. 187-197.

υπ αυτου εν τω ιορδανη: it

εν ιορδανη υπ αυτου: D

εν τω ιορδανη υπ αυτου: W Θ 700

εν τω ιορδανη ποταμω υπ αυτου: A Δ 157 517 579 1342 Fam. 1 Fam. 13
     Fam. Π K¹ Kⁱ Kʳ ς

εις τον ιορδανην υπ αυτου: 28 565

Hiatus: C Ψ' af syᶜ syˢ

1:9   εις τον ιορδανην υπο ιωννου: ℵ B D L Θ 33 517 565 579 700 892 1241 1342
       2427 Fam. 13 bo sa it

εν τω ιορδανη υπ ιωαννου: 28 Fam. 1 bo sa

υπο ιωαννου εις τον ιορδανην: A W Δ 157 Fam. Π K¹ Kⁱ Kʳ ς

Hiatus: C Ψ' af syᶜ syˢ

1:13   και ην εν τη ερημω: ℵ A B D L Θ 33 579 892 1342 2427 bo sa it

και ην εκει εν τη ερημω: W Δ 157 1241 K¹ Kⁱ Kʳ ς

και ην εκει: 28 517 565 700 Fam. 1 Fam. Π syˢ

Omit: Fam. 13

Hiatus: C Ψ' af syᶜ

List II

A. MULTIPLE READINGS IN JOHN 7:18-8:12

7:20   απεκριθη ο οχλος ℵ B L T X 33 sah cop W 𝔓⁶⁶ 𝔓⁷⁵

απεκριθη αυτω ο οχλος syᶜ (dicunt ei homines)

απεκριθη αυτω ο οχλος και ειπεν 1

απεκριθη ο οχλος και ειπεν αυτω 258 1 syrʰ et ᵖᵃˡ

απεκριθη ο οχλος και ειπεν προς αυτον 247

απεκριθη ο οχλος και ειπεν D Γ Δ Λ uncˢ al pler it vg rell

απεκριθησαν οι ιουδαιοι και ειπον αυτω K Π al⁶ syʰ ᵐᵍ

7:31   πολλοι δε (cop ουν, sah om) επιστευσαν εκ του οχλου ℵ D
     sah cop (:: vdtr omnino ex hac lectione ortae reliquae) 𝔓⁶⁶

πολλοι δε εκ του οχλου επιστευσαν ς Γ Δ Λ unc⁷ al pler q syrᶜ et ʰ
     arm go

εκ του οχλου δε K Π al¹⁰ (W ουν, 33 δε after εκ, 69 om)

πολλοι επιστευσαν B K L T X Π al¹⁸ it pler vg eth W 𝔓⁷⁵

7:32   ηκουσαν B L T X Γ Δ Λ unc⁶ al pler b g l q vg cop W 𝔓⁷⁵

ηκουσαν ουν K M U Π 1 28 131 al²⁰ a f ff² sah

ηκουσαν δε ℵ D al pauc c e arm go 𝔓⁶⁶

και ηκουσαν 13 69 124 syᶜ etᵖ etʰ c. ob. eth

7:36   ο λογος ουτος B Dᵍʳ E*ᵛⁱᵈ K L X Π 1 33 69 2ᵖᵉ al⁵ syᶜ arm 𝔓⁶⁶
     W 𝔓⁷⁵

ουτος ο λογος ς ℵ Eᶜᵒʳʳ* Γ Δ Λ unc⁶ al pler it vg syrᵖ et ʰ rell

ο λογος T al⁵ harl

7:39   πνευμα ℵ K T Π 42 91 san fu harl* cop arm 𝔓⁶⁶ corr 𝔓⁷⁵

πνευμα αγιον L X Γ Δ Λ unc⁶ al pler 𝔓⁶⁶* W

πνευμα δεδομενον a b c e ff² g l vgᶜˡᵉ etᶜᵈᵈ pl syrᵖ

το πνευμα αγιον επ αυτοις D f go (eth)

πνευμα αγιον δεδομενον B B 254 e q syrᵖᵃˡ

7:42   κωμης οπου ην Δαυειδ ο χς ερχεται ℵ X Γ Δ Λ Π unc rell al fere omn
     a b f l q go syrᵖ 𝔓⁶⁶ (ην above line)

κωμης Δαυειδ ο χς ερχεται e syrᵖ eth

κωμης οπου ην Δαυειδ ερχεται ο χς B L T 33 c vg syrᵖᵃˡ W 𝔓⁷⁵

κωμης ο χς ερχεται οπου ην Δαυειδ D

7:46 ελαλησεν ουτως ανθρωπος אᶜ B L T X 3 33 𝔓⁶⁶ ᶜᵒʳʳ W 𝔓⁷⁵
ουτως ανθρωπος ελαλησεν א* D 𝔓⁶⁶*
ουτως ελαλησεν ανθρωπος Γ Δ Λ Π uncʔ al pler itᵖˡ vg syrᵖ et ʰ go eth
7:50 προς αυτους א*
προς αυτους ο ελθων νυκτος προς αυτον ς E G H M 028 Γ Λ al pler
προς αυτους ο ελθων προς αυτον νυκτος K U Δ Π 131 157 220 44ᵉᵛ
pˢᶜʳ wˢᶜʳ f l q vg go syrᵖ
προς αυτους ο ελθων προς αυτον προτερον אᶜ B T a e sah syrᵖᵃˡ 𝔓⁷⁵
προς αυτους ο ελθων προς αυτον το προτερον L 𝔓⁶⁶ W
προς αυτους ο ελθων προς αυτον νυκτος το προτερον X c ff² syrʰ c.* arm
προς αυτους ο ελθων προς αυτον το προτερον νυκτος cop eth
προς αυτους ο ελθων νυκτος προς αυτον το προτερον 1 13 33 69 118
124 209 2ᵖᵉ
after εις ων εξ αυτων: ο ελθων προς αυτον νυκτος το πρωτον D

B. MULTIPLE READINGS IN JOHN 1:1–4:40

1:15 ον ειπον (C³ ελεγον) ς אᶜᵇ A B³ D L unc rell al omnᵛⁱᵈ 𝔓⁶⁶ 𝔓⁷⁵
omit ο ειπων א*
ο ειπων אᵃ B* C*
ον ειπον υμιν D² X f am fu eth W

1:19 απεστειλαν οι Ιουδαιοι εξ Ιεροσολυμων ιερεις και Λευιτας ς א C³ L Γ Δ Λ Π
uncʔ al pler 𝔓⁶⁶ W* 𝔓⁷⁵
απεστειλαν προς αυτον οι Ιουδαιοι εξ Ιεροσολυμων ιερεις και Λευιτας
B C* 33 249 al pauc a b c syᶜ et ᵖ cop arm eth
απεστειλαν οι Ιουδαιοι εξ Ιεροσολυμων ιερεις και Λευιτας προς αυτον
A X 13 69 124 al²⁰ aldin e f ff² l q vg syrʰ 𝔓⁶⁶ᶜ

1:21 τι ουν ηλιας ει א L a syrᵖ
τι ουν ηλιας ει συ ς A C³ X Γ Δ Λ Π uncʔ al pler f q vg syrʰ
τι ουν συ ηλιας ει C* 33 e ff² l for foss 𝔓⁶⁶ (τις) 𝔓⁷⁵
συ ουν τι; ηλιας ει B
τι ουν συ ει; ηλιας W

1:26 στηκει B L Tᵇ 1
εστηκει א G (𝔓⁷⁵)
εστηκεν ς A C X Γ Δ Λ Π uncᵂ al pler 𝔓⁶⁶ W

1:27 ουκ ειμι εγω αξιος B Tᵇ X 13 118 𝔓⁶⁶ (ικανος = Mt Mk Lk) W
εγω ουκ ειμι αξιος A Γ Δ Λ Π uncʔ al pler itᵖˡᵉʳ vg theᵖᵖ
ουκ ειμι αξιος εγω a
omit εγω = ουκ ειμι αξιος אC L al ²⁰ fere q cop arm ethʳᵒᵐ 𝔓⁶⁶* 𝔓⁷⁵
(ικανος = Mt Mk Lk)

1:37 οι δυο μαθηται αυτου א B cˢᶜʳ b syrᵖ
οι δυο αυτου μαθηται C* L Tᵇ X 33 W 𝔓⁶⁶ 𝔓⁷⁵
αυτου οι δυο μαθηται ς A C³ P Γ Δ Λ Π unc rell al pler c f l
vg syrʰ

1:39 λεγεται ερμηνευομενον ς א* P Γ Δ Λ Π uncʔ al pler
λεγεται μεθερμηνευομενον אᶜ A B C L X 33 157 249 cˢᶜʳ 𝔓⁶⁶ W 𝔓⁷⁵
ερμηνευεται 1 118 209 cop

1:43 ηγαγεν א B L cop 𝔓⁶⁶* 𝔓⁷⁵
ουτος ηγαγεν G 1 209 arm 𝔓⁶⁶ᶜ
ηγαγεν ουν 15ᵉᵛ b
και ηγαγεν W A X Γ Δ Λ Π uncᵂ al pler itᵖˡᵉʳ vg syrᵒᵐⁿ eth

1:43   εμβλεψας ℵ A B L Γ Π* unc⁸ al plus⁶⁰ aldin arm 𝔓⁶⁶
      εμβλεψας δε ς 028 X Δ Λ Π² b c f l vg cop syrʰ c.* 𝔓⁷⁵
      και εμβλεψας 46 117 15ᵉᵛ a e q syᶜ˙ ᵖ et ʰʳ eth W

1:50 (49) απεκριθη αυτω Ναθαναηλ B L 33. 249 b 𝔓⁶⁶ W 𝔓⁷⁵
      απεκριθη Ναθαναηλ και ειπεν ℵ
      απεκριθη Ναθαναηλ και ειπεν αυτω Γ Δ 245 254 49ᵉᵛ al pauc q
      απεκριθη αυτω Ναθαναηλ και ειπεν X 124 a f ff² l vg arm
      απεκριθη Ναθαναηλ και λεγει αυτως A Λ Π unc⁹ al pler syrᵖ˙ ʰ,
         ᵖᵃˡ cop

2:6   ιουδαιων κειμεναι ℵᶜ B L X 33 eth W 𝔓⁶⁶ 𝔓⁷⁵
      εξ κειμεναι ς A Γ Δ Λ Π unc⁹ al pler c q vg syᵖ˙ ʰ, ᵖᵃˡ
      κειμεναι εξ 69 124 l
      omit κειμεναι ℵ* 13 47ᵉᵛ a e arm

2:12   οι μαθηται αυτου και οι αδελφοι αυτου K Π* 13 28 al² scr al⁶
      omit οι μαθηται αυτου και οι αδελφοι αυτου q
      οι αδελφοι και οι μ αθηται L Tᵇ vid
      οι αδελφοι και οι μαθηται αυτου B c 𝔓⁶⁶* 𝔓⁷⁵
      οι αδελφοι αυτου και οι μαθηται αυτου A X Γ Δ Λ unc⁹ al omnᵛⁱᵈ f vg
         cop syrᵖ˙ ʰ, ᵖᵃˡ eth 𝔓⁶⁶ ᶜᵒʳʳ
      οι αδελφοι αυτου (without και οι μαθηται) ℵ 74* 89* 234 245 249 440
         b ff² l arm
      οι μαθηται αυτου (before και η μητηρ αυτου) W
      οι αδελφοι a e

2:13   εις Ιεροσολυμα ο ῑς ς ℵ B E F K P 028 Tᵇ ᵛⁱᵈ V X Γ Δ Λ Π al pler
      a c f l q am for ing tol syrᵖ˙ ʰ eth W
      ο ῑς εις Ιεροσολυμα G L M U al pauc b ff² vgᶜˡᵉᵐ cop syrᵖᵃˡ arm 𝔓⁶⁶ 𝔓⁷⁵
      ο ῑς εις Ιεροσολυμα ῑς A
      εις Ιεροσολυμα 13 69 124 245 346

2:15   ανεστρεψεν ς A L P Γ Δ Λ Π* unc⁹ al pler 𝔓⁷⁵
      ανετρεψεν B X Π² al plus¹⁰ 𝔓⁶⁶ W
      κατεστρεψεν ℵ 13 16 69ᵐᵍ (ᵗˣᵗ κατορθωσε) 124 157 229* 382 6ᵖᵉ

2:17   εμνησθησαν ℵ B L Tᵇ X cop 𝔓⁶⁶ 𝔓⁷⁵
      εμνησθησαν δε ς A P Γ Δ Λ Π unc⁸ al pler c vg syrᵖ
      εμνησθησαν δε και M
      και εμνησθησαν e f ff² l q foss syrᵖ˙ ᵖᵃˡ eth W
      τοτε εμνησθησαν a arm

3:12   πιστευετε ς ℵ A B E L 028 U V Λ* Π² al plu it vg cop 𝔓⁶⁶
      πιστευσητε G H K M Γ Δ² Π* 1 22 28 69 124 al plus⁵⁰ W
      πιστευετε TᵇΛ al aliq b ff² l foss cop 𝔓⁷⁵

3:20   τα εργα αυτου ς ℵ B Tᵇ Γ Λ unc⁸ al pler it vg rell
      αυτου τα εργα A K Π 1 al¹⁰ W 𝔓⁷⁵
      τα εργα αυτου οτι πονηρα εστιν L Δ 13 33 al¹⁵ cop arr sl 𝔓⁶⁶

4:2   ιησους αυτος ς ℵ B C L Δ unc pler al pler a b e f q 𝔓⁶⁶ W 𝔓⁷⁵
      αυτος ιησους A D Π al¹⁰ ff² l gat mm
      αυτος ο ιησους K al
      omit 251 c vg syrᶜ

4:9   Σαμαριτιδος ουσης ℵ A B C* L Tᵇ 33 𝔓⁶⁶ W
      ουσης γυναικος Σαμαριτιδος ς C³ Γ Δ Λ Π unc⁹ al pler it vg
      omit ουσης D arm
      γυναικος ουσης σαμαρειτιδος 𝔓⁷⁵

4:16   λεγει αυτη B C* 33 a 𝔓⁶⁶ 𝔓⁷⁵
      λεγει αυτη ῑς ℵ* A Π* 1 al pauc
      λεγει αυτη ο ῑς ς ℵᶜ C² D L Γ Δ Λ Π² unc⁹ al pler W

4:21 πιστευε μοι γυναι ℵ B C* L 253 259 g^scr b q sah eth syr^pal 𝔓^66 W 𝔓^75
γυναι πιστευε μοι D
γυναι πιστευσον μοι ς A C³ Γ Δ Λ Π unc⁹ al pler

4:30 εξηλθον A B Γ Δ Π* unc⁸ al¹⁰⁰ a^vid c g am fu for em ing tol arm 𝔓^75
εξηρχοντο L
εξηρχοντο ουν e
εξηλθον ουν ς ℵ Λ 1 69 al mu f l q vg^cle sah 𝔓^66 W
εξηλθον δε Π² cop
και εξηλθον C D b syr^c, p, h, pal eth

List III

DISTINCTIVE READINGS OF THE BETA TEXT-TYPE

A. IN JOHN 7:18-8:12

7:20 απεκριθη ο οχλος ℵ B L T X 33 sah cop W 𝔓^66 𝔓^75
7:33 χρονον μικρον this order ℵ B L T X 69 e q W 𝔓^66 𝔓^75
7:39 οι πιστευοντες] οι πιστευσαντες B L T 18^ev W 𝔓^66 (𝔓^75)
7:42 ουχι] ουχ B³ (B* ουκ) L T 𝔓^66 𝔓^75
7:42 ερχεται ο χριστος [this order] B L T 33 c vg syr^pal W 𝔓^75
7:44 επεβαλεν] εβαλεν B L T P^75
7:46 ελαλησεν ουτως ανθρωπος [this order] ℵ^c B L T X 3 33 W 𝔓^66 corr 𝔓^75
7:46 omit ως ουτος λαλει ο ανθρωπος ℵ^c B L T 225 229* for cop W 𝔓^66 corr 𝔓^75
7:49 επικαταρατοι] επαρατοι ℵ B T 1 33 W 𝔓^66 𝔓^75 (απαρατοι)
7:52 ερευνησον] εραυνησον ℵ B* T W 𝔓^75
7:52 εκ της Γαλιλαιας προφητης [this order] B L T X al pauc vg^cle eth
    𝔓^66* 𝔓^75 (+ ο)

B. IN JOHN 1:1-4:40 [1]

1:18 υιος] θεος ℵ B C* L 33 cop syr^p, h, mg eth^ro W*? 𝔓^66 𝔓^75
1:24 απεσταλμενοι without οι ℵ* A* B C* L cop 𝔓^66 𝔓^75
1:26 απεκριθη] απεκρινατο L T^b U 33 67 248 249
1:26 μεσος without δε ℵ B C* L T^b ff² arm 𝔓^66 𝔓^75
1:28 ο ιωαννης ℵ B C 44^ev W 𝔓^66 𝔓^75
1:30 υπερ ℵ* B C* W 𝔓^66 𝔓^75
1:35 ιπαννης without ο B L al pauc 𝔓^75
1:43 ηγαγεν without copula ℵ B L cop 𝔓^66 𝔓^75
1:46 υιον wthout τον ℵ B 33 𝔓^66 𝔓^75
1:47 ο φιλιππος B L 33 𝔓^66 corr (𝔓^75)
1:50 απεκριθη αυτω Ναθαναηλ without και λεγει B L 33 249 b W 𝔓^66 𝔓^75
2:6 λιθιναι υδριαι this order ℵ B L X 33 c vg 𝔓^66 𝔓^75
2:6 ιουδαιων κειμεναι this order ℵ^c B L X 33 eth W 𝔓^66 𝔓^75
2:15 τα κερματα B L T^b X 33 b q cop arm W 𝔓^66 𝔓^75
2:17 εμνησθησαν without copula ℵ B L T^b X cop 𝔓^66 𝔓^75
2:20 ωκοδομηθη] οικοδομηθη ℵ B* T^b 33 W 𝔓^66 𝔓^75
2:22 ω ειπεν] ον ειπεν ℵ B L T^b 𝔓^66 𝔓^75

---

[1] Ms. D lacks 1:16-3:26.

2:24   ιησους without ο B L 𝔓⁶⁶ 𝔓⁷⁵

3:13   omit ο ων εν τω ουρανω ℵ B L Tᵇ 33 cop eth W 𝔓⁶⁶ 𝔓⁷⁵

3:16   τον υιον without αυτου ℵ* B W 𝔓⁶⁶ 𝔓⁷⁵

3:24   ιωαννης without ο ℵ* B 47ᵉᵛ pˢᶜʳ

3:34   διδωσιν without addition ℵ B C* L Tᵇ 1 33 b e f l W 𝔓⁶⁶ 𝔓⁷⁵

4:5   τω ιωσηφ ℵ B 𝔓⁶⁶ 𝔓⁷⁵

4:15   ερχωμαι] διερχωμαι ℵ* B 𝔓⁶⁶ 𝔓⁷⁵

4:16   λεγει αυτη without ο ι̅ς̅ B C* 33 a 𝔓⁶⁶ 𝔓⁷⁵

4:17   ειπας] ειπες ℵ B*

4:21   πιστευε μοι γυναι ℵ B C* L sah W 𝔓⁶⁶ 𝔓⁷⁵

4:25   παντα] απαντα ℵ B C* 1 W 𝔓⁶⁶ 𝔓⁷⁵

CHAPTER THREE

METHOD IN ESTABLISHING THE NATURE OF TEXT-TYPES OF NEW TESTAMENT MANUSCRIPTS[1]

Recent finds of extensive early manuscript copies of New Testament books have made significant study of this topic possible. The Chester Beatty Papyri and the Bodmer Papyri—to mention no others—take us at least a full century closer to the originals than the previous oldest copies did. The Beatty Gospels ($\mathfrak{P}^{45}$), the Beatty Paul ($\mathfrak{P}^{46}$), the Beatty Apocalypse ($\mathfrak{P}^{47}$), the Bodmer John ($\mathfrak{P}^{66}$), and the Bodmer Luke-John ($\mathfrak{P}^{75}$), while not complete, are extensive enough to establish the text-type they represent for these parts of the New Testament.[2] In date they are close together— all but one from the late second to the early third century, which is significantly earlier than the great parchment codices, Sinaiticus and Vaticanus, from the fourth century.

These documents have revolutionized our understanding of the early history of the manuscript tradition of the Greek New Testament. Present day concepts of the great text-types differ markedly from those held before the publication and study of these documents. The words "Caesarean," "Alexandrian," "Western"—and even "Byzantine" or "Syrian"—have changed their significance as labels for groups of manuscripts in the last twenty-five years.

But before we turn to a study of these changes, a clarification of terminology is essential by way of preface.[3] By text-type I mean the largest identifiable group of related New Testament manuscripts. This is the category familiar under Westcott and Hort's labels as "Neutral," "Alexandrian," "Western," and "Syrian." It is easily distinguished from the "family," the smallest and most intimately

---

[1] Originally published as "The Origin of Texttypes of New Testament Manuscripts," in *Early Christian Origins*, ed. by Allen Wikgren (Chicago, 1961), pp. 128-38.

[2] Frederic G. Kenyon, *The Chester Beatty Biblical Papyri: Description and Texts of Twelve Manuscripts on Papyrus of the Greek Bible* (London, 1933); Victor Martin, *Papyrus Bodmer II* (Cologny-Genève, 1956, and Supplément, 1958); Victor Martin and Rodolphe Kasser, *Papyrus Bodmer XIV and Papyrus Bodmer XV* (Cologny-Genève, 1961).

[3] See the discussion of terminology in Chapter I (above, pp. 11 ff.).

related group—a group whose inter-relationships are so close that its stemma or family-tree can be established with exactness. While the members of a family come from a short span of time and a specific place, the members of a text-type scatter over the centuries and the continents. Nor does the contrast end there. A family is *one* group (e.g., section *a* of the Ferrar Group, fam. 13*a*), but a text-type may be composed of tribes (like the Ferrar Group as a whole) and of sub-text-types (like the two main divisions of the so-called "Caesarean" text-type).

Attribution of a specific manuscript or Church Father to one of these text-types has often been hastily and carelessly done. In Chapter II, I have argued that three steps are necessary for the accurate establishment of relationship: (1) establishing agreement where the evidence splits three or more ways; (2) establishing agreement in readings peculiar to the text-type; (3) establishing agreement in a large majority of the total number of readings where variation exists. The first of these steps is a labor-saving direction finder; it rapidly points to the area of major relationship. The second is the essential demonstration of a significant amount of agreement in the distinctive features of the type. The third is the confirmation of relationship by quantitative demonstration, without which other tests often mislead the student.

When we turn to statements in the handbooks on text-types we find them usually dated as to origin in the end of the third or in the fourth century, and their "making" is usually associated with specific Fathers: Lucian, Hesychius, and Origen. J. L. Hug made this connection in the early nineteenth century, and a dozen others have done likewise.[1] Leon Vaganay in his fine manual repeats this tradition, and usually treats the text-types as the work of an individual.[2] The one big exception is the "Western Text," which he does not attribute to an individual, and which he characterizes as universal, ancient, and lacking in homogeneity. Can this legitimately be called a text-type? One page 118, Vaganay inclines to

---

[1] J. L. Hug in *Einleitung in die Schriften des Neuen Testaments*, summarized by L. Vaganay, *Introduction to the Textual Criticism of the New Testament* (London, 1937), p. 162.

[2] *Ibid.*, p. 115, "The Egyptian or Hesychius' Recension" (4th Century), p. 112; "Lucian's Recension" (4th Century), p. 113; "The Palestinian or Pamphilus's Recension," possibly "the edition, more or less retouched, of Origen's Palestinian text."

differentiate the "Western Text" from the great Greek recensions and the later Vulgate versions.

But Vaganay, somewhat inconsistently, elsewhere (pp. 101 and 113) supposes "the first systematic revisions to have been made in the second century." He bases this directly on a statement by Origen:

> Nowadays, as is evident, there is a great diversity between the various manuscripts, either through the negligence of certain copyists, or the perverse audacity shown by some in correcting the text, or though the fault of those who, playing the part of correctors, lengthen or shorten it as they please (*In Matth.*, xv.14; *P.G.* xiii.1293).[1]

Vaganay elsewhere treats the making of the Hesychian or Alexandrian revision as a process, and he is led to this by his discussion of $\mathfrak{P}^{45}$ in John and Luke.[2]

It must be noted, however, that different scholars exempt a specific text-type from a date-of-origin. Hort's assumption (now held to be invalid) that the Neutral text-type is an unedited preservation of the original placed its origin at the beginning. The counter-blast of early twentieth-century champions of the Western text-type claimed it to be primitive and unedited, hence as "original" in date as Hort's claim for the Neutral. Everyone since the days of Hort has admitted the existence of a date-of-origin for his Syrian text, also called the Byzantine text-type or the *Koine*.

The first action required by the new evidence is to split the fourth-century date for the origin of the text-types in half and to push the halves apart.

All the text-types *began* earlier than we had assumed. The Bodmer John ($\mathfrak{P}^{66}$) and even more the Bodmer Luke-John ($\mathfrak{P}^{75}$) and essentially witnesses to the Beta text-type (Hort's "Neutral"), but are far from being in agreement with the consensus of the later witnesses to this text-type.

But the Bodmer John ($\mathfrak{P}^{66}$) is also a witness to the early existence of many of the readings found in the Alpha text-type (Hort's "Syrian"). Strangely enough (according to our previous ideas), the contemporary corrections in that papyrus frequently change an Alpha-type of reading to a Beta-type of reading (Hort's "Neutral"). This indicates that at this early period readings of both kinds were

---

[1] *Ibid.*, p. 101.
[2] *Ibid.*, p. 119.

known, and the Beta-type were supplanting the Alpha-type—at
least as far as this witness is concerned.

These same points had been noted by Günther Zuntz in his
magnificent study of the text of the Epistles. He located $\mathfrak{P}^{46}$ with
B 1739 sah boh Clem Orig as "proto-Alexandrian." [1]

> The Alexandrian work in the text of the Scriptures (in the
> Epistles) was a long process rather than a single act. Its beginnings
> were inconspicuous, and roughly 150 years passed before it culmina-
> ted in the "Euthalian" edition. Prior to this final achievement, the
> Alexandrian correctors strove, in ever repeated efforts, to keep the
> text current in their sphere free from the many faults that had in-
> fected it in the previous period and which tended to crop up again
> even after they had been obelized. These labours must time and
> again have been checked by persecutions and the confiscation of
> Christian books, and counteracted by the continuing currency of
> manuscripts of the older type. Nonetheless they resulted in the
> emergence of a type of text (as distinct from a definite edition)
> which served as a norm for the correctors in provincial Egyptian
> scriptoria. The final result was the survival of a text far superior
> to that of the second century, even though the revisers, being
> fallible humans, rejected some of its correct readings and introduced
> some faults of their own.

He would put $\mathfrak{P}^{46}$ nearer the beginning than the end of this process.
He locates the publication of the Pauline Corpus in Alexandria
about A.D. 100; and argues cogently that "in the latter half of the
second century the Alexandrian bishopric possessed a scriptorium,
which by its output set the standard for the Alexandrian type of
Biblical manuscript." [2]

Zuntz also found $\mathfrak{P}^{46}$ a witness for the existence of Byzantine (our
Alpha type) readings in the second century. His statement deserves
quotation:

> A number of Byzantine readings, most of them genuine, which
> previously were discarded as "late', are anticipated by $\mathfrak{P}^{46}$.[3] Our
> inquiry has confirmed what was anyhow probable enough: the
> Byzantines did not hit upon these readings by conjecture or in-
> dependent error. They reproduced an older tradition. The existence
> of this tradition was in several cases borne out by some versions
> or patristic quotations; but where such evidence is not forthcoming,

---

[1] Günther Zuntz, *The Text of the Epistles* (Oxford, 1953), p. 156.

[2] *Ibid.*, pp. 271-3.

[3] The same is true of the sister-manuscript $\mathfrak{P}^{45}$; see, for example, Matt.
26:7 (*Chronique d'Égypte*, XXVI [1951], 200) and Acts 17:13. [True also
of $\mathfrak{P}^{66}$].

the inference proved no less certain. How then—so one is tempted to go on asking—where no Chester Beatty papyrus happens to vouch for the early existence of a Byzantine reading? Are all Byzantine readings ancient? In the cognate case of the Homeric tradition G. Pasquali [1] answers the same question in the affirmative; and, indeed, it seems to me unlikely that the Byzantine editors ever altered the text without manuscript evidence. They left so many hopelessly difficult places unassailed! Their method, I submit, was selection rather than conjecture.[2]

Thus $\mathfrak{P}^{46}$ argues for the Beta text-type as a process, and argues further for an early date for the beginning of that process and for the antiquity of Byzantine readings—though not necessarily for their originality.

One of the Beatty papyri ($\mathfrak{P}^{45}$) in the Gospel of Mark has had the same effect on the Caesarean text-type which had been established by the work of Streeter and of Lake, Blake, and New.[3] The discerning eye of Ayuso saw that $\mathfrak{P}^{45}$ split the Caesarean witnesses into two groups: $\mathfrak{P}^{45}$ fam 1 28 W Orig; and Θ fam 13 565 700.[4] Here also the papyrus witness established a proto-group. Here also it went with "weaker" members against the "leaders" of the type—a fact which Zuntz noted of some of the readings of $\mathfrak{P}^{46}$ within the Alexandrian group. Here also some of the readings of $\mathfrak{P}^{45}$ anticipated Alpha-type readings found in the Textus Receptus.

The Beatty papyrus of the Apocalypse ($\mathfrak{P}^{47}$) had an equally important influence on the writing of the history of the manuscript tradition of that book. The writing of that history has been the monumental work of Josef Schmid. This is now available in a series of monographs and volumes which are indispensable for any student of this subject.[5] He establishes four text-types of the Apocalypse.

---

[1] *Storia del tradizione* (1934), p. 241.

[2] *Op. cit.*, p. 55.

[3] Burnett Hillman Streeter, *The Four Gospels: A Study of Origins* (New York, 1924), Chap. IV.

[4] T. Ayuso in an article in *Biblica*, XVI (1935), 369-415; this grouping was accepted by the Lakes (in *Studies and Documents*, V [1937], 4, n. 5; and in *Revue Biblique*, XLVIII [1939], 497-505), and this revision of Caesarean grouping is reviewed by Metzger in *Journal of Biblical Literature*, LXIV (1945), 457-89; LXVI (1947), 406-7.

[5] *Der Apokalypsetext des Arethas von Kaisareia und einiger anderer jüngerer Gruppen* (Athens, 1936); "Untersuchungen zur Geschichte des griechischen Apokalypsetextes. Der *K*-Text," *Biblica*, XVII (1936), 11-44, 167-201, 273-293, 429-460; *Studien zur Geschichte des griechischen Apokalypse-Textes*, 1. Teil: *Der Apokalypse-Kommentar des Andreas von Kaisareia, Text* (Munich, 1955); *Einleitung* (Munich, 1956); 2. Teil: *Die alten Stämme* (Munich, 1955).

Before his study, previous scholars had made one group of the old uncials A, C, ℵ. Schmid is able with the help of 𝔓⁴⁷ to split these into two types: A and C; 𝔓⁴⁷ and ℵ. The other two types are the Andreas type and the *Koine* (Alpha or Byzantine). Schmid demonstrates the superiority of the AC type to all others, the superiority of 𝔓⁴⁷ ℵ to the largely "corrected" types, Andreas and *K*.

Josef Schmid in his final volume [1] is reconstructing the history of the manuscript tradition. This final structure stands on the foundation of his earlier careful studies of groupings of manuscripts within the major groups; and also—importantly—on his study of the Greek idiom of the Apocalypse. It is not extravagant to say that in comprehensiveness and careful accuracy he has surpassed all previous studies of the Greek manuscript tradition of any part of the New Testament, including the fine work of Ropes on Acts, of the Lakes and their associates on Mark, and of von Soden on the *pericope adulterae*. He has related existing codices to each other in families, occasionally in tribes, and in text-types. His work carries our knowledge beyond the stage to which the labors of Hoskier carried it, and it is the library to which the student of any newly discovered manuscript of the Apocalypse must turn for guidance. It may be that Schmid was influenced toward caution by Hoskier's failure; at any rate, he leaves the last chapter unwritten.

His summary of results [2] starts off very crisply in numbered paragraphs, which stay brief through number 4.

> In brief, the established results are now put together. In part they consist of clear and certain knowledge; in part they involve problems for which a definite solution is not possible.
>
> 1. The entire Greek tradition of the Apocalypse-Text divides into four stems, namely AC, 𝔓⁴⁷ ℵ, Aν, and *K*.
> 2. Aν and *K* are two sharply distinct recensions. Their peculiar readings consist for the most part of corrections.
> 3. Aν and *K* are not completely independent of each other (as Bousset and von Soden insisted). They have a common stem which though not extensive is clearly recognizable in a number of common corrections. In several places they contain the original Text against A(C) (𝔓⁴⁷)ℵ. It follows from this that they are not merely later forms of the 'older' Text extant in AC and 𝔓⁴⁷ℵ.

---

[1] *Studien zur Geschichte des griechischen Apokalypse-Textes*, 2. Teil: *Die alten Stämme*.

[2] *Ibid.*, pp. 146-51.

4. The 'older' Text divides again into two Text forms, AC and
𝔓⁴⁷ℵ, which are to be clearly distinguished. Of these, 𝔓⁴⁷ℵ
contains a not insignificant number of corrections, while these
are almost entirely lacking in the archetype of AC. In one
single passage 𝔓⁴⁷ℵ alone have the original Text (9:20, οὐδέ).[1]

But paragraph 5 is as long as the first four together. It begins
with the statement that the AC text-type (which includes Oecume-
nius and the Vulgate) outranks all others in the value of its evidence,
but it takes a long paragraph to state that AC is not identical with
the Ur-text.

His sixth conclusion is equally lengthy. It argues that since
"each of the text-types has preserved the Ur-text in at least some
passages, . . . the text-types which stand farthest from the original
are not to be understood as later, revised forms of their elders in the
textual tradition."

In the seventh place, Schmid, recognizing the existence of an
interconnection between all text-types and their constituent parts,
concludes "that it is not possible to establish the present connections
of the major text-types of the Greek Apocalypse Text-tradition with
complete accuracy, and to arrange them all in a *Stemma*." All the
text-types, Schmid concludes, are older than the mss. A and C and
reach back at least into the fourth century.

His final (eighth) point reaffirms the relative value of the
witnesses in descending order A, C, 𝔓⁴⁷, ℵ.

Schmid is weak where Zuntz is strong: in the clear recognition
of the implication of the data for the interrelationship of the major
text-types. Schmid overrates agreement in the original reading as
evidence for common lineage. He underrates the possibility of
coincidental agreement in error; e.g. 13:7 where in AC, 𝔓⁴⁷, Aν an
entire sentence has fallen out as the result of homoeoteleuton. The
presence of the sentence in ℵ and *K* shows no more than that the
error has not occurred there. As a matter of fact, this omission is
not universal in Aν (cf. Schmid's edition of the Andreas Commentary
[p. 139, apparatus to line 1] which cites three Andreas families and
two other Andreas mss. against the omission), nor is it universal
in *K*.

But the major mistake is made in thinking of the "old text-types"
as frozen blocks, even after admitting that no one manuscript is a
perfect witness to any text-type. *If* no one manuscript is a perfect

---

[1] *Ibid.*, pp. 146-7.

witness to any type, then all witnesses are mixed in ancestry (or individually corrupted, and thus parents of mixture). The mixture was, we are certain, partial.[1] It did not remove all original readings; it did not remove all the distinctive readings of the text-type to which the codex belonged. Beyond this we now recognize that the text-types developed, they grew, they are a process starting in the second century and proceeding by selection from available readings, from available "good, old mss.," and proceeding also into new paths under local standards of excellence in syntax and in doctrine.

Quae cum ita sint, agreement of the late text-type *K* with an early text-type or manuscript in the original reading is due to the survival of that original reading in some one of the various channels that make up the complex ancestry of *K*. Agreements of this kind do *not* move *K* as an entity (as a text-type) back to the date of the earlier text-type or manuscript. Even if—and it is too big an if— every reading found in *K* existed somewhere in the second century, *K* did not exist in the second century. If the term "text-type" means anything, it means the entire complex of readings in its total pattern which we refer to as "the Alpha text-type" or "the Byzantine text" or "the *K* text-type." This did not exist as the dominant element in any manuscript in the second century. It does exist in the ninth century and later. The clinching evidence for the date of a text-type is a datable manuscript *belonging* to it, or a Church Father who uses it as Cyprian used the "Western" type found in the Old Latin witness *k*.

Schmid's first five conclusions are solidly established, and the ranking of the four oldest witnesses in his eighth seems equally sound. But the claim in number 6 that the later text-types are not revised forms of their elders seems doubtful. All that has been proved is that they are not *entirely* derived from their elders. If, however, there stands "at the beginning of the text a text handled by humble piety and therefore a text with little unity," all text-types must derive from this and/or from each other plus a modicum of "new" editorial contribution. What needs clarification in Schmid's sixth conclusion is not only the meaning of "later" with reference to a text-type, but also the meaning of a "revised form" of an older text-type. Revision almost universally proceeded on a documentary basis. Manuscripts from outside the text-type were used to revise it.

---

[1] *Ibid.*; Schmid gives evidence for this again and again in the course of his work.

This opened a door through which Ur-text readings could be added just as surely as it opened the door to alien corrections and corruptions.[1] This challenges also his seventh conclusion that a stemma of text-types cannot be made. I am confident that he has supplied the data that makes this possible—at least in large outlines.

To focus the material surveyed here into sharp statement as a basis for criticism and further study is the purpose of the following propositions:

1. *A text-type is a process, not the work of one hand.*

Scholars have been forced to the conclusion that a text-type is a process not from the study of the loosely-connected "Western" witnesses but from the study of the Beta text-type—Hort's "Neutral." This was implicit in Hort's own identification of his "Alexandrian" text, intimately related to his Neutral. Vaganay's argument for process came from his study of the relationship of $\mathfrak{P}^{45}$ to the Beta text-type in Luke and John. Zuntz's argument has been quoted above (pp. 48-49). Schmid sharply differentiates Aν and *K* from AC and $\mathfrak{P}^{47}$ א, and the differentiation includes the recognition of process as more extensive in AC and $\mathfrak{P}^{47}$ א than in the other two types. My own earlier study of the Beta text-type in Mark drove me to the recognition of "process" in the formation of a text-type.[2]

2. *The vulgate versions were the work of one hand and were editions as well as translations.*

3. *The Greek vulgate—the Byzantine or Alpha text-type—had in its origin no such single focus as the Latin had in Jerome. Like Jerome's Vulgate it had several revised editions.*

4. *Origen did not make an edition (i.e., create a text-type) of the Greek New Testament.*

5. *The so-called Western text or Delta text-type is the uncontrolled, popular text of the second century. It has no unity and should not be referred to as the "Western text."*

(*a*) Even Zuntz (with whom I find it hard to differ) once refers to the text of the New Testament in the second century as if it were a

---

[1] But before Schmid's argument for a fourth-century date for Aν is rejected, the evidence (which Schmid refers to) of the agreement of א^a (the fourth century corrector of Sinaiticus) with Aν must be explained (Schmid, *op. cit.*, p. 129). Schmid's argument here rests on his acceptance of the conclusions drawn by Bousset (*Studien*, pp. 42-4). Bousset's work should be reviewed in the light of current understanding of the history of text-types.

[2] See Chapter V (below, pp. 63-83).

unity: "The final result was the survival of a text far superior to that of the second century. . ." (quoted above, p. 48). Schmid did not work out the inter-relations of his four types except that he grouped the first two (AC and $\mathfrak{P}^{47}$ ℵ) as closer to each other than they were to the last two (Aν and K), and the last two as closer to each other than they were to the first two. (*b*) Schmid's work is limited to the Greek tradition, which does not contain the equivalent of codex Bezae. Without D and the versions in the Gospel of John, where would we find this text-type(s) ? (*c*) If the answer is "the Fathers," Schmid's findings still seem to exclude "Western" types. Origen's text is generally identical with $\mathfrak{P}^{47}$ ℵ, Hippolytus of Rome with AC Oec. Irenaeus seems not very different from AC Oec; and Clement of Alexandria, Eusebius, Methodius have few, inconclusive quotes (pp. 156-171). (*d*) Did the Apocalypse enjoy widespread popular usage in the second century ?

Is it far-fetched to regard his type $\mathfrak{P}^{47}$ ℵ as a stage on the way from the second-century types to the "better" Beta text-type of AC Oec ? As such a stage $\mathfrak{P}^{47}$ ℵ Orig would contain a number of readings which earlier nomenclature would have labelled as "Western," meaning early non-Neutral. Schmid, by his separation of $\mathfrak{P}^{47}$ℵ Orig from the "Neutral" AC Oec, is saying the same thing. He will not call them "Western" in a geographical sense because of the absence of Latin support. But Western has long since ceased to be a geographical term.

6. *The Beta text-type (Hort's "Neutral") is a "made" text, probably Alexandrian in origin, produced in part by the selection of relatively "good old mss." but more importantly by the philological editorial know-how of Alexandrians.* Zuntz's reconstruction of this process is superb.

7. *The so-called Caesarean text-type is not Caesarean and is at least two types, the earlier of which is a proto-type, an early stage in the process which produced the mature Beta and Delta text-types.*

8. *It follows from number 1, as also from the textual data, that the earliest witness to a text-type is never the archetype of the text-type.*

Thus Schmid tells us that P is not the archetype of Aν, and Q even less the archetype of K.[1] He shows that $\mathfrak{P}^{47}$ and ℵ, though earlier than A and C, are not as good witnesses as the later manuscripts. The Lakes identified Θ, 700, and 565 as the strongest Caesarean

---

[1] *Op. cit.*, pp. 64-66.

witnesses in Mark, but $\mathfrak{P}^{45}$ is the earliest and agrees with the weaker witnesses. A in the Gospels is the earliest member of the Alpha text-type, but it does not fit into any of the major editions of that type, not even Family Π, as Silva Lake has shown. $\mathfrak{P}^{66}$ and $\mathfrak{P}^{75}$ can be claimed for the Beta text-type in John but neither is the center of the group. Zuntz put $\mathfrak{P}^{46}$ with 1739 and B as, at times, a proto-Beta text-type in the Epistles. His inclusion of B is, in my judgment, an error. *Some* of the readings of B are derived from the proto-Beta text-type of which $\mathfrak{P}^{46}$ is a member, but we cannot relocate an entire manuscript on the basis of a small minority of its readings.

9. *The textual history of the New Testament differs from corpus to corpus, and even from book to book; therefore the witnesses have to be re-grouped in each new section.*

Schmid shows this in striking fashion for the Apocalypse vis-à-vis the Praxapostolos:

> Bei der über 80 Hss umfassenden *K*-Gruppe lässt sich feststellen, dass Schwester-Hss im Apk-Text dies fast niemals auch im Praxapostolos sind, und dass umgekehrt Schwester-Hss im Praxapostolos fast nie in der Apk unmittelbare Schwestern sind.

He then gives more than half-a-dozen examples.[1]

10. *As in dating documents, so in dating text-types what is needed is a datable witness to the type, not only to some of its readings, for the overwhelming majority of readings were created before the year 200. But very few, if any, text-types were established by that time.*

The agreement of Origen with $\mathfrak{P}^{47}$ in the Apocalypse and with $\mathfrak{P}^{45}$ in Mark exhorts us to pay more attention to date in interpreting the history of the tradition. Therefore, in writing the history of the text-types we should begin with the earliest witnesses, as Zuntz did in his study of the Epistles.

---

[1] *Op. cit.*, pp. 37-38. See my examples of alternations of type even within one manuscript (above, pp. 22-23).

CHAPTER FOUR

METHOD IN ESTABLISHING QUANTITATIVE RELATIONSHIPS BETWEEN TEXT-TYPES OF NEW TESTAMENT MANUSCRIPTS [1]

(WITH ERNEST W. TUNE)

The study of manuscript relationships in the last fifty years has made extensive use of quantitative data. The use of these data has usually taken the form of "the total number of agreements in variations from Stephanus," or "the percentage of agreements in the total variations from Stephanus." The amount of difference established in either of these areas has often been statistically insignificant—either because of the small amount of difference, or because of the incompleteness of the statistics. Moreover, these studies have frequently been naïve in the determination of the variants which are to be counted in these totals or percentages.

This chapter argues that refinement in method is needed. Sound method requires (*a*) that in any area of text which is sampled the total amount of variation be taken into account—not just the variants from some text used as a "norm"; [2] (*b*) that the gross amount of agreement and difference in the relationships of manuscripts must be large enough to be significant; (*c*) that all variants must be classified as either genetically significant or not.

The need for such refinement in method has been obvious in certain instances. Some scholars have presented statistics of difference that assumed importance for very small amounts. [3] On the other hand, there has been an increasing awareness of the need for taking total variation into account and at the same time exercising discrimination in regard to what is counted. Harold Murphy [4]

---

[1] Originally published as "The Quantitative Relationships Between MS Text-Types," in *Biblical and Patristic Studies in Memory of Robert Pierce Casey*, ed. by J. N. Birdsall and R. W. Thomson (Freiburg im Breisgau, 1963), pp. 25-32.

[2] See Chapter II, (pp. 31 ff. above).

[3] D. W. Riddle, *The Rockefeller McCormick New Testament*, II: *The Text* (Chicago, 1932), pp. 126 ff.; Edgar Goodspeed, *The Newberry Gospels* (Chicago, 1902), pp. 26-28.

[4] Harold S. Murphy, "Eusebius' NT Text in the *Demonstratio Evangelica*," *Journal of Biblical Literature*, LXXIII (1954), 167.

recognized clearly the former of these needs, and Bruce Metzger [1] has urged discrimination before tabulation.

In computing the quantitative relationship between manuscripts we have decided to use only those places in the text where the manuscripts involved occur in text-type groupings; i.e., in Double, Triple, or Quadruple Readings. The steps which lead to this decision are as follows.

1. A broad cross-section of manuscripts must be used which will include representatives of all text-types. We are not completely satisfied with the comprehensiveness of our list, but it is in our judgment adequate for a sample demonstration.[2]

2. The section of text used should be large enough to give several hundred places of variation—the more the better. We have used the 11th chapter of the Gospel of John.

3. In any given place of variation by one manuscript from any other manuscript, all the varieties of readings at that place should be listed using all the manuscripts in the set of representative manuscripts and recording them with the particular variant which they support.

4. In order not to blur the picture of relationships we then eliminated readings which occur *commonly* in manuscripts as the result of scribal error or habit, even if supported by more than one manuscript, since such agreement was probable as coincidence, either in common scribal error, in spelling habits, or the like. This left us with 205 places where our manuscripts support divergent readings.

5. For tabulation purposes we then eliminated those places where the vast majority of manuscripts agree *and each of the few disagreeing manuscripts has a unique reading*.

In 86 places all but one manuscript agree.[3] This means that in 40 per cent of the places, the existence of manuscript variation is due to the presence of a unique reading in a single manuscript.

---

[1] See "The Caesarean Text of the Gospels," *Journal of Biblical Literature*, LXIV (1945), 489.

[2] Versions are omitted deliberately. The statistical problems involved in citing them on the same base as the Greek we leave for more skilled investigators. Their relationship can be established only by the use of distinctive text-type readings, and the use of judgment based on special knowledge concerning agreements in non-distinctive readings.

[3] For this count wherever the work of a corrector was encountered each hand was treated as if a separate manuscript. This occurred eight times.

In 14 more places all but two manuscripts agree and these two each have a unique reading.

In 5 more places all but three manuscripts agree and these three each have a unique reading.

In a total of 105 places, the existence of variation is due to unique readings in one, two, or three manuscripts.

These readings are particularly meaningless for this study, because

(1) They tell us nothing about manuscript relationship, since they leave a manuscript unrelated to others.

(2) They inflate the quantitative relationship of the other manuscripts by making it *appear* that the others agree at a place with real differences, when this is not the case. This results in a distortion of the evidence.

(3) Unless at least one other manuscript can be found to agree, these readings have a high probability of being no more than scribal error.[1]

6. We use for tabulation the remainder—those places where all manuscripts divide into groups of manuscripts which support two or more variant readings, with at least two supporting each variant.[2] These total 100 places.

In a total of 93 places, we found Double Readings. In 29 of these, there was one other unique reading. In 10 more, there were two other unique readings.

In a total of 6 places, we found Triple Readings. In 3 of these, there was one (or more) other unique reading.

In only 1 place did we find a Quadruple Reading.

7. Using then these places where group (text-type) division occurs, the number of times any certain manuscript reads with any other manuscript out of a given number of places can now be tabulated and converted into percentages. All manuscripts with singular readings are treated as if they had lacunae at these places. (Extrapolation is used to obtain a corrected agreement between any manuscripts with lacunae). Also, for the case of a corrected reading

---

[1] In the case of unique firsthand readings corrected to agree with all the others, it is clear that we are observing the correction of scribal error.

[2] In addition to these group readings, one or more manuscripts may have a singular reading. Care has been exercised in grouping the manuscripts especially for readings which, though not identical, yet are so definitely related that it might be misleading to treat them as unique readings.

which supports a group, if the first-hand is a singular reading, the corrected reading is recorded as if it were the first-hand reading— otherwise both the first-hand and the corrected reading are recorded as if different manuscripts.

8. If the above percentages of agreement between all the manuscripts in our set are computed, it is then possible to obtain a reasonably accurate picture of the quantitative difference between individual manuscripts and also of the quantitative difference of text-type groupings.

In order to indicate the relevance of these procedures, we present in Table I (see p. 60) statistics of agreement based on tabulations *before* these eliminations were made.

In Table II (see p. 60) statistics of agreement based on Double, Triple, or Quadruple Agreements are presented. Compare this with results based on raw data in Table I.

Various groups or text-types clearly appear in Table II. The Beta text-type consists of $\mathfrak{P}^{75}$ B W $\aleph$, with Ψ skirting the bottom fringes of the group. This group is separated from its nearest neighbors by about a 10 per cent gap. The group agrees within itself in a range of 70± per cent to 92 per cent in the case of $\mathfrak{P}^{75}$ and B.

The Alpha text-type consists of ς Ω C^{R} A Ψ, with 565 skirting the bottom of the group. This group also is separated from its nearest neighbors by about a 10 per cent gap. The group agrees within itself in a range of 70± per cent to 93 per cent in the case of Ω and ς.

The Delta text-type consists of D $\mathfrak{P}^{45}$ and $\mathfrak{P}^{66}$. But the range of agreement is only from 58 per cent to 68 per cent. And for $\mathfrak{P}^{66}$ three manuscripts (B, W, Ψ) intrude between D and $\mathfrak{P}^{45}$. These facts leave a serious question whether or not this is a text-type.

Of the Gamma text-type (so-called) only Θ and 565 are included in our set. Manuscript Θ has a narrow range of agreement. It agrees with all others except D from about 52 per cent to 62 per cent! Thus Θ may be said to contain the lowest common denominator of Alpha and Beta. But 565 agrees more closely with all of the Alpha text-type than with Θ, and should probably be identified here as a weak member of the Alpha text-type group.

This suggests that the quantitative definition of a text-type is a group of manuscripts that agree more than 70 per cent of the time and is separated by a gap of about 10 per cent from its neighbors. Both these elements seem to us to be significant.

TABLE I

This table gives the percentage of agreements between MSS in John 11 at 205 places of variation which include singulars (readings attested by only one MS).

	ς	𝔓45	𝔓66	𝔓66c	𝔓75	ℵ	ℵc	A	Ac	B	D	W	Wc	Θ	Ψ	Ω	CR	565
ς		68	64	67	74	73	78	83	82	75	51	73	74	70	85	95	83	80
𝔓45	68		65	66	64	62	63	65	65	61	55	60	61	60	62	66	66	63
𝔓66	64	65			66	63	67	66	66	69	50	66	66	58	72	65	62	62
𝔓66c	67	66			69	66	70	69	69	73	52	69	69	60	74	68	65	65
𝔓75	74	64	66	69		81	82	72	72	92	49	78	80	67	80	73	66	72
ℵ	73	62	63	66	81			73	72	79	46	78	79	63	76	73	67	71
ℵc	78	63	67	70	82			77	76	83	50	83	84	66	82	78	72	73
A	83	65	66	69	72	73	77			73	49	72	73	65	83	83	79	76
Ac	82	65	66	69	72	72	76			73	50	71	73	65	82	82	78	76
B	75	61	69	73	92	79	83	73	73		53	77	78	65	81	74	67	71
D	51	55	50	52	49	46	50	49	50	53		48	48	41	52	50	47	47
W	73	60	66	69	78	78	83	72	71	77	48			63	79	71	69	70
Wc	74	61	66	69	80	79	84	73	73	78	48			65	81	73	70	71
Θ	70	60	58	60	67	63	66	65	65	65	41	63	65		68	68	63	71
Ψ	85	62	72	74	80	76	82	83	82	81	52	79	81	68		84	78	79
Ω	95	66	65	68	73	73	78	83	82	74	50	71	73	68	84		80	80
CR	83	66	62	65	66	67	72	79	78	67	47	69	70	63	78	80		74
565	80	63	62	65	72	71	73	76	76	71	47	70	71	71	79	80	74	

TABLE II

This table gives the percentage of agreements between MSS in John 11 at 100 places of variation which exclude singulars (readings attested by only one MS).

	ς	𝔓45	𝔓66	𝔓66c	𝔓75	ℵ	ℵc	A	Ac	B	D	W	Wc	Θ	Ψ	Ω	CR	565
ς		56	47	46	52	58	61	76	74	52	42	57	58	63	73	93	78	65
𝔓45	56		69	67	48	51	51	59	57	44	68	52	52	52	48	54	64	44
𝔓66	47	69			57	58	58	59	58	60	58	62	63	55	66	51	55	45
𝔓66c	46	67			57	57	57	58	57	61	59	60	61	52	63	50	52	43
𝔓75	52	48	57	57		77	73	57	56	92	43	72	73	60	65	52	47	49
ℵ	58	51	58	57	77			65	63	75	40	82	83	56	67	60	58	51
ℵc	61	51	58	57	73			66	64	74	42	85	86	58	72	63	61	53
A	76	59	59	58	57	65	66			57	45	64	65	60	76	77	78	64
Ac	74	57	58	57	56	63	64			57	47	62	63	58	74	75	76	62
B	52	44	60	61	92	75	74	57	57		49	69	70	54	67	53	48	50
D	42	68	58	59	43	40	42	45	47	49		44	43	37	46	44	44	30
W	57	52	62	60	72	82	85	64	62	69	44			57	73	56	62	55
Wc	58	52	63	61	73	83	86	65	63	70	43			58	74	57	63	57
Θ	63	52	55	52	60	56	58	60	58	54	37	57	58		59	60	56	61
Ψ	73	48	66	63	65	67	72	76	74	67	46	73	74	59		74	71	63
Ω	93	54	51	50	52	60	63	77	75	53	44	56	57	60	74		75	67
CR	78	64	55	52	47	58	61	78	76	48	44	62	63	56	71	75		69
565	65	44	45	43	49	51	53	64	62	50	30	55	57	61	63	67	69	

The adjoining tables provide the data on which the preceding generalizations are based. Note that membership in a group is established by taking *in succession* each possible member of the group as the base of comparison. Thus if we begin with Θ as the base, ς and 565 appear as the closest relatives; but when we turn to 565 as the base, manuscripts C^R Ω ς A and Ψ are all closer kin to 565 than Θ is. When we turn to ς, Ω is incomparably closer than all others; and manuscripts C^R A Ψ and 565 are closer than Θ. Q.E.D., Θ does *not* form a group with ς and 565 *as the single comparison with Θ as a base might suggest.* The statistical Tables were prepared before the publication of *Papyrus Bodmer II, Supplément: Évangile de Jean, Chap. 14-21*, Nouvelle édition augmentée et corrigée avec reproduction photographique complète du manuscrit (chap. 1-21) (Cologny-Genève, 1962). A collation of the photographs with the original edition in chap. 11 of John increased the number of corrections from first-hand readings, increased the number of singular readings, and also the number of obvious errors by the first hand.

Sources

The manuscript evidence for this study was obtained from facsimiles in the case of: 𝔓^45 𝔓^75 ℵ A B D W Θ Ψ 565.

A transcription, collation, or printed edition was used for the remainder:

ς: — The *Textus Receptus* as printed by Stephanus in his third edition of 1550.

𝔓^66: — V. Martin, ed., *Papyrus Bodmer II, Évangile de Jean, chap. 1-14* (Cologny-Genève, 1956).

Ω: — Kirsopp Lake and Silva New, eds., *Six Collations of New Testament Manuscripts* (Cambridge, Mass., 1932) (Mary W. Winslow collated codex Ω, pp. 1-25).

C^R: — Ian Moir, ed., *Codex Climaci Rescriptus* (Cambridge, 1956).

APPENDIX: THE WORK OF CORRECTORS

A total of 56 corrections is noted for the text of John 11 in our group of manuscripts (here 𝔓^66 is taken from the facsimile edition): 𝔓^45 (1) 𝔓^66 (29) 𝔓^75 (0) ℵ (15) A (3) B (2) D (1) W (3) Θ (2) Ψ (0) Ω (0) C^R (0) 565 (0). Only 𝔓^66 and ℵ would seem to have a number large enough to be significant in percentage relationships with other manuscripts.

But the value of these corrections for establishing relationships among manuscripts becomes even less after individual examination. *Seventy per cent* of these corrections seem to be merely the removal of scribal errors which occurred in producing the manuscript; that is, they are the correction of *singular* readings. For example, 23 of the corrections in $\mathfrak{P}^{66}$ are corrections from a singular reading. When the correction from these singular readings to a group reading is ignored the figures become:

$\mathfrak{P}^{45}$ (0) $\mathfrak{P}^{66}$ (6) $\mathfrak{P}^{75}$ (0) ℵ (5) A (2) B (1) D (0) W (1) Θ (0) Ψ (0) Ω (0) C^R (0) 565 (0), or a total of 12 corrections when the correction involves a change from one group-reading to another group-reading. (No doubt some of these are coincidences, which would reduce the number even further).

It is interesting to note that the bulk of singular readings occur in $\mathfrak{P}^{66}$ and ℵ (careless scribes?). $\mathfrak{P}^{66}$ has two uncorrected singular readings in 11:35 and 11:38 that justify calling the scribe careless. The largest single cause of the singulars in our set of readings is the omission or the contraction of words (about 65 per cent of the instances). In order, the other causes are: spelling or inflectional differences, substitution of other words, and addition of other words (seldom). There is no change of word-order involved in these corrections.

CHAPTER FIVE

GENEALOGICAL METHOD: ITS ACHIEVEMENTS AND ITS LIMITATIONS[1]

Since Westcott and Hort, the genealogical method has been the canonical method for restoring the original text of the books of the New Testament. It dominates the handbooks. Sir Frederic Kenyon, C. R. Gregory, Alexander Souter, and A. T. Robertson are a few of the many who declare its excellence.[2] Von Soden used it as Hort had used it, and Streeter's theory of local texts is built upon it.

Hort's exposition of method gives the palm to the genealogical method. He prefers it in both its branches (genealogical study of manuscripts and genealogical study of groups of manuscripts) to the study of internal evidence—whether of documents or of readings. He claims that it adds a new set of data to the evidence of readings or of single manuscripts and that it is, therefore, more objective and dependable.

Yet genealogical method as defined by Westcott and Hort was not applied by them or by any of their followers to the manuscripts of the New Testament. Moreover, sixty years of study since Westcott and Hort indicate that it is doubtful if it can be applied to New Testament manuscripts in such a way as to advance our knowledge of the original text of the New Testament.

The classic definition of genealogical method is that given by Westcott and Hort:

> The proper method of Genealogy consists . . . in the more or less complete recovery of the texts of successive ancestors by analysis

---

[1] Originally published in *Journal of Biblical Literature*, LXVI (1947), 109-133.

[2] Caspar René Gregory, *The Canon and Text of the New Testament* (New York, 1907); Frederic G. Kenyon, *Handbook to the Textual Criticism of the New Testament*, 2nd ed. (London, 1912; reprinted 1926); Frederic G. Kenyon, *Our Bible and the Ancient Manuscripts*, 4th ed. (New York, 1940); Kirsopp Lake, *The Text of the New Testament*, 6th ed., revised by Silva New (London, 1928); Archibald Thomas Robertson, *An Introduction to the Textual Criticism of the New Testament* (New York, 1925); Alexander Souter, *The Text and Canon of the New Testament* (New York, 1913); Benjamin B. Warfield, *An Introduction to the Textual Criticism of the New Testament* (London, 1886).

and comparison of the varying texts of their respective descendants, each ancestral text so recovered being in its turn used, in conjunction with other similar texts, for the recovery of the text of a yet earlier common ancestor.[1]

This definition implies that the student of New Testament manuscript history will carry on his work by constructing a family tree, or stemma, of the New Testament manuscripts, beginning with the mass of late codices and working back through successive generations of ancestors to the original text. That this is actually what Westcott and Hort meant when they spoke of "the proper method of genealogy" is shown by the diagrams which they employed as illustrations.

Note first their example of simple or divergent genealogy:[2]

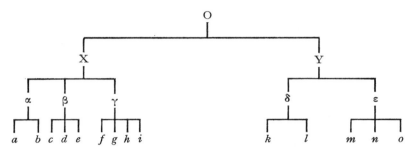

The lower case English letters represent extant manuscripts; all other symbols indicate reconstructions. It should be noted that this pedigree is analogous to the family tree of a human family in which descent is traced *through males alone*.

Westcott and Hort wrote with two things constantly in mind: the Textus Receptus and the codex Vaticanus. But they did not hold them in mind with that passive objectivity which romanticists ascribe to the scientific mind. That is to say, they did not hold them in mind as a chemist might hold two elements constantly in the focus of his attention. The sound analogy is that of a theologian who writes on many doctrines but never forgets Total Depravity and the Unconditional Election of the Saints. As in theology, so in Hort's theory, the majority of individuals walk through the broad gate and are lost souls; only a few are the elect. Westcott and

---

[1] Brooke Foss Westcott and Fenton John Anthony Hort, *The New Testament in the Original Greek: Introduction and Appendix* (New York, 1882), p. 57.

[2] *Ibid.*, p. 54.

Hort preferred the text supported by a minority, by codex Vaticanus and a few friends; they rejected the reading supported by the vast majority of witnesses.

As the justification of their rejection of the majority, Westcott and Hort found the possibilities of genealogical method invaluable. Suppose that there are only ten copies of a document and that nine are all copied from one; then the majority can be safely rejected. Or suppose that the nine are copied from a lost manuscript and that this lost mansucript and the other one were both copied from the original; then the vote of the majority would not outweigh that of the minority. These are the arguments with which Westcott and Hort opened their discussion of genealogical method.[1] If diagrammed, they look like this:

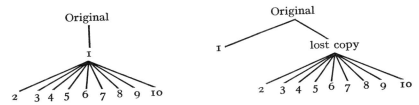

They show clearly that a majority of manuscripts is not *necessarily* to be preferred as correct. It is this *a priori* possibility which Westcott and Hort used to demolish the argument based on the numerical superiority urged by the adherents of the Textus Receptus.

That Westcott and Hort did not apply this method to the manuscripts of the New Testament is obvious. Where are the charts which start with the majority of late manuscripts and climb back through diminishing generations of ancestors to the Neutral and Western Texts? The answer is that they are nowhere. Look again at the first diagram, and you will see that *a, b, c*, etc., are not actual manuscripts of the New Testament, but hypothetical manuscripts. The demonstrations or illustrations of the genealogical method as applied to New Testament manuscripts by the followers of Hort, the "Horticuli" as Lake called them, likewise use hypothetical manuscripts, not actual codices. Note, for example, the diagrams and discussions in Kenyon's most popular work on textual criticism, including the most recent edition.[2] All the manuscripts

---

[1] *Ibid.*, pp. 40 ff.
[2] Frederic G. Kenyon, *Our Bible and the Ancient Manuscripts*, 3rd ed.

referred to are imaginary manuscripts, and the later of these charts was printed sixty years after Hort. One exception has come to my attention. A reviewer of Westcott and Hort, writing in *The Church Quarterly Review* in 1882, substitutes for the Hortian diagram an actual family tree of a specific group of manuscripts, but a footnote informs the reader that the family tree is that of the manuscripts of Catullus as edited by Mr. Robinson Ellis.[1]

That genealogical method was a secondary element in the procedures by which Westcott and Hort established their text can be seen from their frank statements of its limitations, and from a recognition of their continual reliance upon the Internal Evidence of Documents and Groups of Documents as the primary evidence. The decisive factor in Hort's method is the high appraisal of a manuscript or group of manuscripts which can be shown in some of their readings to be the best available witness. That this appraisal rests basically upon the internal evidence of readings rather than upon genealogical method can be seen from a careful reading of Hort's argument.

Westcott and Hort clearly perceived and clearly stated the two serious limitations upon the application of genealogical method to the text of the New Testament. The first of these limitations is a radical one. Commenting on their diagram (see above, p. 64), they say:

> Given only the readings of X and Y, Genealogy is by its very nature powerless to show which were the readings of O . . . When O has come to mean the autograph, we have, in reaching the earliest known divergence, arrived at the point where Genealogical method finally ceases to be applicable, since no independent documentary evidence remains to be taken up. Whatever variations survive at this ultimate divergence must still stand as undecided variations. Here therefore we are finally restricted to the Internal Evidence of single or grouped Documents and Readings, aided by any available external knowledge not dependent on Genealogy.[2]

That is to say, genealogical method can trace the tree down to the

---

(London, 1903), p. 9; 4th ed., revised, rewritten and enlarged (New York, 1940), p. 22. Years before this, Sanday had restated the method in Hortian style without reference to a single actual family of manuscripts. See Edward Miller, *The Oxford Debate on the Textual Criticism of the New Testament held at New College on May 6, 1897* (London, 1897), p. 22.

[1] "Westcott and Hort's Greek Text of the New Testament," *The Church Quarterly Review*, XIII (January, 1882), 420-451.

[2] Westcott and Hort, *op. cit.*, pp. 56 f.

last two branches, but it can never unite these last two in the main trunk—it can never take the last step. To quote Westcott and Hort again:

> Where the two ultimate witnesses differ, the genealogical method ceases to be applicable, and a comparison of the intrinsic general character of the two texts becomes the only resource.[1]

The nature of this limitation can be easily illustrated. Common ancestry is indicated by agreement in reading; if there are two brothers and a cousin, the agreement of one brother with the cousin will establish the parental nature even where the brothers differ; but if the two brothers have no cousins and disagree, genealogy can assert nothing as to which trait comes from the father.[2]

Westcott and Hort do not explicitly say that all genealogies will end in two branches, but this is the inescapable implication of their argument and discussion. The difficulty created by a two-branched tree might be surmounted by finding a three-branched tree, but Westcott and Hort do not escape that way. They found a two-branched tree, and their language indicates that they regarded this as inevitable. If genealogical method takes the investigator only as far as the penultimate station, his reconstruction cannot justifiably be described as achieved by the genealogical method.

I have stated above that Hort's principal reliance was upon the Internal Evidence of Documents and Groups of Documents. When, in the passage quoted, Hort comes to the two-branched tree, to what does he turn? "Here," he says, "we are finally restricted to the Internal Evidence of single or grouped Documents and Readings. . . ."

The second limitation upon the application of the genealogical method to the manuscripts of the New Testament springs from the almost universal presence of mixture in these manuscripts. Westcott and Hort recognized both the extent and the disastrous influence of mixed ancestry upon the genealogical method. Mixture was created when a text copied from one exemplar was corrected by a different exemplar. "Insofar as mixture operates," say Westcott and Hort, "it exactly inverts the results of the simpler form of

---

[1] *Ibid.*, p. 42.

[2] For a full exposition of this limitation, see Paul Collomp, *La critique des textes* (Paris, 1931), pp. 107 ff.

transmission, its effect being to produce convergence instead of divergence."

The genealogical diagram printed above (p. 64) from Westcott and Hort shows what happens *when there is no mixture*. When there *is* mixture—and Westcott and Hort state that it is common, in fact almost universal in some degree—then the genealogical method *as applied to manuscripts* is useless.

Without mixture a family tree is an ordinary tree-trunk with its branches—standing on the branches with the single trunk (the original text) at the top. The higher up—or the further back—you go from the mass of late manuscripts, the fewer ancestors you have!

With mixture you reverse this in any series of generations. The number of possible combinations defies computation, let alone the drawing of diagrams. The mixture could be consistent in its intrusion. Then the chart would be symmetrical and can easily be obtained by turning our first chart upside down.

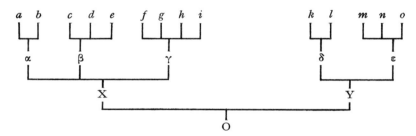

But here O represents one late manuscript which has a constantly mixed ancestry. This ancestry three generations earlier would consist of *a b c d e f g h i k l m n o*. But where would you go from there? This is a family tree in which the further back you go, the more ancestors you have. This manuscript genalogy is comparable to human genealogies, where the individual has two parents.

The difficulty that confronts the user of genealogical method in mixed texts may be paraphrased in human terms thus. My mother was of German origin through the "Pennsylvania Dutch." My father was born in the south of England. My wife's mother was of French descent through the Huguenots who settled in the Carolinas. Her father was born in the north of England. We have two children. By studying them, could you reconstruct us; or if we were missing —as is usually the case with New Testament manuscripts—could you reconstruct our parents and so on back to Adam? When the children agree in some British trait, are they agreeing with us or with their grandparents or with some proto-Briton?

Just to make it interesting, mixture occurs occasionally as well as regularly. The intermarriage of manuscripts knows no more restrictions than exist in the human race. A late manuscript may be corrected by an early one of the type from which the late manuscript is descended. Or it may be corrected by a manuscript of any other type from any earlier generation. Mixture might take place in a particular line of manuscripts in every third generation. The diagram of its ancestry would look like a boa-constrictor which had swallowed a calf every forty-five minutes.

Another and simpler type of mixture is that in which one section of a manuscript has one ancestry and another section of the same manuscript has a different ancestry. This is well known in the case of the Washington Codex of the Gospels, which in six sections presents four different text-types. Similar cases of mixture "in packages" occur in later manuscripts. Elsewhere I have discussed Gregory 574, a four gospels codex which had eight ancestors in the first generation! [1]

Westcott and Hort knew all this. They admitted that mixture makes the use of genealogical method impossible. They admitted that mixture occurred early and generally. They recognized this second limitation as clearly as the first.

Yet they championed the genealogical method. They escaped from the first limitation only by abandoning the method. This they did—as we have seen—openly. They admitted the limitation, and still claimed that the method was good up to the final stage of the task.

In the case of mixture, the genealogical method is saved by a robust hero who comes riding in on a white horse—much in the style of the Lone Ranger. His name is "conflate readings."

The existence of a particular type of variant reading called conflate readings saved the genealogical method. As Westcott and Hort stated the case:

> Evidently no resource can be so helpful, where it can be attained,
> as the extrication of earlier unmixed texts or portions of texts from

---

[1] Ernest Cadman Colwell, "The Complex Character of the Late Byzantine Text of the Gospels," *Journal of Biblical Literature*, LIV (1935), 211-21; and *History and Text*, Vol. I of *The Four Gospels of Karahissar*, ed. by E. C. Colwell and H. R. Willoughby (2 vols. [Chicago, 1936]), pp. 216-222.

the general mass of texts now extant. The clearest evidence for tracing the antecedent factors of mixture in texts is afforded by readings which are themselves mixed, or, as they are sometimes called, 'conflate', that is, not simple substitutions of the reading of one document for that of another, but combinations of the readings of both documents into a composite whole. . . .[1]

Thus, they argue, if documents habitually support the conflate readings, mixture must have had a large share in producing their text; if documents lack conflate readings, they are witnesses to texts antecedent to mixture.

But this final conclusion is not sound. Westcott and Hort listed only eight conflate readings (all in the gospels) to justify the characterization of an entire text as "antecedent to mixture" or as subsequent to mixture.[2] But, as they recognized, mixture usually resulted in the substitution of one reading for another rather than in conflation. More important is the fact that there is no unmixed text in existence, nor any manuscript with an unmixed text. Codex Vaticanus lacks the conflate readings of the "Syrian text," but it has conflate readings of its own.[3] The "Neutral text" lacks the Syrian conflations, but it has other conflate readings, and the "Western non-interpolations" are clear evidence of mixture in that text.

No text or document is homogeneous enough to justify judgment on the basis of *part* of its readings for the rest of its readings. This was Hort's Achilles' heel. He is saying here that since these

---

[1] Westcott and Hort, *op. cit.*, p. 49.

[2] Mark 6:33; 8:26; 9:38; 9:49; Luke 9:10; 11:54; 12:18; 24:53 (*ibid.*, pp. 51, 93 ff.).

[3] See, e.g., Mark 1:28 where ευθυς πανταχου is read by B C L Fam 13 543 837 892, while ευθυς πανταχου is omitted by ℵ* Θ Fam 1 28 33 349 474 517 565 700 *c ff* Sy⁵ Cop^bo Geo² Arm, ευθυς is read by A D Γ Δ Π Σ Φ E F G H K M S U V Y Ω 22 157 1071 1241 al.pler. *f g² l* vg Sy^pesh hi, and πανταχου is read by W 579 *b e q* Geo¹ Eth; or Mark 1:40 where οτι is read by ℵ A Γ Δ Π Φ 090 E F G H K M S U V Y Ω Minusc. pler. *a* Sy⁵ pesh(aliq.) hl Cop^bo (aliq.) Geo¹, while κυριε is read by C L W Θ Σ 579 700 892 *c e ff* vg (plur.), οτι is omitted by D 238 *b f g¹' ² l* vg (plur. *et* WW) Sy^pesh. (plur.) Aug, and κυριε οτι is read by B.

The ending of the story concerning the plucking of grain on the Sabbath is another case in point. Codex Vaticanus with most manuscripts and versions reads και ελεγεν αυτοις το σαββατον δια τον ανθρωπον εγενετο και ουχ ο ανθρωπος δια το σαββατον ωστε κυριος εστιν ο υιος του ανθρωπου και του σαββατου (Mark 2:27, 28). Codices D *a c e ff i*, however, read λεγω δε υμιν κυριος εστιν ο υιος του ανθρωπου και του σαββατου; and codex 2427 and the Bohairic manuscript K* read και ελεγεν αυτοις το σαββατον δια τον ανθρωπον εγενετο και ουχ ο ανθρωπος δια το σαββατον.

eight conflate readings occur in the Syrian text that text as a whole is a mixed text; if a manuscript or text lacks these readings, it is in its other readings a witness to a text antecedent to mixture.

Westcott and Hort state this fallacy very clearly in their argument for the importance of the evidence of a document as over against readings:

> Where then one of the documents is found habitually to contain these morally certain or at least strongly preferred readings, and the other habitually to contain their rejected rivals, we can have no doubt, first, that the text of the first has been transmitted in comparative purity, and that the text of the second has suffered comparatively large corruption; and next, that *the superiority of the first must be as great in the variations in which Internal Evidence of Readings has furnished no decisive criterion as in those which have enabled us to form a comparative appreciation of the two texts.*[1]

This would be true if we knew that there was no mixture involved and that manuscripts and texts were rigorously homogeneous. Everything we have learned since Hort, however, confirms the opposite position. Thus Hort's argument by extension from the presence or absence of conflate readings to the presence or absence of mixture in a text is unconvincing.

J. Rendel Harris issued a strong caveat against this type of generalization as it had been applied to the "Western Text":

> [The Western Text] may be justified in select readings even where it cannot be justified as a whole. And this means that there is nothing against which we need to be so much on our guard as the seductive supposition that the cause of certain variants is necessarily the cause of the remainder, or that we can, because we have explained two or three obscure changes in the text, use the Newtonian *vera causa* over the remainder.[2]

The risk involved in claiming uniform quality for a text has once again been stressed in a recent publication by Kilpatrick who urges more reliance on internal evidence.[3]

But Hort turns rapidly from the confusion caused by mixture to a resource which he called the Internal Evidence of Groups of Documents. In the one volume edition, he follows the discussion of mixture with this statement:

---

[1] Westcott and Hort, *op. cit.*, p. 32 (italics mine).

[2] J. Rendel Harris, *Four Lectures on the Western Text of the New Testament* (London, 1894), p. 66.

[3] G. D. Kilpatrick, "Western Text and Original Text in the Gospels and Acts," *Journal of Theological Studies*, XLIV (1943), 25 f., and 33.

But this seeming confusion is seldom productive of real and permanent difficulty in determining what lines of transmission did or did not contain *a given reading* in ancient times.[1]

He is thinking primarily of separate readings or groups of readings as supported by groups of documents. In the same way that generalizations are made on all the readings of one document, generalizations can be made on all the readings of a group of documents. In the case of a document with a mixed text its several lines of ancestry are indicated by the several groups which it joins in different readings. Thus Westcott and Hort claim that this method is applicable to mixed and unmixed texts alike.

A serious objection to this type of generalization is the lack of exact definition for the phrase "a group of documents." The groups themselves are unstable and mixed. In the light of our experience of several years study of the Neutral text, we would affirm that it is often "really and permanently" difficult to determine "what lines of transmission did or did not contain a given reading in ancient times." Within a text-type as supposedly close-knit as the Neutral, there are large variations. Those manuscripts, for example, which are alleged to be witnesses to this text-type (א B C L Δ Ψ 33 157 517 579 892 1241 1342 2427) show the following groupings in the Markan account of the cursing of the fig tree (Mark 11:12-14) and the cleansing of the Temple (Mark 11:15-19):

Mk 11:12 και τη επαυριον εξελθοντων αυτων απο βηθανιας: א B C L Δ Ψ 33 157 517 579 892 1342
και τη επαυριον εξελθοντων απο βηθανιας: 1241
και τη επαυριον εξελθοντων εκ βηθανιας: 2427

επεινασεν: א^c B C L Δ Ψ 33 157 517 579 892 1241 1342 2427
Omit: א*

13 και ιδων συκην μακροθεν εχουσαν φυλλα: 157 892 1241
και ιδων συκην απο μακροθεν εχουσα φυλλα: Δ 517
και ιδων συκην απο μακροθεν εχουσαν φυλλα: B C L Ψ 33 579 1342 2427
και ιδων συκην μιαν απο μακροθεν εχουσαν φυλλα: א

ηλθεν ει αρα ευρησει τι εν αυτη: 157
ηλθεν ει αρα τι ευρησει εν αυτη: א B C L Δ Ψ 33 517 579 1342 2427
ηλθεν ει αρα τι ευρησει επ αυτην: 892
ηλθεν αρα ευρησει τι εν αυτη: 1241

και ελθων επ αυτην ουδεν ευρεν ει μη φυλλα: א B C* Δ Ψ 157 517 1241 1342 2427

---

[1] Brooke Foss Westcott and Fenton John Anthony Hort, *The New Testament in the Original Greek* (New York, 1885), p. 546 (italics mine).

Mk 11:13 και ελθων επ αυτην ουδεν ευρεν ει μη φυλλα μονον: C^c 33
και ουδεν ευρεν εν αυτη ει μη φυλλα μονον: 579
και ουδεν ευρεν ει μη φυλλα: 892
και ελθων επ αυτην ουδεν ουχ ευρεν ει μη φυλλα: L

ου γαρ ην καιρος συκος: C 33 157 517 1241
ο γαρ καιρος ουκ ην συκων: ℵ B L Δ Ψ 892 1342 2427
Omit: 579

14 και αποκριθεις ο ιησους ειπεν αυτη: 157 517
και αποκριθεις ειπεν αυτη: ℵ B C L Δ Ψ 33 579 892 1241 1342 2427

μηκετι εκ σου εις τον αιωνα μηδεις καρπον φαγοι: 33 157 579 1241
μηκετι εις τον αιωνα εκ σου μηδεις καρπον φαγοι: ℵ B C L 892 1342 2427
μηκετι εις τον αιωνα εκ σου μηδεις καρπον φαγη: Ψ
μηκετι εις τον αιωνα εκ σου καρπον φαγοι: Δ
μηκετι εκ σου εις τον αιωνα μηδεις καρπον φαγη: 517

και ηκουον οι μαθηται αυτου: ℵ B C L Δ Ψ 33 157 892 1241 1342 2427
και ηκουσαν οι μαθηται αυτου: 517 579

15 και ερχονται εις ιεροσολυμα: ℵ B L Δ Ψ 33 157 579 1241 1342 2427
και ηρχοντο εις ιεροσολυμα: C
και ερχονται παλιν εις ιεροσολυμα: 517 892

και εισελθων ο ιησους εις το ιερον: 157 517 892 1241
και εισελθων εις το ιερον: ℵ B C L Δ Ψ 33 579 1342 2427

ηρξατο εκβαλλειν τους πωλουντας: ℵ B C L Δ Ψ 33 157 517 579 892 1241 1342 2427

και αγοραζοντας εν τω ιερω: Δ Ψ 33 157 579
και τους αγοραζοντας εν τω ιερω: ℵ B C L 517 892 1241 1342 2427

και τας τραπεζας των κολλυβιστων: ℵ B C L Δ Ψ 33 157 517 579 892 1241 1342 2427
και τας καθεδρας των πωλουντων τας περιστερας κατεστρεφε: ℵ^c B C L Δ Ψ 33 157 517 579 892 1241 1342 2427
κατεστρεψεν και τας καθεδρας των πωλουντων τας περιστερας: ℵ*

16 και ουκ ηφιεν ινα τις διενεγκη σκευος δια του ιερου: ℵ B C L Δ Ψ 33 157 517 892 1342 2427
και ουκ ηφιεν ινα τις διενεγκη σκευος δια το ιερον: 579
και ουκ ηφιεν ινα τις διενεγκει σκευος δια του ιερου: 1241

17 και εδιδασκε λεγων αυτοις: 33 157 517 579 1241
και εδιδασκεν και ελεγεν αυτοις: ℵ C L Δ 892 1342
και εδιδασκεν και ελεγεν: B Ψ 2427

ου γεγραπται: ℵ B C L Δ Ψ 33 157 517 892 1241 1342 2427
γεγραπται: 579

οτι ο οικος μου οικος προσευχης κληθησεται πασι τοις εθνεσιν: ℵ B L Δ 33 157 517 892 1241 1342 2427
ο οικος μου οικος προσευχης κληθησεται πασι τοις εθνεσιν: C Ψ 579

υμεις δε εποιησατε αυτον σπηλαιον ληστων: ℵ C 157 892 1241
υμεις δε αυτον εποιησατε σπηλαιον ληστων: 33 517 579
υμεις δε πεποιηκατε αυτον σπηλαιον ληστων: B L Δ Ψ 1342
υμεις δε πεποιηκατε σπηλαιον ληστων: 2427

18 και ηκουσαν οι γραμματεις και οι αρχιερεις: 157 1241 1342*
και ηκουσαν οι αρχιερεις και οι γραμματεις: א B C L 33 579 2427
και ηκουσαν οι γραμματεις και οι φαρισαιοι: 517
και ηκουον οι αρχιερεις και οι γραμματεις: Ψ' 892
και ηκουον αρχιερεις και οι γραμματεις: Δ

και εζητουν πως αυτον απολεσουσιν: Δ 2427
και εζητουν πως αυτον απολεσωσιν: א B C L Ψ' 33 157 517 579 892
1241 1342

εφοβουντο γαρ αυτον: א B C L Δ Ψ' 33 157 517 579 892 1241
εφοβουντο γαρ ο λαον: 1342
εφοβουντο γαρ: 2427

οτι πας ο οχλος εξεπλησσετο επι τη διδαχη αυτου: L 157 517 1241
οτι πας ο οχλος εξεπλησσοντο επι τη διδαχη αυτου: 579
οτι πας ο οχλος εξεπλησσετο εν τη διδαχη αυτου: 33
πας γαρ ο οχλος εξεπλησσετο επι τη διδαχη αυτου: B C Ψ' 1342
πας γαρ ο οχλος εξεπλησσοντο επι τη διδαχη αυτου: א Δ 892
πας γαρ ο οχλος εξεπλησσετο επι τη διδαχη: 2427

19 και οτε οψε εγενετο: 157 517 1241
και οταν οψε εγενετο: א B C L Δ Ψ' 33 579 892 1342 2427

εξεπορευετο εξω της πολεως: א C 33 157 517 579 892 1241 1342
εξεπορευοντο εξω της πολεως: B Δ Ψ' 2427
εξω της πολεως: L

A much more dramatic cleavage within this group is to be found in the second chapter of Mark, where C and Δ depart from the majority of the "Neutral" witnesses in the direction of the Byzantine text, while B and 2427 leave the majority in a different direction. Thus, we have here a tripartite division within the Neutral Text itself. Until the genealogical method has demonstrated with reference to actual manuscripts what some of these "groups" are, we have no touchstone by which to identify the several strands of ancestry in a mixed text.

A distinguished classicist, Louis Havet, has issued a much needed warning concerning this Hortian general approval of the readings of the best groups. He urges that the use of a symbol for a group of manuscripts should not be taken as adequate representation of *all* the readings of the group. The genealogical determination of an archetype, he points out, may overlook the better reading preserved by a single manuscript. Thus for Plautus, manuscripts V E J have one ancestor different from that of B and that of D. It would seem that a good reading could *not* occur in J against V E *and* B *and* D. But it does. The genealogical prejudice is thus, M. Havet remarks, convinced of excess.[1]

---

[1] Louis Havet, *Manual de critique verbale appliquée aux textes latins* (Paris, 1911), §§ 1618-1622, pp. 424 f.

Finally, a caveat should be entered concerning our ignorance of the inter-relationships of groups. Westcott and Hort's claim that the Neutral text is "neutral" is now generally repudiated. That repudiation involves the assumption of a rather complex ancestry for the text-type formerly called Neutral and better designated by Kenyon's colorless symbol "Beta." There are both "Western" and "Syrian" readings within the Beta text-type. We surely err if we assume the isolation of one text-type from another. This was what Hort claimed for the Beta text-type, and it is this claim that has been abandoned.[1] We must realize that its abandonment forces the abandonment of the groups-of-documents touchstone also, and without this, genealogical method cannot be applied to mixed texts. Until we know more about "groups of documents," we cannot use them as road signs to guide us through the tangled jungle of mixture. When we do know more, it is probable that the new knowledge will illuminate the history of the text to a limited degree, and will thus aid all studies in textual criticism, but will render only general and not direct assistance to the problem of overcoming mixture.

Yet Westcott and Hort's genealogical method slew the Textus Receptus. The *a priori* demonstration is logically irrefutable. It was supported in the minds of the readers of Westcott and Hort by their knowledge that it worked (as Hort claimed) when applied to the manuscripts of the classics. It sounded convincing against the appeal of Burgon and Scrivener to the majority of the witnesses.

In the nearly ninety years since Westcott and Hort, some scholars have made effective use of the genealogical method and all have come to a clearer understanding of its limitations. Kirsopp and Silva Lake have used the method in reconstructing the text of certain families of documents. It was used effectively in the edition of Fam. 1 [2] and of Fam. II,[3] and somewhat less effectively in the study of Fam. 13 (where they built upon foundations laid

---

[1] See, e.g., Frederic G. Kenyon, *Recent Developments in the Textual Criticism of the Greek Bible* (London, 1933), pp. 67 ff.

[2] Kirsopp Lake, *Codex 1 of the Gospels and its Allies* ("Texts and Studies," VII [Cambridge, 1902]).

[3] Silva Lake, *Family II and the Codex Alexandrinus; The Text according to Mark* ("Studies and Documents," V [London, 1936]).

down by Ferrar).[1] In these and other areas [2] the Lakes have made valuable use of this method.

Less valuable was the use made by A. C. Clark, who emphasized the role of accidental loss of lines in transmission as a clue to the descent of manuscripts.[3] It was unfortunate that he wrote before the Beatty Papyri were published. Thus he chose the line-length of the Purple Codices of the sixth century as normal for the primitive period. But a glance at the Beatty Papyri shows lines-that vary greatly in length and do not conform to Clark's pattern. He claimed also that the only abbreviations used were the *nomina sacra*. But our studies have shown that primitive usage of the *nomina sacra* was irregular and differed widely from the usage of his norm—the Purple Codices.[4] Even without the Beatty Papyri, New Testament scholars have generally regarded Clark's technique as a will-o'-the-wisp bound to mislead its users. The flexibility of the line-unit and its multiples is so high that the scholar who employs it can use it in a subjective fashion to endorse any conclusion he desires.

At the other extreme lies Dom Quentin's rigorous effort to make the genealogical method one hundred per cent objective.[5] He argued that community in error is not enough to establish genealogy. Therefore he set forth what he called a Rule of Iron, and applied it to the reconstruction of the text of the Latin Vulgate of the Old Testament. There he reported complete success with his method.

The method is to take the list of variant readings in a particular book or passage as one datum. Then take up the manuscripts in turn in groups of three until all possible groups of three have been employed. The internal agreements and disagreements of these manuscripts are tabulated as follows:

---

[1] Kirsopp and Silva Lake, *Family 13 (The Ferrar Group)*; *The Text according to Mark with a Collation of Codex 28 of the Gospels* ("Studies and Documents," XI [London, 1941]).

[2] E.g., Silva New, "A Patmos Family of Gospel Manuscripts," *Harvard Theological Review*, XXV (1932), pp. 85 ff.

[3] Albert Curtis Clark, *The Primitive Text of the Gospels and Acts* (Oxford, 1914); *The Descent of Manuscripts* (Oxford, 1918); *The Acts of the Apostles: A Critical Edition with Introduction and Notes on Selected Passages* (Oxford, 1933).

[4] E. C. Colwell, "Some Unusual Abbreviations in MS. 2427," *Studia Evangelica*, ed. Kurt Aland *et al.* (Berlin, 1959), pp. 778-92.

[5] Henri Quentin, *Mémoire sur l'établissement du texte de la Vulgate* ("Collectanea Biblica Latina," V, 1 [Paris, 1922]); *Essais de critique textuelle (Ecdotique)* (Paris, 1926). See also the bibliography given by Paul Collomp, *op. cit.*, pp. 72 f.

$$A < B \quad C = 20$$
$$A > B < C = 0$$
$$A \quad B > C = 11$$

The "zero" line indicates the manuscript through which the other two are related. In the data given above, A and C are related through B. The relationship might be either:

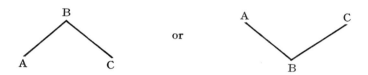

or

When all groups of three have been run through, you have the data for the stemma and the determination of the archetype of these manuscripts. Quentin emphasizes the possibility that this archetype may not be the original text.

We felt that this deserved a test on New Testament manuscripts. Some years ago, therefore, Dr. William N. Lyons applied this method to the members of Fam. 13 in the Gospel of Mark. We were forced to be more subjective than Quentin in at least one respect. We found all sorts of spelling errors in the manuscripts of this family that we judged could be personal to a scribe no matter what his exemplar read. We eliminated them as "insignificant" variants. (Had they been included in the final results, those results would have been less rather than more significant).[1] To the residue, we applied the Rule of Iron and tabulated the results on hundreds of cards. *There was but one zero line among eighty-four groups of three manuscripts!*

To indicate the nature of the results, I quote the nearest thing to zeros that we obtained:

---

[1] The authority of Père Lagrange can be cited for the discarding of such variants. He says of "iotacism," "Ces nuances doivent être notées dans une collation de mss., mais ce ne sont pas des variantes qui permettent de juger de la valeur d'un texte ni même ordinairement du groupe dans lequel on doit le ranger"; and in a footnote, he adds, "Hoskier (*Codex B and its Allies*, I, xi) a noté comme divergences entre B et Oxyr. 2; pour B: υιου, Δαυειδ, αμεινα δαβ(bis) etc., et pour Ox, ῡῡ, δαυιδ, αμμιναδαβ(bis). Cela ne suffirait pas pour nier l'accord des deux textes" (Marie-Joseph Lagrange, "Projet de critique textuelle rationnelle du N.T.," *Revue Biblique*, XLII [1933], 483).

$$543 < 788 \quad 826 = 10$$
$$543 > 788 < 826 = 59$$
$$543 \quad 788 > 826 = 0$$

$$346 < 543 \quad 826 = 40$$
$$346 > 543 < 826 = 3$$
$$346 \quad 543 > 826 = 7$$

$$543 < 826 \quad 828 = 8$$
$$543 > 826 < 828 = 3$$
$$543 \quad 826 > 828 = 26$$

We are convinced that if the Rule of Iron will not help us with manuscripts that we know to be related, it will be of no help in the areas of broader relationship or in free exploration. The amount of labor involved is enormous; the results are meaningless. I hope that Dr. Lyons will publish a critique of this method based on the work he has done.

But subsequent study of Fam. 13 softens this indictment of Quentin's "Rule of Iron." In two out of the three cases listed above the totals point to ms. 826 as the one through which the others are related. In Geerlings' publications of Fam. 13 he says of ms. 826 in Fam. 13a in Matthew: It "is the only member of group *a* which could itself be the archetype of the others." [1] Of ms. 826 in Luke he says, "826 is almost but not quite the archetype although by far the best representative of it." [2] In John, he points out that ms. 826 "closely approximates . . . the Family 13 text as it has been printed." [3] Thus while Quentin's Rule lacked the inflexibility of iron, it could have pointed us in the right direction. But Metzger is right in his negative appraisal of the method.[4]

Like Quentin, the French scholar Bédier recognized the inadequacy of the agreement-in-error test. He wrote savage indictments of the genealogical method as applied to the classics and to Old French literature. His particular *bête noire* was the two-branched family tree. He collected statistics as to the number of times editors

---

[1] Jacob Geerlings, *Family 13—The Ferrar Group: The Text According to Matthew* ("Studies and Documents," XIX [Salt Lake City, 1961]), p. 11.

[2] Jacob Geerlings, *Family 13—The Ferrar Group: The Text According to Luke* ("Studies and Documents," XX [Salt Lake City, 1961[), p. 8.

[3] Jacob Geerlings, *Family 13—The Ferrar Group: The Text According to John* ("Studies and Documents," XXI [Salt Lake City, 1962]), p. 1.

[4] Bruce M. Metzger, *The Text of the New Testament* (New York and London, 1964), p. 165.

constructed a two-branched tree rather than a multiple-branched tree. In one account, he lists 110 editions of classical works, in 105 of which the editor constructed a tree with two branches.[1] Bédier cynically comments that the editors make it come out this way on purpose, for with a two-branched tree genealogy is no help and the editor is free to put in the reading he prefers. If he had three branches, Bédier points out, he would have to follow the manuscripts.

This cynicism is to be deplored. I much prefer the more generous judgment of A. E. Housman who says:

> ... An editor of no judgment, perpetually confronted with a couple of manuscripts to choose from, cannot but feel in every fibre of his being that he is a donkey between two bundles of hay. What shall he do now? Leave criticism to critics, you may say, and betake himself to any honest trade for which he is less unfit. But he prefers a more flattering solution: he confusedly imagines that if one bundle of hay is removed he will cease to be a donkey.[2]

The work of Bédier has been picked up and systematized by Paul Collomp. He explores the implications of mixture for the use of the genealogical method with a thorough industry and a French lucidity that make his book invaluable.[3] Like Bédier, he tends to favor internal evidence as against genealogical method. I owe to Collomp the insight that the opponents of objective methods, including the genealogical, are really obsessed with the method that favors using "the best manuscript" or the best family. He says that actually Bédier and the other subjective critics favor this more than do the objectivists.[4] The difference is one of slight degree. Westcott and Hort favored a best manuscript and a best family. Their recent critic, Kilpatrick, referred to above (p. 71, note 3), regards "the Alexandrian text and especially B as our best authorities" and asks only that other sources be allowed to contribute something. Sanders and others simply transfer allegiance to the Western Text as "the best." Lagrange, one of the most judicious critics of the genealogical method, favored internal evidence versus objective evidence. But instead of using this "rational" criticism to determine the

---

[1] See the preface to Joseph Bédier's edition of *Lai de l'Ombre* (Paris, 1913), and his "La tradition manuscrite du Lai de l'Ombre: reflections sur l'art d'éditer les anciens textes," *Romania*, LIV (1928), 161-181, 321-356.

[2] A. E. Housman (ed.), *M. Manilii Astronomicon; Liber Primus*, 2nd ed. (Cambridge, 1937), p. xxxi.

[3] Collomp, *op. cit.*

[4] *Ibid.*, pp. 82 ff.

original form of a particular reading, he used it to determine which
is the best recension and its best manuscript.[1] In this he, in fact
though not in theory, is doing what Hort did. Of only a few critics,
among them J. Rendel Harris and F. C. Burkitt, can it be said that
there is no obsession with the best manuscript or the best group.[2]

No discussion of genealogical method today can afford to ignore
the work of Vinton A. Dearing. Metzger summarizes Dearing's
method of editing a text by statistical analyses, and traces his
dependence upon Sir Walter W. Greg, Quentin, and Archibald
A. Hill. Metzger shows no enthusiasm for Dearing's distinction
between bibliographical and textual stemmata, and in general is
sceptical as to the future application of this method.[3] Yet Dearing's
continued work in theory and application and his pioneering in the
use of the computer hold real promise for the improvement of our
methods.[4]

The discovery of papyrus texts both of the classics and of the
New Testament has done much to upset the genealogists. In both
these fields there has been a growing eclecticism as to method. Yet
within this eclecticism internal evidence increasingly outweighs
the external in the judgment of the critics. This can be seen, for
example, in the major work of Lagrange in this field.[5] Lagrange
turned first to the area of theory and method. He holds to the
major grouping of manuscripts in "texts." But he does not urge the
application of genealogical method to the reconstruction of the
original from these. On the contrary, he selects the "best" manuscript as a type of each text and discusses it.

The study of these text-types leads to an appraisal of one of
them as the "best"—with a consequent high appraisal of its best
manuscript. In this appraisal process he gives the major role to
"rational" criticism based on internal evidence.[6] When the text-

---

[1] Marie-Joseph Lagrange, *La critique rationnelle*, Vol. II, Part 2 of *Introduction à l'étude du Nouveau Testament* (Paris, 1935), pp. 25 ff.

[2] See, e.g., F. C. Burkitt, "The Chester Beatty Papyri," *Journal of
Theological Studies*, XXXIV (1933), 363-68.

[3] Metzger, *op. cit.*, pp. 165-69.

[4] Dearing's most recent publication on this subject (which appeared
while the present volume was passing through the press) is his article,
"Some Notes on Genealogical Methods in Textual Criticism," *Novum
Testamentum*, IX (1967), 278-297.

[5] Lagrange, *La critique rationnelle*, and "Projet de critique textuelle
rationnelle du N.T.," *Revue Biblique* XLII (1933), 493 ff.

[6] Lagrange was influenced by the important work of Louis Havet (see

types have been appraised, Lagrange will not tolerate any appeal to majority vote (or genealogical method). He then urges "rational criticism" based on internal evidence as the ground for decision as to the original reading.

The most serious limitation on the use of the genealogical method is the complexity of the pattern of transmission in the New Testament. This has been recognized not only by theorists like Collomp but also by such veteran workers in the vineyard as the Lakes. In their publication of Fam. 13, they present in tentative fashion certain general conclusions which deserve the widest consideration. These conclusions of theirs concern the definition of terms, and the usefulness of method.

They point out that we have groups of manuscripts in at least three magnitudes. There are small homogeneous groups which might be called "families." The manuscripts that make up Fam. 1 comprise such a family; and—in their judgment—at least one and possibly two of the sub-groups of the so-called "Fam. 13" are distinct families. The third sub-group is not, and "Fam. 13" itself is not a family.[1]

At the other extreme are the large aggregates that Westcott and Hort, for example, called the Neutral Text, or the Syrian Text. The "Caesarean Text" as initially discussed by Lake, Blake, and New [2] and by Streeter [3] is a similar aggregate. These "texts"

---

above, p. 81, note 6). In this work, Havet pointed out four traps in genealogical method: (1) instead of diverging constantly, it happens that the branches of the tree converge (as an example, Havet notes Manuscript E of Terence whose complex relationships cannot be represented by any pattern or design); (2) different sections of a manuscript have separate genealogies; (3) agreements often have nothing to do with ancestry—especially in orthography; (4) glosses and notes are capable of multiple interpretations which go counter to genealogy. (§ 1610, p. 418). And Havet himself gives the ultimate vote to internal evidence: "Si en effet il y a conflit entre le critère qu'offre l'autorité des mss. et les critères qu'offre le texte pris en lui-même, la présomption est en faveur des derniers" (§ 1595, pp. 413 f.).

[1] Silva Lake, *Family II and the Codex Alexandrinus*; *The Text according to Mark* ("Studies and Documents," V [London, 1936]), p. 5, footnote 12, and Kirsopp and Silva Lake, *Family 13—The Ferrar Group*: *The Text according to Mark with a Collation of Codex 28 of the Gospels* ("Studies and Documents," XI [London, 1941]), pp. viii ff.

[2] Kirsopp Lake, Robert P. Blake, and Silva New, "The Caesarean Text of the Gospel of Mark," *Harvard Theological Review*, XXI (1928), 208-404.

[3] Burnett H. Streeter, *The Four Gospels*: *A Study of Origins* (New York, 1924), pp. 77 ff.

are in no sense families, and the title should never be applied to them.

Between these extremes are groups more loosely related than families, but more closely related than texts.

In earlier studies of a "Neutral" manuscript at Chicago, we were seriously hampered by the lack of definite titles and meanings for these various groups. Significantly enough, our definition of a "family" rests on the method by which its existence is demonstrated. We suggest that "a family is a group of manuscripts so closely related that the text of the archetype can be reconstructed by the use of the genealogical method applied to manuscripts rather than to readings. Members of a family seldom contain mixed texts. Members of a family are not widely separated from each other by missing generations."

For the medium-sized group we propose the use of the term "Clan." For the largest we urge the use of "Text-type" instead of the more ambiguous "Text." We do not believe that genealogical method is applicable to either the Clan or the Text-type. We tentatively share the Lakes' scepticism as to whether or not a Text-type can be reconstructed. It may be that a text-type is an apparatus rather than a text. We have every confidence in our ability to identify the witnesses to a Text-type. But we have as yet little confidence that we can reconstruct *the original form* of a Text-type—even of the "Neutral." We are confident that we can establish the Beta text-type in the sense that it is the text supported by the majority of primary witnesses. The publication of such a text-type must be accompanied by an apparatus containing the dissent of all witnesses to the text-type. Although this reconstructed text would not be the original form of the text-type, it would be an average of the text-type. It would represent the Neutral text-type, for example, better than Hort's modification of B does. It would contribute substantially to the illumination of our knowledge of the history of the text.

In any case, it is clear that in a field where no manuscripts have parents, where centuries and continents separate witnesses, the genealogical method is not of primary importance. Its importance lies in the realm of provincial history. It can chart the history of transmission in an area narrowly limited in time and space. Within that area it sheds a bright light. But in the larger realm where the larger questions are settled, it still has to demonstrate its value for the reconstruction of the original text of the Greek New Testament.

I can quote without reservation one of F. C. Burkitt's last paragraphs:

> I have, frankly, no constructional hypothesis to offer. But a textual theory which is to hold the field must be able to answer all objections. Above all, B and "the neutral text" are not synonymous. It is easier, from some points of view, to reconstruct the original than some half-way house like the "neutral" or the "Caesarean" text, that contains some corruptions but not all.[1]

The task that confronts the serious student of New Testament textual criticism is the creation of "the constructional hypothesis" to which Burkitt referred. No patching will preserve the theory of Westcott and Hort. Kirsopp Lake called it "a failure, though a splendid one" as long ago as 1904,[2] and Ernst von Dobschütz felt that its vogue was over when he published his introduction.[3] But the crowd has not yet followed these pioneers—von Soden, Streeter, and Sanders worked in Hort's framework. Nor did these men themselves make a systematic replacement for the Hortian theory.[4]

A new theory and method is needed. Those who work at it must clarify the concept "text" or text-type as in the phrase "the Western text" or "a local text." To those who work in this vineyard I recall the warning uttered by Miller in 1897, "Sub verbo text dolus latet." [5] I add the futher warning that the theory of so-called local texts is a snare and a delusion. Our dilemma seems to be that we know too much to believe the old; we do not yet know enough to create the new.

---

[1] *Journal of Theological Studies*, XXXIV (1933), 367.

[2] Kirsopp Lake, *The Influence of Textual Criticism on the Exegesis of the New Testament* (Oxford, 1904), p. 3.

[3] Ernst von Dobschütz, *Eberhard Nestle's Einführung in das griechische Neue Testament*, 4th ed. (Göttingen, 1925).

[4] For example, the Lakes in 1939 blamed Hort for a too-inclusive rejection of Western readings, and for this alone; Kirsopp and Silva Lake, "De Westcott et Hort au Père Lagrange et au-delà," *Revue Biblique*, XLVIII (1939), 495-505.

[5] Edward Miller, *The Oxford Debate on the Textual Criticism of the New Testament held at New College on May 6, 1897* (London, 1897), pp. 11 f. Miller urged—and rightly—that Hort had strained the theory of texts. His own definition was, "Text is merely a collective word denoting a number of readings in the particular part of the world to which it refers. Besides these it includes also other readings which belong to the true text. . . ."

CHAPTER SIX

METHOD IN THE STUDY OF GOSPEL LECTIONARIES [1]

Do the majority of the Greek lectionaries of the gospels agree with one another so consistently that it is possible to speak of their text as "the lectionary text"? It has generally been assumed that the text of lectionaries does not merit serious attention, and that even if they should agree in text, the quality of that text would not justify its study.[2] But the discussion of the quality and significance of this text may reasonably be postponed until its existence has been established.[3]

The complete proof that there is a distinct lectionary text must await the collation of a considerable number of manuscripts, but enough evidence can be advanced to show that the existence of such a distinct text is highly probable, if not certain.[4] This evidence was obtained by sampling the text of a fair number of lectionaries—twenty-six lections [5] in from five to fifty-six manuscripts having been

---

[1] Originally published as "Is There a Lectionary Text of the Gospels?" *Harvard Theological Review*, XXV (1932), 73-84.

[2] This is the position, for instance, of von Soden (*Die Schriften des Neuen Testaments*, I, i, 19 f.), who excluded lectionaries from his studies.

[3] The Department of New Testament and Early Christian Literature of the University of Chicago inaugurated an investigation of the text of the lectionaries. In 1933 preliminary studies were published in the volume, *Prolegomena to the Study of the Lectionary Text of the Gospels* ("Studies in the Lectionary Text of the Greek New Testament"), edited by Ernest Cadman Colwell and Donald W. Riddle (University of Chicago Press). Professor Allen P. Wikgren replaced the original editors, and in 1963 published a review and summary of a dozen publications and papers that have carried this study further. See Allen P. Wikgren, "Chicago Studies in the Greek Lectionary of the New Testament," in *Biblical and Patristic Studies in Memory of Robert Pierce Casey*, ed. by J. Neville Birdsall and Robert W. Thompson (Freiburg, 1963), pp. 96-121. Wikgren concludes that the method expounded in the present chapter has been shown to be sound by these subsequent studies.

[4] A large part of the evidence which follows was collected in the summer of 1930 during a three-months' study of the lectionaries in the Bodleian Library, the British Museum, the John Rylands Library, and the Bibliothèque Nationale.

[5] By "lection" is meant the section of the gospels read at one service; thus, the "lection" for Easter Sunday is John 1:1-17.

collated against Charles Lloyd's edition of the Textus Receptus (Oxford, 1894). These twenty-six passages fall into three groups on the basis of the extent of their difference from Stephanus. (1) In seven of these sample lections the variants from Stephanus are neither considerable enough nor consistent enough to imply the existence of a lectionary text except insofar as that text is practically identical with Stephanus. (2) In fourteen lections the variants are not very numerous or decisive, and yet occur regularly enough to suggest a lectionary text distinct from Stephanus. (3) In five lections the variants are so numerous and consistent as to demonstrate the existence of a lectionary text distinct from that of Stephanus.

(1) The rather neutral evidence of the first group of seven lections must be interpreted in the light of the evidence of the two following groups. When so interpreted, it plainly indicates the existence of the lectionary text here also, but shows that it practically coincides with the text of Stephanus in these lections. Three [1] of these lections are from the Synaxarion (for the movable year), and four [2] are from the Menologion (for the fixed year). In each of these lections the agreement of the lectionaries with each other is too close to be accidental, and the number of variants from Stephanus is trifling. Almost any one of the manuscripts which contain the text of Stephanus would be found to differ more from the printed text than do the forty lectionaries here used. This can easily be illustrated from the collations published by Scrivener (20 manuscripts), which, for the lections in question, show an average departure of three readings each from the printed text. As is well known, the printed text of Stephanus as a whole is not a perfect reproduction of the readings of any New Testament codex.

TABLE I

β' of γ' ἐβδ. of John (4:46-54) in 40 lectionaries

Total number of variants	57
Average number of variants per lectionary	$1\frac{1}{3}$
No variant from Stephanus in	12 lectionaries
One variant from Stephanus in	12 lectionaries

---

[1] β' of γ' ἐβδ. of John (4:46-54); σαββατον γ' of John (15:17-16:2); σαββατον γ' of Matthew (7:24-8:4).

[2] κυριακη προ των φωτων (Mark 1:1-8); September 3 (John 10:9-16); June 24 (Luke 1:1-15); and εωθινον γ' (Mark 16:9-20).

TABLE II

In the tables, x indicates that the MS. shows the variant. The letters, a, b, c, etc., indicate a different variant (given in the notes below the table). The absence of any sign indicates agreement with Stephanus' text of 1550. Since the lectionaries were collated once only, there are probably some errors in detail. 'Incip(it)' is the opening formula, the adaptation of the text necessary for the beginning of an independent section.

β' of γ' ἑβδ. of Matthew (Matt. 9:36-10:8) in 26 lectionaries

Other support	Variants from Stephanus	2	7	8	9	10	12	14	15	69	70	150	184	191	203	233	318	319	322	332	333	336	361	371	374	930	1499
o ι̅ς̅ G al	Incip. τ. κ. ε. ειδεν ο ιησους πολυν οχλον και εσπλαγχνισθη επ αυτους οτι	x	x	a	b	x	x	x	x	x	x	x	x	x	x	x	c	x	x	x	x	x	b	x	x	x	x
all exc L al	9: 36 εσκυλμενοι	x	x	a		x	x	x	x	x	x	x	x	x	x	x	x	x	x	x	x	x	x	x	x	x	x
CDFLM al 40	9: 36 ως for ωσει	x	x		x	x	x	x	x	x	x	x	x	x	x	x	x	x	x	x	x	x	x	x	x	x	x
II 33 al	9: 36 omit και ερριμμενοι								x		x						x	x									
EFL al 50	10: 1 add κατα before πνευματων							x		x																	
C³L al mu	10: 1 add ο ι̅ς̅ before τους				x	x	x	x	x	x	x	x	x	x	x	x	x	x	x		x	x		x	x	x	x
	10: 1 omit δωδεκα			x																x							
L al 30 fere	10: 2 εισιν for εστι	x	x	x	x	x	x	x		x	x	x	x	x	x	x	x	x	x		x	x	x	x	x	x	x
	10: 2 tr. ο λεγ. Σιμ. Πετρος																			x		x				x	
DF al 2	10: 3 omit ο ι⁰		x																								
C 476	10: 4 ισκαριωθ for ισκαριωτης		x																								
L fam 13 al	10: 4 ος παρεδωκεν for ο παραδους										x	x	a					a							a	x	
F	10: 5 αποστειλας for απεστειλεν												x				x										
ℵᵇC³ unc¹² al	10: 6 omit μαλλον																										x
plus 150, vers	10: 8 omit νεκρους εγειρετε	x	x	x	x	x	x	x	x	x	x	x	x	x	x	x	x	x	x	x	x	x	x	x	x	x	x

Incip. a = περι αυτου for επ αυτους.   b = αυτους for επ αυτους.   c = τ(ω) κ(αιρω) ε(κεινω) ιδων ο ιησους τους . . . :   9: 36 a = εσκελυμμενοι.
10: 4 a = παραδιδους.

Similar figures could be given for the other six lections of this group. In four of them the average variation from the text of Stephanus is less than one variant per lectionary; the highest amount of variation, in σαββατον γ' of Matthew, is 1.6 variants per lectionary. This seems to indicate that the text of the great body of lectionaries is a unit even in those areas where it differs least from Stephanus.

(2) The fourteen lections in which the lectionary text differs enough from the Textus Receptus to suggest its existence as a separate entity without completely establishing it are drawn from both parts of the lectionary, but mainly from the Synaxarion.[1] The extent of agreement among lectionaries in these sections can be seen in the lection for Monday of the third week of Matthew (see Table II on page 86).

The twenty-six lectionaries used date from the 10th through the 14th century.[2] One other lectionary, Gregory's 364, was studied, but it contains a different section of the gospel at this point. The table shows plainly the majority of the lectionaries supporting four variants in addition to the opening formula. Only one of these four variants is supported by the majority of contemporary non-lectionary manuscripts, as adduced by Tischendorf.

Similar phenomena can be seen in almost every one of these lections, most strikingly perhaps in the lection for Tuesday of the third week of Luke (see Table III).

TABLE III

γ' of γ' ἑβδ. of Luke (6:37-45) in 23 lectionaries

Variants from Stephanus	Other support
6:44 βατων for βατου (16 lects.)	U al pauc (Lect. 49)
6:44 tr. σταφυλην τρυγωσιν (16 lects)	ℵ B C D L X Ξ 13 33 69 346 al⸗pauc (Lect. 49)
6:45 omit του 3° (15 lects)	ℵ A B D E H K S V X Δ Ξ Λ Π al 20
6:45 omit της 3° (13 lects.)	ℵ A B D Ξ al plus 10
6:45 omit αυτου 3° (17 lects.)	CF al 20 fere

---

[1] κυριακη δ' of John (5:1-15); β' of γ' ἑβδ. of Matthew (9:36-10:8); κυριακη ια' of Matthew (18:23-35); γ' of γ' ἑβδ. of Luke (6:37-45); κυριακη ε' of Luke (16:19-31); δ' of ιε' of Luke, Mark (11:23-27); σαββατον β' of Lent, Mark (1:35-45); κυριακη ε' of Lent, Mark (10:32-45); αγια γ' πρωι, Matthew (22:15-25[-46]); ωρα γ', Mark (15:16-41); αγια γ' λειτ., Matthew (24:36-25:13); January 6 ορθρος, Mark (1:9-11); παθος θ', John (19:25b-37);ο παθος ς', Matthew (27:33-54).

[2] The numbers given to the manuscripts in the Table are Gregory's lectionary numbers.

These five variants are all found in the same thirteen lectionaries; seven of the thirteen contain no other variant.

In addition, 13 variants occur (seven of these being unrecorded by Tischendorf), of which 9 are found in one lectionary each, 2 in two lectionaries, 1 in three lectionaries, and 1 in five lectionaries.

These two lections are typical of the entire group of fourteen; in these lections the lectionaries agree in a text which differs slightly from that of Stephanus and is not found in any known non-lectionary codex.

(3) In the next group of lections (five in number) the variants from Stephanus are so numerous and so consistently supported that their evidence is decisive.

The evidence of three of these is given in full (Tables IV-VI).

Table IV (on p. 89) shows that of the twenty-four lectionaries whose text is known for this lection, seventeen agree quite consistently in supporting eleven significant variants. This consistency is the more remarkable in view of the diverse character of the other attestation. Of the remaining lectionaries, three (7, 101, 15) agree in a text that differs slightly from Stephanus and largely from the lectionary text as found in the group of seventeen. Three more (76, 14, 86) agree with Stephanus; and one (8) seems to have a lectionary text which has been partially corrected to conform to the Textus Receptus.

The most valuable material for a check on the study of the text of late manuscripts is Lake's collation of about 120 such for Mark, chapter 11.[1] The difference between lectionaries and other manuscripts can be easily seen by comparing them in this section of Mark. Lake remarks upon the large number of variants and the absence of close relation between codices. But the astonishing thing about lectionaries is the very close relation between them. Seventeen out of twenty-four lectionaries support quite faithfully eleven variants in this lection, Mark 11:11-23. That this agreement is not accidental can be seen by noting the number of lectionaries and the number of codices reported by Lake that support these eleven variants.

Variant number	1	2	3	4	5	6	7	8	9	10	11
Out of 24 lectionaries	17	17	16	16	18	16	17	19	16	19	15
Out of Lake's 120 codices	1	2	9	16	0	12	2	60	0	45	24

[1] *Harvard Theological Review*, XXI (1928), 349-357.

TABLE IV

γ′ of ιε′ ἑβδ. of Luke (Mark 11: 11–23) in 24 lectionaries

(The statements about 251 and 260 are drawn from Muralt).

Other support	Variants from Stephanus	7	8	9	10	12	14	15	69	70	76	80	98	101	150	184	161	233	251	260	333	361	364	371	374
	Incip. τ. κ. ε. εισηλθεν ο ις εις ιεροσ. και εις	o	x	x	x	x	o	o	x	x		x	o	o	x	x	x	x			x	x		x	x
565 minn	11 παντας for παντα	x						x																	
אABCDLMNΔΘ fam 1 fam 13 28 565 700 al plus 20	13 add απο before μαχροθεν		x		x	x			x	x		x			x	x		x			x	x		x	x
אABCLMNΔΠ W fam 1	13 tr. τι ευρησει		x		x	x			x	x		x			x	x		x			x	x		x	x
28 al	14 omit ο ιησους	o	x		x	x	o		x	x		x		x	x	x	x	x		x	x	x	x	x	x
אABCKLΔΠ Caesarean Mss.	14 φαγει for φαγοι	x	x		x	x	o	o	x	x	x	x			x	x	x	x			x	x		x	x
DUW fam 1 fam 13 28 al	15 add παλιν after ερχονται	x	x		x	x		o	x	x		x	o	x	x	x	x	x		x	x	x	x	x	x
N al (Lect. 49)	15 add τους before αγορας	x	x		x	x			x	x		x	o	x	x	x		x			x	x		x	x
אABCKLMNUΠ al 20 fere	17 omit οτι	x						x						x											
CD al pauc	17 tr. αυτον εποιησατε	x	x		x	x			x	x	x	x		x	x	x	x	x		o	x	x	x	x	x
AMΘΠ 33 fam 1 565 700	18 add κ. οι φαρ. after γρ.	x	x		x	x			x	x		x		x	x	x	x	x		x	x	x	x	x	x
pauc (Lects. 18 19 49)	18 απολεσωσιν for -ουσιν	x	x		x	x			x	x		x		x	x	x	x	x			x	x		x	x
אABCEGHD al 50 Caesarean mss.	20 tr. παραπορευομενοι πρωι	x	x		x	x			x	x		x		x	x	x	x	x		x	x	x	x	x	x
	21 ειπεν for λεγει		x									x													
syr sin Θ 565 700 (M 33)	21 τω ιησου for αυτω																						x		
אBCDLΔW 33 fam 1 28	22 add ο before ιησους	x	x	x	x	x			x	x		x		x	x	x	x	x		x	x	x	x	x	x
unc omn min plu Caesarean Mss.																									
XΓ al mu	23 πιστευσει for -ση	x	x		x	x	x	x	x	x		x	x	x	x	x	x	x			x	x		x	x

Incip. o = εις ιεροσ. ο ιησους ο ις εις. 76 is torn here, and the evidence for 251 and 260 is not available. 14 o = φαγη. 17 o = omit αυτον. 23 o = πιστευει.

The following variants have no (or very litle) support elsewhere:

13 add εν αυτη after ευρεν 9
13 add και before ηλθεν 233
14 70 has a variant which I have lost
15 τραπεζας for καθεδρας 184, 364
15 εισηλθεν και for εισελθων 150
15 om εις 361
16 δε for και 7
18 και for οτι 80
21 εξηρανται for εξηρανται 8, 364, 14
23 add μη before πιστευση 70

The uniformity of lectionary support for these variants and the wide variation in the support found among other codices show that here there is a lectionary text distinct from that of late manuscripts in general.

Another striking instance of the agreement of lectionaries is found in another lection in this group of five, that from the Gospel of John for September 14 (see Table V on p. 91).

The entire lection, John 19:6-35, was collated in the forty-four manuscripts, but only the first half of the lection is shown in the Table. In this first half, the following variants have no (or very little) support elsewhere:

19:6 omit πιλατος 152	19:17 γαβαθα for γολγοθα 328
19:6 tr. αιτιαν εν αυτω 318	19:17 εξηλθον for εξηλθεν 7, 188, 373
19:11 omit κατ εμου 369	19:17 τοπον for τον 2° 13, 16
19:14 omit δε ωσει 366	

One lectionary (329) differs so widely from the rest that its text cannot easily be shown in the same table.

In the second half of the lection, which does not appear in the Table, the chief variants with their support are as follows (the total number of lectionaries supporting the variant, and not the numbers of individual lectionaries, is given):

19:17 εαυτου for αυτου (29 lects.) A IU Y min (Lect. 135)
19:20 tr. ο τοπος της πολεως (40 lects.) ℵª A B Dˢᵘᵖᵖ I L X Y Γ Λ Π unc⁶
      minn longe plu
19:21-25 (εποιησαν) omit (42 lects.) no others
19:26 ιδε for ιδου (44 lects.) B Dˢᵘᵖᵖ M Tᵈ X Λ al 80 fere
19:27 ημερας for ωρας (37 lects.) A Eˡ ᵛⁱᵈ al 40
19:27 add εκεινος after μαθητης (42 lects.) U Γ al 50
19:28 ταυτα for τουτο (33 lects.) U al 30
19:28 omit ηδη (41 lects.) fam 1 565 al plus 30
19:28 add περι αυτου after τετελεσται (40 lects.) U Mᵐᵍ al pl 20
19:28 (ινα τελεσθω) — 30 (τετελεσται) omit (44 lects.) no others
19:34 ευθεως for ευθυς (44 lects.) Dˢᵘᵖᵖ G M U Y Γ al plus 60
19:35 tr. εστιν η μαρτυρια αυτου (44 lects.) H Y al 60

In this lection the agreement of the lectionaries is most striking. In twenty-nine verses the majority of the forty-five lectionaries collated agree in twenty-five variants. If the four variants which involve the omission of ten and a half verses be disregarded, there remain twenty-one variants in eighteen and a half verses. Only four lectionaries differ from the majority sufficiently to be classified as having other than the lectionary text, and the text of three of these (2, 16, 366) is indicated in Table V (on p. 91). Furthermore it should be noted that here, as elsewhere, the highly divergent

TABLE V

Liturgy, September 14 (John 19: 6-17) in 44 lectionaries

Manuscript columns (reading left to right across the grid):
1, 7, 7, 2, 8, 11, 12, 13, 14, 15, 16, 17, 25, 64, 69, 70, 71, 76, 150, 151, 152, 184, 188, 189, 193, 318, 319, 326, 328, 331, 333, 335, 364, 365, 366, 367, 369, 372, 373, 374, 930, 1231, 1491, 1492

Other support	Variants from Stephanus
none	Incipit
none	7-9 a (πραιτωριον) omit
ΣΓΔΛ 127 al 25	7 tr. θεον υιον
Mᵐᵍ²	9 ο πιλατος for και 2°
ℵ*ABE*	10 tr. απολυσαι...σταυρωσαι
ℵ*A 28 69 124 346 435 al 25	10 omit ουν
BDˢᵘᵖᵖEHKSUXY*ΓΠ al 50	11 omit ο 1°
Δ*28 80 235 254 al	11 omit ουδεμιαν
none	11 omit δια...12 end
none	13 τοτε ουν ο for ο ουν
HΓΠ minn 60 (Lect. 135)	13 γαβαθα for γαββαθα
ℵABDˢᵘᵖᵖLMUXΔΠ al 60 (Lect. 135)	14 ην for δε 2°
min (Lect. 135)	15 εκραζον for εκραυγασαν
U fam 13 al 15 (Lect. 135)	15 add λεγοντες after εκραυ-γασαν
ℵᶜ UΠ² al 20 (Lect. 135)	16 παραλαβοντες for παρελα-βον
ℵ*⁺ᶜMUΠ² fam 1 al (Lect. 135)	16 omit και
127 131 (Lect. 135)	16 ηγαγον for απηγαγον
MUΓ 127 262 299 al permu	16 add εις το πραιτωριον after απηγαγον
ℵABK 157 440 al 20 (Lect. 135)	17 ο for ος

Incipit = τ. κ. ε. συμβουλιον εποιησαν οι αρχιερεις και οι πρεσβυτεροι κατα του ιησου οπως αυτου απολεσωσιν και παρεγενοντο προς πιλατον λεγοντες αρον αρον σταυρωσον αυτον λεγει. Incip. o = υπηρεται for πρεσβυτεροι, omit οπως...πιλατον, και ελεγον for λεγοντες. Incip. + = add του λαου after πρεσβυτεροι...ωστε θανατωσαι αυτον...9 o = και ο πιλατος 9+ = ουν ο πιλατος 11—12 o = omit κατ εμου 11—12 + = εαυτον for αυτον 13 o = τοτε ο 14 o = omit δε 14+ = ως τριτη for ωσει εκτη 15 o = εκραυγαζον 16 o = omit και απηγαγον.

character of the supporting attestation throws the close agreement of the lectionaries into bold relief.

Of the two preceding lections one comes from the Synaxarion and one from the Menologion. The following lection comes from the Easter season and shows the same high agreement of lectionaries.

TABLE VI

Liturgy, παθος ϛ′ (Mark 15:16-32 a)

Incip. τ.κ.ε. οι στρατιωται απηλαγον τον ιησουν εις την αυλην του καιαφα ο (44 lects.)

15:18 ο βασιλευς for βασιλευ (50 lects.) A C² E F G H K N U Γ Π al plu 110
15:24 διαμεριζονται for διεμεριζον (36 lects.) ℵ A B C D L P X Γ Δ Π unc⁹ fam 1 al plus 130
　　　　[διεμεριζοντο (7 lects.) 69 124 al 15 fere]
15:28 omit verse (48 lects.) ℵ A B C¹ ⁺ ³ D X al 25 fere item Eus canon ut vdtr
15:32 add αυτω after πιστευσωμεν (39 lects.) C³ D F G H M¹ P V² Γ Π² al 80
　　　　[add εις αυτον (5 lects.) al pauc]

In addition to these, the lectionaries show approximately 38 variants, of which 33 are supported by fewer than 5 lectionaries. The other five variants are supported by from 5 to 21 lectionaries. It is worthy of note that the two variants which are supported by the highest number of lectionaries are very differently supported by non-lectionary manuscripts, the first being supported by more than 110, and the second by about 25. Here again the lectionaries agree with one another in readings where contemporary non-lectionary manuscripts do not agree with one another.

The agreement of lectionaries with one another can also be shown by comparing some collations made in Paris in 1930 with published collations of lectionaries. In Mark 5:1-20 I collated the text of four lectionaries selected at random in the Bibliothèque Nationale. Table VII (on p. 94) shows the agreement of these four with the text of five lectionaries published by Scrivener and Muralt. One of the five is 184, British Museum, Burney 22, which Scrivener, Gregory, and Hort regarded as having an unusually good text. Yet this lectionary has in this lection, out of twenty-two variants, only two which are not supported by other lectionaries.[1] The

---

[1] A study of the variants read by 184 in Tables II and IV will show the same high agreement with other lectionaries; the same is true in six out of eight other lections in which a comparison is possible.

only one of the nine lectionaries to disagree with the majority
is 260, and its disagreement lies in the possession of eight variants
in addition to eighteen variants supported by the other lectionaries.

A further hint as to the extent of the agreement of lectionaries
is found in the text of two lectionaries, 12 and 70, selected at
random, which were collated throughout Mark, insofar as the text
of Mark appears in 52 lections for week-days in the Synaxarion.
Codex 12 has 302 variants from Stephanus; codex 70 has 352; and
they agree in 288 variants. About one-tenth of the variants in
which they agree have no attestation of any kind in Tischendorf's
apparatus criticus.

Thus we see that lectionaries agree with one another in lections
taken from the Synaxarion and in lections taken from the Menologion. They agree in lections where their text is practically identical
with the Textus Receptus, and they agree where their text differs
widely from the Textus Receptus. Whether a small number of
lectionaries are compared in a large number of lections or a large
number of lectionaries are compared in a small number of lections,
the result is the same: they agree with one another. This agreement
is the more significant when it is noted that the support from
non-lectionary manuscripts varies in both kind and amount; and
even where there is no other support, the agreement of lectionary
with lectionary is as close as ever. Such agreement justifies speaking
of the text of lectionaries as "the lectionary text."

Several years ago the British and American Committees of the
International Greek New Testament Manuscript Project agreed to
publish the readings of this "lectionary text" under a siglum which
would represent the agreement of the vast majority of lectionary
manuscripts. These readings will be established by a carefully
selected limited sample of "middle-of-the-road" lectionary manuscripts. These committees have further agreed to cite completely as
single witnesses a number of lectionary manuscripts whose text
diverges from that of the dominant lectionary text. The first step
will make the evidence of *the* lectionary text available; the second
will contribute to the writing of the history of that text's encounters
with and modifications by other elements in the transmission of the
Greek New Testament throughout the later manuscript period.

TABLE VII

Comparison of two sets of lectionaries

Lectionaries 12, 70, 69, and 10 are here cited from fresh collations. 150 is H of Scrivener (*Exact Transcript of the Codex Augiensis* 1859), and 185 is Scrivener's z (*A Full and Exact Collation*, 1853). 184 is Scrivener's y (ibid.) 251 (Greg.) is 3 of Muralt, and 260 (Greg.) Muralt's 10. The column headed IIτ gives the evidence of the Patriarchate Greek New Testament (Constantinople, 1904), which is based on lectionaries.

Only those variants of WH from Stephanus which are also found in one or more lectionaries are noted in the Table. There are 10 other variants of WH not here noted.

Lectionary 260 is the only one of the lectionaries consulted which seriously departs from the "lectionary text"; to a remarkable degree its departures are agreements with WH. Its readings are known only through a collation sent to Muralt from Odessa, and the present location of the lectionary itself is unknown.

ε′ of ιδ′ έββ. of Matthew (Mark 5:1-20)

Other support	Variants from Stephanus	Codex 12	70	69	10	150	185	184	251	260	IIτ	WH
		Cent. xiii	xiii	xii	xii	xiii	x	xi	xiv	?		
LUΔ 1 28 33 118 131 209 565 al 20	1 γεργεσηνων for γαδαρηνων	x	x	x	x	x	x	x	x	x	x	o
א BCLΔ 1 13 33 69 118 124 131 209 346 565 al 10 fere	2 εξελθοντος αυτου											
א BCDGLΔ 1 13 28 69 al 20	2 υπηγγησεν for απηγγησεν	x	x	x		x	x			x	x	x
א ABCLΔII unc⁸ al longe plu	3 μνημασι for μνημειοις	x	x	x		x	x	x		x		x
א ABCDLΔII unc⁶ minn 50	3 εδυνατο for ηδυνατο				x	x				x	x	x
BC*L 33 565	3 αλυσει for αλυσεσιν								x			x
א ABCKLMUΔ al 20	4 tr. ισχυεν αυτον	x	x	x	x	x	x			x	x	x
א ABCKLMUΔXII al 60	5 tr. εν τ. μν. κ. εν τ. ο.	x	x	x	x	x	x			x	x	x
א BCLΔ 1 28 69 131 346	6 και ιδων for ιδων δε	x	x	x				x	x	x	x	x
AKLMII al plus 30	6 omit απο							x	x	x		[x]
ABCLΔ al 15	6 αυτον for αυτω	x	x				x	x	x	x		x
א ABCKLΔ al plus 30	7 λεγει for ειπε	x	x	x	x	x	x	x	x	x		x
א ABCKLMΔΠᵗˣᵗ al plus 25	9 tr. ονομα σοι	x	x	x	x	x	x	x	x	x	x	x

TABLE VII (*Continued*)

Variants:

9 λεγει αυτω for απεκριθη λεγων
10 tr. αποστειλη αυτους
11 τω ορει for τα ορη
11 tr. προς τω ορει to end
11 omit μεγαλη
13 αυτους for αυτοις
13 omit ευθεως ο ιησους
13 omit ησαν δε
14 και οι for οι δε
14 αυτους for τους χοιρους
14 απηγγειλαν for ανηγγειλαν
14 omit εις 2°
14 ηλθον for εξηλθον
15 omit καθημενον
15 omit και ιματισμενον
18 εμβαινοντος for εμβαντος
18 tr. μετ αυτου η
19 και for ο δε ιησους
19 απαγγειλον for αναγγειλον
19 tr. ο κυριος σοι
19 πεποιηκεν for εποιησε

Manuscripts:

אABCKLMΔΠ txt al plus 25
AM al 20
unc omn minn 150
AKΠ txt al plus 15
DLU 131 al pauc
U al
אBCLΔ 1 28 102 118 131 209 al pauc
BC¹DLΔ 1 565
אABCDLMΔ al 25
אBCDLΔ 13 69 124 346 565
אABCDKLMII al 35
no attestation
א^e ABKLMUII* 33 al 30
Δ 472
M¹
אABCDKLMΔΠ 1 33 124 al 25
אBCKLMUΔΠ txt 1 28 33 69 al 25
אABCKLMΔΠ 1 33 102 al 30
אBCΔ al pauc
BCΔ
אABCLII unc⁸ al 100

10 a = αποστειλη αυτον

The only other variants in these mss. are without support elsewhere; they are:

3 κατοικιαν 185
4 συντριφθαι 185
9 μου for μοι 70
10 omit ινα 251
11 το ορος for τα ορη 184
13 omit εισηλθον 260
16 omit πως εγενετο 70
18 add πολλα after αυτον 260

CHAPTER SEVEN

METHOD IN CLASSIFYING AND EVALUATING VARIANT READINGS [1]

(With Ernest W. Tune)

When one begins to speak of variant readings, he is immediately confronted with the question, "Variant from what?" The very word "variant" implies a deviation or change from something else taken for a norm. Yet we use this word blithely in New Testament textual studies, not always making clear just what norm we have in mind.

Certainly we cannot define a variant reading in terms of variation from the original Greek autographs. So what is commonly done in practice? Some particular text is chosen—often at random—for the norm. Either we use a printed text such as the Textus Receptus, sometimes an edition by Tischendorf, Westcott-Hort, or Nestle; or, we may use the text of a particular manuscript whose textual affinities are already known, e.g., Vaticanus or Alexandrinus. It is against these norms that other Greek texts are usually compared. And it is this process of comparison which gives rise to a set of variant readings for the text under consideration.

For the present moment, the exact manner, purpose, and terminology involved in the comparison just mentioned is beside the point. The important fact to be noticed is that such a set of variant readings, produced by the process of comparison, has only a relative validity. It is only between the particular Greek texts being compared that this peculiar set of differences exists. And any inference or conclusion which involves additional manuscripts should be made with caution.

All this may appear to be only a stating of the obvious. It may even be difficult at first glance to see how any problem could arise over the interpretation of data obtained in this fashion. Nevertheless, it is the opinion of the authors of the present chapter that the careless use of variant readings to establish manuscript

---

[1] Originally published as "Variant Readings: Classification and Use," *Journal of Biblical Literature*, LXXXIII (1964), 253-61.

relationships often renders inaccurate the conclusions of an otherwise fine text study.[1] This is especially so for studies to determine
manuscript kinship where the manuscripts involved have large
differences in their texts.

If then a clearer definition of a variant is needed, the beginning
of wisdom is to attempt such a definition. We should like to suggest
the following.

A unit-of-variation or a variation-unit could be described in
terms of that passage or section of the Greek New Testament where
our manuscripts do not agree as to what the Greek text is. By
variation-unit we do not mean an individual variant reading in a
particular manuscript. Rather we are referring to a length of the
text wherein our manuscripts present at least two variant forms;
it is that passage in which differences occur.

Thus in John 11:29, Tischendorf indicates that manuscripts
disagree in three places in this verse. This means there are three
variation-units in this verse. Outside of these three places in the text,
the manuscripts all agree and show no differences. The first
variation-unit contains these three alternative readings: και εκεινη,
εκεινη δε, and εκεινη. Some invariable text follows (ως ηκουσεν)
in which all manuscripts agree; then the second set of differences
occurs: εγειρεται and ηγερθη. More invariable text follows (ταχυ
και) until the third variation-units occur. Here manuscripts read
either ερχεται or ηρχετο. The remaining invariable text (προς αυτον)
concludes the verse. All of these data (the three variation-units
containing manuscript alternatives, and the invariable text)
could be diagrammed as follows:

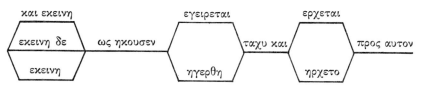

When one manuscript is compared with another to establish
kinship, it is important to know the total number of variation-
units which exists in that portion of the text being used. This
is always a larger number than the number of variant readings that
exist between any two witnesses, or the number of variant readings
secured by collating an individual manuscript with a printed text.

---

[1] See Chapter IV (pp. 56-62 above) for further elaboration of this point.

Such lesser totals are only a partial citation of the evidence of kinship between manuscripts. The total range of existing variation must be taken as the only adequate basis of comparison.

Take as an example the important Bodmer Papyrus $\mathfrak{P}^{75}$. It is relatively meaningless to ask, "How many times in John 11 does manuscript $\mathfrak{P}^{75}$ differ from Stephanus?" The important question is, "How many units-of-variation are there in this chapter?" and then to find the maximum agreement of $\mathfrak{P}^{75}$ with any other witnesses in this total record of the units-of-variation. Nor will the task of locating $\mathfrak{P}^{75}$ be completed solely by collating $\mathfrak{P}^{75}$ with codex Vaticanus to which it is closely related. The task of the appraiser of $\mathfrak{P}^{75}$ requires that he locate this new witness within the total amount of manuscript variation in the 11th chapter of John, if that is the sample to be analyzed.

According to our figures, with the set of manuscripts being used for this sampling, there are (conveniently) 100 variation-units in John 11. At 92 of these variation-units, $\mathfrak{P}^{75}$ has the same variant readings as Vaticanus. There is no other manuscript with which it agrees so frequently. It agrees with the Textus Receptus at only 52 of these 100 places. But please note, if we had the figures of agreement, which were respectively 92 and 52, without any knowledge of the total variants possible, we could easily be misled. If the total number of possible variations were 200, instead of 100, the figures 92 and 52 would not mean what they do in the actual case before us. These figures point out why we need to have such a distinction as the variation-unit in text criticism, regardless of what we ultimately call it.

When we say "our manuscripts present at least two variant forms," we mean ideally all known manuscript evidence. But in the interest of accuracy, careful workers will want to recheck citations of manuscript evidence in existing apparatuses. This limits the number of manuscripts whose evidence can be cited. We believe that the minimum number to be cited must include representatives of the known major types of text, and, if possible, representatives of well-established family groups.

A further problem in the definition of a unit-of-variation is its extent. One scholar may subdivide what another scholar regards as a single unit. Does this destroy the accuracy of tabulation of agreements in variation-units? The answer to this question is yet to be determined, but we believe the problem can be satisfactorily solved.

Definition of the extent of the unit-of-variation should be made empirically by observing what occurs in the manuscript tradition. When we find the change in a conjunction at the beginning of a sentence is always accompanied by the use of a participle rather than a finite verb, it becomes clear that the unit-of-variation includes both the conjunction and the verbal form, i.e., that they are one unit-of-variation, not two. In other words, the general rule for the recognition of a total variation-unit is by noticing those elements of expression in the Greek text which regularly exist together.

Thus, for example, in Tischendorf's edition at John 1:50 the variant reading βασιλευς ει is cited together with the variant reading ει ο βασιλευς. This is preferable to citing βασιλευς over against ο βασιλευς as one unit-of-variation, and then adding a second unit-of-variation for βασιλευς ει and ει ο βασιλευς. There is only one unit-of-variation here, since the presence or absence of the article accompanies the transposition in word order in the individual witness cited. It is what goes together in the individual witnesses that establishes the unit-of-variation.

There is another advantage to using such a variation-unit. We are working in a period when the data for textual criticism will inevitably be translated into mathematics. In fact it is doubtful that New Testament textual critics can really hope to relate all of the data now available to them without the aid of computers. Our suggested definition of a variation-unit could easily be translated into mathematics. The individual manuscript variants could also be easily identified numerically in such a scheme.[1]

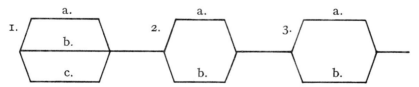

How does all of this help us to define a variant? That is the question we started out to answer. Perhaps it might be formulated as follows. A variant (or variant reading) is one of the possible

---

[1] James William Ellison in his doctoral dissertation of 1957 at Harvard Divinity School, *The Use of Electronic Computers in the Study of the Greek New Testament Text*, has shown in detail how a numerical code can be used to indicate variant readings in the Greek text. He uses Luke 10:1-15 as a sample passage for demonstrating his method.

alternative readings which are found in a variation-unit. This definition avoids defining a variant relative to any single manuscript or printed text. Rather it establishes the variant reading empirically as part of the total scheme of differences known to exist in the manuscript tradition.

But now we should like to turn and look at the individual variant readings which make up the variation-unit. This is the second essential step. All other parts of this study are sequential and rest upon the study of variant readings. This is true both of the description of an individual manuscript and of the grouping of manuscripts. Moreover the construction of a useful and dependable *apparatus criticus* presupposes a careful classification of variant readings.

Not all variant readings deserve continued study if the goal of that study is either to write the history of the manuscript tradition or to reconstruct the original wording of the Greek New Testament. The identification of a reading as a variant reading does not predetermine its inclusion in the later phases of manuscript study. Only if our goal were to make available all data needed for *any* future study of any part or all of the existing manuscript copies (however inconceivable that study may be to us) can we justify the inclusion of *all* variant readings beyond the first stage of textual criticism. No such goal commends itself as defensible in the textual criticism of the Greek New Testament. Two facts prevent its adoption: (*a*) The vast mass of material (literally thousands of manuscripts) makes it impracticable; (*b*) the number and range of variant readings which have no significance for history or original text would confuse and defeat all study directed toward those goals.

Variant readings should be classified so as to make possible the elimination of insignificant variant readings from the subsequent stages of this study. This classification should be objective-descriptive where that is possible, but should not hesitate to rely on judgment based on a careful survey of differences.

Binary classifications of the clear either/or type lack general validity. Thus the classification of all variant readings as "errors" or "correct readings" lacks the requisite complexity and accuracy. So also a simple classification into "intentional variations" or "unintended variations." Each of these four classes has an area of valid application, but not as one of only two possible classes.

In the remainder of this chapter we shall present the beginnings of a system for classifying variant readings.[1] A few categories are suggested which the authors believe may prove stimulating to further work in this area. The examples cited are all chosen from three of our earliest papyri, $\mathfrak{P}^{45}$, $\mathfrak{P}^{66}$, $\mathfrak{P}^{75}$.

The Nonsense Reading. This is the extreme case of the unintended error. It is the one clear, objectively demonstrable error. It is, by definition, that variant reading which does not make sense, and/or cannot be found in the lexicon, and/or is not Greek grammar.

It is to be rejected—not only as one of the claimants to be the original text but also from further study; therefore, it is to be excluded from the critical apparatus.

This decision rests upon the high historical probability that neither the original author nor a scribe wrote nonsense, except by inadvertence. It rests on the second probability that scribes were more prolific than authors in the production of nonsense. The external evidence for this conclusion is strong; it lies in the existence of other variant readings that make sense out of those passages in which a Nonsense Reading makes nonsense.

The soundness of the judgment that the Nonsense Reading is insignificant as claimant to be the original reading has never been challenged by the scholars who work in this field.

But the judgment that the Nonsense Reading is insignificant for the writing of the history of the manuscript tradition has been challenged. Carl Lachmann pointed out that agreement in error indicates a common ancestry. Since his day, scholars have used agreement in error to build the *stemma* (the family tree) of the manuscripts containing a literary work from classical antiquity. This genealogical method—which reconstructs the history of the manuscript tradition through construction of the family tree or genealogy—became dominant in the textual criticism of the classics by the last quarter of the nineteenth century.

Fenton John Anthony Hort used "genealogical method" to overthrow the rule of the late Byzantine type (the Alpha-type of text) in his edition of *The New Testament in the Original Greek* (1881).[2] But he used another of Lachmann's principles, that where

---

[1] The authors are carrying this study further and what follows should be considered only a beginning.

[2] See Chapter V (pp. 63-83 above).

errors cannot be used, the agreement of all readings indicates a common ancestry. Hort's knowledge of the manuscripts of the New Testament was encyclopedic, and his judgment was sound. He based his method upon agreement in readings, not upon agreement in error.

The course of New Testament textual criticism since Hort's day has endorsed his rejection of the "agreement in error" criterion. The reasons for this are empirically sound. No one has been able to establish the existence of even a small family of New Testament manuscripts by using agreement in error. Errors seem to have had a short life in the manuscript period. In circumstances where individual scribes had great freedom (and thus could produce errors), their freedom seems to have included the freedom to correct obvious errors—the Nonsense Reading. In circumstances where a dominant type controlled the tradition, scribes were not free to introduce Nonsense Readings into it. In any case, the facts are that Nonsense Readings are frequent in some individual manuscripts, but they are not common to families, tribes, or types of text. Therefore the Nonsense Reading can be safely ignored.

The following are examples of some of the common types of Nonsense Reading:

John   3:27   ου δυναται ανθρωπος λαμβανει ουδε ἑν
($\mathfrak{P}^{75}$)   (λαμβανει for λαμβανειν by error)
John   3:29   ο εχων τη νυμφην
($\mathfrak{P}^{66*}$)   (omission of letter)
John 11:1   μαριας και μαριας
($\mathfrak{P}^{66*}$)   (harmonization to immediate context)
John 11:11   λαζαρος η φιλος ημων
($\mathfrak{P}^{75}$)   (η for ο)
Luke   9:31   ελεγον την εξοδον αυτου ην εμελλον
($\mathfrak{P}^{45}$)   (plural for singular)
Luke   9:32   διεγρηγορη(σαν)τες
($\mathfrak{P}^{45}$)   (impossible form; N.B. -τες begins new line)
Luke 10:19   δεδωμι
($\mathfrak{P}^{45}$)   (impossible form)

The Dislocated Reading. This might more properly be called the Dislocated Scribe. The scribe has taken his eye off the exemplar. When he looks at it again, his eye falls upon a word identical with (or similar to) the last word he copied, but—alas!—located some distance before or after the last word he copied.

If it is some distance before the last word he copied, he copies a passage over again. For example, in John 11:2-3 the scribe of $\mathfrak{P}^{75}$ wrote:

ησθενει απεστειλαν ουν αι αδελφαι προς
was sick. The sisters then sent to
αυτον λεγουσαι κυριε ιδε ον φιλεις
him saying, Lord, Behold he whom you love
ασθενει απεστειλαν ουν αι αδελφαι προς
is sick. The sisters then sent to
αυτον
him

The error is clear. The scribe lost his place after he had written "is sick" (ασθενει). When he looked back, he found the first "sick" (ησθενει), and started over on "The sisters." Another example is Luke 9:57 in 𝔓⁴⁵.

Alternatively, if the scribe's eye falls upon a word identical with (or similar to) the last word he copied but located some distance after the last word he copied, he omits a passage. For example, in John 3:17 the scribe of 𝔓⁶⁶ wrote:

ου γαρ απεστειλεν ο θεος τον υιον εις τον
For God sent not the Son into the
κοσμον αλλ ινα σωθη ο κοσμος
world, but in order that the world

The error is clear. The exemplar read:

ου γαρ απεστειλεν ο θεος τον υιον εις τον
For God sent not the Son into the
κοσμον ινα κρινη τον
world, in order that he might condemn the
κοσμον αλλ ινα σωθη ο κοσμος
world, but in order that the world

The scribe lost his place after the first "world," and erroneously found it again after the second.

The Dislocated Reading belongs with the Nonsense Reading in the general group of errors that involve unintended variation. Here, too, the error is clear, and usually demonstrable; though in both these matters the Dislocated Reading is definitely second to the Nonsense Reading. But it is like the Nonsense Reading in that it is to be excluded from the subsequent stages of textual criticism. Readings of this class should not be included in a critical apparatus; they are clearly insignificant readings. It may be worth noting that each of the examples quoted here was corrected by the scribe who made it. Neither affected the content of copies.

The Singular Reading. While the Nonsense Reading and the Dislocated Reading may be singular readings, they occasionally find support through casual agreement in error. They are to be differentiated from the Singular Reading also by the greater range of the latter class. Some Singular Readings make sense, and some are not dislocated. But all are to be ignored in the subsequent stages of manuscript study.

The Singular Reading is prevented by its very nature from usefulness in establishing group relationships of manuscripts. And if it be argued (as it sometimes is) that a Singular Reading may be the original reading, a sufficient answer lies in the high probability that in a tradition so richly evidenced as that of the New Testament, the original reading has survived in some group or type of text.

It may be argued that the Singular Reading should be cited because future discoveries may include a manuscript which shares this Singular Reading. If this Singular Reading has not been recorded in the *apparatus criticus*, shall we not be hampered in the establishment of relationship? The answer is "No." Group relationships are demonstrated by agreement in those readings which are peculiar *to the group*, and by the percentage of agreement in the total mass of variants. Once a relationship has been established, any agreement in Singular Readings can be picked up by reference to facsimile or to collation. The Singular Reading should not be allowed to clutter up the apparatus or to waste the scholar's time.

Yet the Singular Readings have a value in the initial appraisal of the work of the scribe in a particular manuscript. If his pages are crowded with them, he is a careless or rash workman. Moreover a study of his singular readings will reveal habits and inclinations that will aid in the appraisal of his readings which are not singulars.

In his edition of $\mathfrak{P}^{45}$, Kenyon passed lightly over the astonishingly large number of Singular Readings in that papyrus. He says, "Further it has a considerable number of readings which are either singular or have very slight support elsewhere, though most of these only affect the order of the words or other small details. The most notable new readings are in Luke 9:50, 11:15, 11:42, 12:4 and 13:32 [which he quotes]."[1] His lists contain a total of 254 Singular Readings.

In Chapters 11-12 of Luke, Singular Readings were found in 74 verses. Add those lost in gaps, and the average is almost one to a verse. If, furthermore, the small size of many fragmented pages is taken into account, one must compute a total of from 2,000 to 3,000 Singular Readings in $\mathfrak{P}^{45}$, or an average of 10 to 15 or more to a page.

---

[1] *The Chester Beatty Biblical Papyri*, Fasc. II, *The Gospel and Acts, Text*, pp. xiv f.

Again, Kenyon's reference to transpositions is misleading. We found twice as many omissions or shortened forms as transpositions; many more substitutions; and as many additions. The transpositions were only one-sixth of the singular readings counted.

The most remarkable fact about the text of $\mathfrak{P}^{45}$ is this mass of Singular Readings. $\mathfrak{P}^{45}$ is an undisciplined text, obviously not subject to learned or to ecclesiastical control. A survey of these readings gives one a clear impression of a scribe who felt free to modify the text in matters of detail. $\mathfrak{P}^{45}$ is a maverick, as Westerners would say; it runs wild. When its relationship to the Caesareans is reconsidered (as it should be), this important element of its nature should be given serious consideration. For example, in Singular Readings in the preference for short readings, the scribe often uses the simple verb as against the compound verb of the total tradition. When then in agreement with others he uses the simple verb rather than the compound, what weight can be given to this agreement? Is $\mathfrak{P}^{45}$ here following his group? Or is he again expressing his preference for the simple verb even though his archetype had the compound?

For one interested in pursuing the study of the significance of Singular Readings, attention is called to manuscript 1546 of Family II. From a study of the Gospel of Luke, 1546 seems to rival $\mathfrak{P}^{45}$ in the number of singular readings.

But what conclusion do we draw from all this? No doubt some will want to object to it. But it is the writers' opinion that the Singular Reading, like its cousins the Nonsense Reading and the Dislocated Reading, should not be used as one of the possible alternative readings which go to make up the variation-unit. It is not genealogically significant; it should not be counted.

The data submitted here justify further investigation of the concept of the variation-unit. Moreover these data clearly promise that the extension of the list of types of alternative readings will be of service in future studies of the manuscript tradition of the Greek New Testament.

CHAPTER EIGHT

METHOD IN EVALUATING SCRIBAL HABITS: [1]

A STUDY OF $\mathfrak{P}^{45}$, $\mathfrak{P}^{66}$, $\mathfrak{P}^{75}$

The dead hand of Fenton John Anthony Hort lies heavy upon us. In the early years of this century Kirsopp Lake described Hort's work as a failure, though a glorious one. But Hort did *not* fail to reach his major goal. He dethroned the Textus Receptus. After Hort, the late medieval Greek Vulgate was not used by serious students, and the text supported by earlier witnesses became the standard text. This was a sensational achievement, an impressive success. Hort's success in this task and the cogency of his tightly reasoned theory shaped—and still shapes—the thinking of those who approach the textual ciriticism of the New Testament through the English language.

I do not mean to suggest that this influence is undeserved. Hort's second volume is still the best statement of theory and method in this field of study. His knowledge was comprehensive, and his judgments were marked by a wisdom so unusual as to merit the word "unique." Any one who would think constructively here must first rethink Hort's thoughts.

But I would be the last to suggest that his system was a perfect one. Many years ago I joined others in pointing out the limitations in Hort's use of genealogy, and the inapplicability of genealogical method—strictly defined—to the textual criticism of the New Testament. Since then many others have assented to this criticism, and the building of family trees is only rarely attempted. Therefore we might assume that the influence of Hort's emphasis upon genealogical method is no longer a threat. But this assumption is false.

Hort's brilliant work still captivates our minds. So when confronted by a reading whose support is minimal and widely divorced in time and place, we think first and only of genealogical relationships. Hort has put genealogical blinders on our eyes that keep us from recognizing the major role played by scribal corruption.

---

[1] Originally published as "Scribal Habits in Early Papyri: A Study in the Corruption of the Text," in *The Bible in Modern Scholarship*, ed. by J. Philip Hyatt (Nashville, 1965), pp. 370-389.

True, Hort's basic dictum was "identity of reading implies identity of origin," but he at times slips into the argument that identity in *a* reading implies identity of origin. This is not true, nor is it Hort's real position. He recognized the importance of extensive agreement in numerous readings, as also of agreement in distinctive readings.[1] But the followers of Hort commonly fall into the fallacy of assuming that any agreement in readings demands the assumption of a common ancestry. We forget to ask, "How much agreement is significant?"

From his study of the manuscript tradition of Cyprian, Bévenot emphasizes the importance of quantity in agreements: "But whether correct or not," he says, "and whether recognizably correct or not, a great number of such common readings reveals a *connexion* between these two manuscripts, either by direct transcription or by borrowing, whereas a small number of such common readings indicates little or no connexion." [2]

The influence of Hort limits our vision in another way. For him the external evidence of documents was as important as it was for the champions of the Textus Receptus. His prudent rejection of almost all readings which have no manuscript support has given the words "conjectural emendation" a meaning too narrow to be realistic. In the last generation we have depreciated external evidence of documents and have appreciated the internal evidence of readings; but we have blithely assumed that we were rejecting "conjectural emendation" if our conjectures were supported by some manuscripts. We need to recognize that the editing of an eclectic text rests upon conjectures. If these conjectures are to be soundly based, they must rest upon transcriptional probability as well as intrinsic probability. If the conjectures as to transcriptional probability are to be soundly based, they must rest upon a knowledge of scribal habits.

A careful study of what scribes actually did, with a resultant catalogue of readings produced by scribes, is essential for textual criticism. Two outstanding scholars have emphasized this need. Maas claims that, "To reach firm ground in this field it would be necessary to prepare a catalogue of all peculiar errors arranged in classes according to the different periods of history, types of

---

[1] For a discussion of these criteria for the grouping of manuscripts see Chapter II (pp. 26-44 above).

[2] Maurice Bévenot, *The Tradition of Manuscripts* (Oxford, 1961), p. 128.

literature, and the scripts used in the different localities. . . ." [1]
And Dain, after praising Havet's work on Latin texts, admits
that in an effort to apply this to Greek texts he found nothing
new except minor matters of historical character.[2] But the degree
of our specialization is such that until we have the equivalent of
Havet with Greek data, critics of the Greek New Testament will be
handicapped and inadequate in struggling to remove corruptions
from the text.

THE PRESENT STUDY

The present chapter is an initial step toward meeting the needs
which have been mentioned. Its primary purpose is to gain knowledge of an individual scribe's habits, and thus to increase skill in the
evaluation of that manuscript. Also its purpose is to gain knowledge
of the habits of scribes in general—of the processes of corruption—
and thus to increase skill in the evaluation of readings. Ultimately
it will sharpen tools for establishing the kinship of manuscripts;
it will disencumber the *apparatus criticus*, and will support both
conjectural emendation broadly defined and an increased use of
external evidence.

The singular readings of $\mathfrak{P}^{45}$, $\mathfrak{P}^{66}$, and $\mathfrak{P}^{75}$ constitute the material
for this study.[3] Since in most readings the student cannot determine
whether or not the scribe copied or originated the reading, this
study is restricted to singular readings (readings without other
manuscript support) on the assumption that these readings are
the creation of the scribe. The restriction of this study to singular
readings can be made with confidence in view of the wealth of
manuscript attestation for the Greek New Testament. A singular
reading has been defined as a reading which has no Greek support in
the critical apparatus of Tischendorf's 8th edition. It is true that
some witnesses unknown to Tischendorf may support some of these
readings, but it is also highly probable that many readings with

---

[1] P. Maas, *Textual Criticism*, tr. B. Flower (Oxford, 1958), p. 14.

[2] A. Dain, *Les Manuscrits* (Paris, 1949), pp. 38 ff., with reference to L.
Havet, *Manuel de critique verbale appliquée aux textes latins* (Paris, 1911).
Dain presents from the teaching of Desrousseaux a superb analysis of
copying as four acts: reading, remembering, saying it to oneself, and writing.

[3] *The Chester Beatty Biblical Papyri: The Gospels and Acts, Text*, ed. by
Frederic G. Kenyon, fasc. 2 (London, 1933); *Papyrus Bodmer II*, Nouvelle
édition augmentée et corrigée (Cologny-Genève, 1962); and *Papyrus Bodmer
XIV-XV*, 2 vols. (Cologny-Genève, 1961).

minor support in Tischendorf are scribal creations. Where the support of recent finds was known, the reading was eliminated from our list; but no rigorous effort was made to go beyond the evidence of Tischendorf's apparatus.

Before turning to statistical summaries, one word of caution: in many passages a clear decision as to the presence of a singular reading is not possible. In some cases this is due to the gaps in the papyrus and the hypothetical reconstruction of the text. The density of singular readings is the greatest where the text is complete. Thus our figures probably understate the case. In other cases the complex nature of the attestation and the difficulty of identifying the unit of variation made decisions difficult and statistics only approximately accurate. But no major conclusion of this study depends upon an absolutely exact tabulation.

The total number of readings in these three papyri but unsupported by Greek witnesses in Tischendorf is 1,649: 482 in $\mathfrak{P}^{66}$, 275 in $\mathfrak{P}^{45}$, and 257 in $\mathfrak{P}^{75}$ (plus 635 itacisms to which we shall come presently).

The primary classification of these readings must be based upon their genesis—not upon formal descriptive categories, nor upon the presence or absence of intention, nor upon the bodily organ responsible for error (whether eye, ear, or mind). "Sound textual criticism [is] founded on knowledge of the various classes of facts which have determined variation," said Hort.

But since the process of study of a manuscript of the New Testament usually began by collating the manuscript against the Textus Receptus (or some other edition) taken as a base, readings were classified in formal descriptive categories as (a) omission, (b) addition, (c) transposition, or (d) substitution. When the classification of readings is based upon these descriptive categories, the student has tacitly assumed knowledge of the original text (or of the text used by the scribe), a knowledge which he has not yet attained. Thus the common use of these categories is to be abandoned. Moreover, the use of these categories does not aid in the removal of the wrong reading, which is the primary goal of textual criticism. To speak of omissions, transpositions, and the like does not help us to understand the habits of scribes. Scribes were not addicted to omission or addition or transposition or substitution as such.

To base a primary classification of readings upon the presence or absence of intention is to anticipate the establishment of probabilities which must be established in other ways. There is always the risk of reading deliberate intention into unintended error. A secondary classification of readings based upon the presence or absence of intention plays a valuable role in textual criticism but only if it itself rests upon a classification based upon the genesis of readings.

WHY SINGULAR READINGS?

We begin, then, with the difficult question of "Why?" Why did the scribes of these papyri create this mass of singular readings? The first reason is their lack of ability to spell. Their spelling in certain restricted areas is regularly irregular.

Scholars have long known that one cause of corruption is the spelling habits of the individual scribe. These show up clearly in his singular readings where the interchange of similar sounds in diverse spellings is frequent. The three early papyri studied here underline the insignificance of variant readings of this type.

These "itacistic spellings" are numerous. More than 635 have been tabulated in the three papyri: $\mathfrak{P}^{45}$ has approximately 90, $\mathfrak{P}^{75}$ about 145, and $\mathfrak{P}^{66}$ has 400. Exact comparisons as to frequency are difficult, due primarily to the consistently fragmentary nature of the pages of $\mathfrak{P}^{45}$, and to the wide variation in the amount of text per page. If number of pages be taken as a base, $\mathfrak{P}^{45}$ has 60 (all more or less imperfect), $\mathfrak{P}^{66}$ has 148, and $\mathfrak{P}^{75}$ has 199. If the number of verses be taken as a base, $\mathfrak{P}^{45}$ has 795 (at least in part), $\mathfrak{P}^{66}$ has 808, and $\mathfrak{P}^{75}$ has 1,406. In general $\mathfrak{P}^{75}$ has the fewest itacisms per square inch, and $\mathfrak{P}^{66}$ has the most.

These papyri differ also in their favorite spellings. Tischendorf's 8th edition was taken as the base for identifying divergence, an admittedly arbitrary procedure. But lest it be too easily assumed that the recorded divergences are only the "regular" spelling for the scribe in question, note that every word in a particular papyrus which is spelled in divergence from Tischendorf is also spelled in agreement with Tischendorf in the same papyrus. Accurate generalization as to spelling customs in the second century will require very extensive and careful study.

Some general comments on these itacisms may be of value. $\mathfrak{P}^{45}$ and $\mathfrak{P}^{75}$ agree (against $\mathfrak{P}^{66}$) in changing iota to epsilon-iota in approximately three-fourths of all their itacisms. In these two papyri, no other single change of spelling is frequent.

In $\mathfrak{P}^{66}$, on the other hand, the most frequent variation is from epsilon to alpha-iota, with the change from epsilon-iota to iota running it a close second. These two variations total about two-thirds of the itacisms of $\mathfrak{P}^{66}$. But there is another frequent change in $\mathfrak{P}^{66}$, namely, from iota to epsilon-iota, about 70 times. It may be worth noting that the interchange of omicron and omega is very infrequent: 10 times in $\mathfrak{P}^{75}$, 5 times in $\mathfrak{P}^{66}$, one time in $\mathfrak{P}^{45}$.

The differences are striking. $\mathfrak{P}^{75}$ has alpha-iota for epsilon once, $\mathfrak{P}^{45}$ none, $\mathfrak{P}^{66}$ at least 150 times. Whereas $\mathfrak{P}^{45}$ and $\mathfrak{P}^{75}$ move from iota to epsilon-iota, $\mathfrak{P}^{66}$ moves the reverse direction from epsilon-iota to iota. Since the documents come from the same period and from the same general area, these differences may be identified as scribal in origin and of little significance for the history of the text. The removal of all such spelling variations from the critical apparatus to the realm of special studies would give us more valuable editions of the Greek New Testament. If the itacisms are to be cited at all in our *apparatus criticus*, they should all be cited, since the availability of a comprehensive survey of evidence is essential in such a highly variable area. But stop and think what that means. If these three papyri, fragmentary as they are, give us more than 600 itacisms to record, the total for all witnesses would crowd hundreds of pages with relatively insignificant lore that would be a stumbling block to the reconstruction of the original text and the establishment of manuscript relationships.

Let us then remove these itacisms from our list of Singular Readings in $\mathfrak{P}^{45}$, $\mathfrak{P}^{66}$, and $\mathfrak{P}^{75}$. The total of 1,649 is reduced to 1,014: $\mathfrak{P}^{66}$ has 482, $\mathfrak{P}^{45}$ has 275, $\mathfrak{P}^{75}$ has 257 singular readings exclusive of itacisms.

For the sake of increasing our acquaintance with the individual manuscripts, let us digress to note the distribution of their Singular Readings between Sensible Readings and Nonsense Readings. The Nonsense Readings include words unknown to grammar or lexicon, words that cannot be construed syntactically, or words that do not make sense in the context.

In $\mathfrak{P}^{66}$, two out of five Singular Readings are Nonsense Readings—
    40 per cent;
  in $\mathfrak{P}^{75}$, one out of four—25 per cent;
  in $\mathfrak{P}^{45}$, less than one out of ten—10 per cent.
If these Nonsense Readings were to be removed from consideration, the number of Sensible Singular Readings remaining would be:

in 𝔓⁶⁶, 289; in 𝔓⁴⁵, 250; in 𝔓⁷⁵, 190.

Thus 𝔓⁷⁵ (the most extensive manuscript) has the fewest, and 𝔓⁴⁵ in spite of its fragmentary nature almost equals the longer 𝔓⁶⁶. Another way of saying this is that when the scribe of 𝔓⁴⁵ creates a singular reading, it almost always makes sense; when the scribes of 𝔓⁶⁶ and 𝔓⁷⁵ create singular readings, they frequently do not make sense and are obvious errors. Thus 𝔓⁴⁵ must be given credit for a much greater density of intentional changes than the other two.

How shall we begin a classification of the Singular Readings of the manuscripts based upon the nature of the origin of the readings? Dain in his invaluable manual states that the most frequent scribal errors are (1) the leap from the same to the same (homoeoteleuton and homoeoarcton) and (2) the omission of short words.[1] New faults tend to accumulate from copy to copy—but books destined for libraries alter little. Our scribes have a worse than average record.

The leap from the same to the same is a familiar phenomenon to all students of manuscripts. It is really the case of the misplaced scribe. The scribe loses his place, looks around and finds the same word, or at least the same syllable or letter, and starts from there. If he looks ahead to find his place, the result is a gap in the text. If he looks back, the result is a text twice written (dittography). A special case of a gap caused by the leap is that where a word, or at least a syllable or a letter, is repeated immediately in the text. The writing of only one of these (haplography) causes the loss of the other.

𝔓⁶⁶ has 54 leaps forward, and 22 backward; 18 of the forward leaps are haplography.

𝔓⁷⁵ has 27 leaps forward, and 10 backward.

𝔓⁴⁵ has 16 leaps forward, and 2 backward.

From this it is clear that the scribe looking for his lost place looked ahead three times as often as he looked back. In other words, the loss of position usually resulted in a loss of text, an omission.

HARMONIZATION

Our manuals all mention the scribal habit of harmonizing the text with parallel passages. The importance of the Synoptic Problem and the concentration of textual studies upon the Gospel of Mark,

---

[1] Dain, *op. cit.*, pp. 43 f.

under the influence of the Lakes and Streeter and the Caesarean text, have led to a focus upon remote parallels, parallel passages in other Gospels, or in the Old Testament.

HARMONIZATION TO REMOTE PARALLELS

Although they are not frequent, harmonizations to remote parallels do occur. Ten occur in our manuscripts. Peter's confession in John (6:69, $\mathfrak{P}^{66}$) is enriched by adding "the Christ" from Matthew 16:16. In Luke (11:12, $\mathfrak{P}^{45}$) the hungry son asks for Matthew's bread, while Matthew's "birds of the air" (6:26) are added to Luke's ravens (12:24, $\mathfrak{P}^{45}$). In both $\mathfrak{P}^{66}$ and $\mathfrak{P}^{75}$ the Baptist's statement of his unworthiness in John uses the language of the Synoptic Gospels.

HARMONIZATION TO THE IMMEDIATE CONTEXT

Our three papyri show clearly that scribes were much more addicted to *harmonization to the immediate context*. The influence of a neighboring word, of a balancing clause in the same sentence, of the familiar phraseology of the Gospel in question, was evidently inescapable. Harmonization to immediate context is usually mentioned incidentally in our manuals. It needs to be given headlines on the front page. There are 104 cases of harmonization creating singular readings in our three papyri, and 83 of them are harmonizations to immediate context.

These run the gamut from a change of tense in the answer to a question to harmonize with the tense in the question (John 11:27, $\mathfrak{P}^{66}$), to adding a verb to the second clause of a sentence to balance the verb in the first clause (Matt. 25:43, $\mathfrak{P}^{45}$), to picking "Herod" out of the context to replace the title "King" (Mark 6:22, $\mathfrak{P}^{45}$). They include changing the genitive (υμων) to the dative (υμιν) after the εν of εσωθεν (Luke 11:39, $\mathfrak{P}^{75}$), repeating the prepositional prefix of a verb after the verb (Luke 13:13, $\mathfrak{P}^{75}$), changing "door" to "shepherd" (John 10:7, $\mathfrak{P}^{75}$), changing the case of a noun to agree with the case of the following possessive pronoun (John 11:5, $\mathfrak{P}^{75}$). Harmonizations range to writing πανθρωπον for ανθρωπον (John 1:9, $\mathfrak{P}^{66}$) under the influence of the preceding word, παντα, or μεψαντα for πεμψαντα (John 7:18; 7:33; 13:20, $\mathfrak{P}^{66}$) under the influence of the word which follows (με), which $\mathfrak{P}^{66}$ liked so well he did it three times.

HARMONIZATION TO GENERAL USAGE

A third type of harmonization is equally well attested, occurring eleven times. This leads to "correctional formulas." Καὶ εγενετο is added before an infinitive phrase in Luke (9:36, 𝔓⁴⁵). In John (6:57, 𝔓⁷⁵) the bare words "the Father" have the usual possessive "my" added. In Jesus' interview with Nicodemus the "Amen, Amen, I say to thee" is harmonized to the prevailing plural "I say to you" (John 3:3, 𝔓⁶⁶).

Harmonization of all kinds occurs; but the dominant type to which the textual critic needs to be especially alert is harmonization to immediate context.

THE INDIVIDUAL SCRIBE: ATTITUDES AND HABITS

The characterization of these singular readings can go no further until the individual scribes have been characterized. Their peculiar readings are due to their peculiarities. This has been well said by Dain.[1] He reminds us that although all scribes make mistakes and mistakes of the same kind, yet each scribe has a personal coefficient of the frequency of his mistakes. Each has his own pattern of errors. One scribe is liable to dittography, another to the omission of lines of text; one reads well, another remembers poorly; one is a good speller; etc., etc. In these differences one must include the seriousness of intention of the scribe and the peculiarities of his basic method of copying.

On these last and most important matters, our three scribes are widely divided. 𝔓⁷⁵ and 𝔓⁴⁵ seriously intend to produce a good copy, but it is hard to believe that this was the intention of 𝔓⁶⁶. The nearly 200 nonsense readings and the 400 itacistic spellings in 𝔓⁶⁶ are evidence of something less than disciplined attention to the basic task. To this evidence of carelessness must be added those singular readings whose origin baffles speculation, readings that can be given no more exact label than carelessness leading to assorted variant readings. A hurried count shows 𝔓⁴⁵ with 20, 𝔓⁷⁵ with 57, and 𝔓⁶⁶ with 216 purely careless readings. As we have seen, 𝔓⁶⁶ has, in addition, more than twice as many "leaps" from the same to the same as either of the others.

---

[1] *Ibid.*, p. 46.

INFLUENCE OF SIMILAR FORMS

These are surprisingly few in number. Here the progression goes from the fewest in 𝔓⁴⁵ through 𝔓⁷⁵ to 𝔓⁶⁶, which has the greatest number. There are a bare half dozen in 𝔓⁴⁵. Two seem to be the textbook type of visual confusion, the misreading of very similar forms. In Acts 13:46 αυτους is read for εαυτους. And in Acts 15:4 the finite verb followed by τε becomes the participle ending in τες. In two cases words with similar beginnings are confused—the more interesting occurring in Luke 10:30, where Jericho becomes a priest. In another case the augment of the finite verb is added to the participle. But the total of these cases is so small in this manuscript as to be insignificant.

In 𝔓⁷⁵ there are no examples of misreading very similar forms through visual confusion. In this papyrus, only one letter is involved, more often a vowel than a consonant. Basically these are errors due to carelessness or perhaps fatigue; and the role of the similar word or form is simply that of giving some superficially responsible form to the misread or misremembered word. Eighteen times in 𝔓⁷⁵ a similar word has influenced the shape of the error. In Luke 11:11 fish (ιχθυν) has become strength (ισχυν); and in John 3:8 the verb "blows" has been turned into the *nomina sacra* type of abbreviation for "spirit" (πνει for πνει). In thirty-six other passages in 𝔓⁷⁵ the *form* of a word has been changed to a similar form.

In 𝔓⁶⁶ it is necessary to distinguish carefully between readings involving confusion with similar words or forms and a great number of changes which are very similar but lack any possible reference to confusion with similar words. Here (as in 𝔓⁴⁵) there are two cases of possible visual misreading as the basic cause of a variant. In John 12:1, 𝔓⁶⁶ reads "five days before the Passover" instead of "six days before. . . ." Père Boismard felt that this possibly represents an ancient tradition.[1] But it is more easily explained as a misreading of "six." Scribes in this period used a bold rough breathing with a long horizontal stroke over confusable forms such as "six" (εξ). If "six" were thus written in the exemplar of 𝔓⁶⁶, the horizontal stroke above the letter epsilon would easily suggest the numeral "five" to the scribe of 𝔓⁶⁶, and he would write "five" (πεντε). Half a dozen times, 𝔓⁶⁶ confuses similar words; e.g.,

---

[1] M.-É. Boismard, review of *Papyrus Bodmer II* in *Revue Biblique*, LXX (1963), 120-33.

in John 20:14 he changes "Jesus" to "Lord." A dozen times, he writes a similar form of the word. Thus, in John 18:34, he writes "he said" (ειπεν) for "they said" (ειπον), even though the subject is clearly plural.

On the avoidance of careless error, $\mathfrak{P}^{45}$ would be given top rating. But if we look at the basic method of copying, the rating of the three papyri changes. In general, $\mathfrak{P}^{75}$ copies letters one by one; $\mathfrak{P}^{66}$ copies syllables, usually two letters in length; $\mathfrak{P}^{45}$ copies phrases and clauses.

The accuracy of these assertions can be demonstrated. That $\mathfrak{P}^{75}$ copied letters one by one is shown in the pattern of his errors. He has more than sixty readings that involve a single letter *and* not more than ten careless readings that involve a syllable. But $\mathfrak{P}^{66}$ drops sixty-one syllables (twenty-three of them in "leaps") and omits as well a dozen articles and thirty short words. In $\mathfrak{P}^{45}$ there is not one omission of a syllable in a "leap" nor is there any occurrence of "careless" omissions of syllables. $\mathfrak{P}^{45}$ omits words and phrases.

Another clue to the nature of a scribe's work can be obtained from a study of his transpositions. Since word order in Greek is very free, it may be assumed that most changes in word order are due to scribal error. I suggest three causes of transposition: (*a*) By a leap the scribe jumps over a word, copies the following word, looks back at his exemplar, catches his error, and writes in the omitted word out of order. I have noted five of these in $\mathfrak{P}^{45}$,[1] four in $\mathfrak{P}^{66}$,[2] and four in $\mathfrak{P}^{75}$.[3] (*b*) Even more rarely, a scribe omits a word, the corrector interlines it slightly out of order, and the next copyist produces the transposition. One of these in-the-making occurs in these papyri. (*c*) The third and commonest cause of transpositions is carelessness as to word order.

In carelessness as to word order $\mathfrak{P}^{45}$ comes first with 37 instances, $\mathfrak{P}^{66}$ second with 21, and $\mathfrak{P}^{75}$ last with 11 (these are in addition to transpositions due to "leaps").

The transpositions in $\mathfrak{P}^{66}$ and $\mathfrak{P}^{75}$ are explicable as abortive omissions, caught in the act and immediately corrected. These are errors, lapses on the part of the scribe—as usual more frequent in $\mathfrak{P}^{66}$, less frequent in $\mathfrak{P}^{75}$.

---

[1] Luke 10:38; 12:11; 12:36; Acts 10:32; 16:37.
[2] John 5:6; 10:4; 10:31; 13:34.
[3] Luke 14:10; John 4:9; 7:18; 14:19.

But the transpositions in $\mathfrak{P}^{45}$ are capable of a very different explanation. This scribe does not actually copy words. He sees through the language to its idea-content, and copies that—often in words of his own choosing, or in words rearranged as to order. The length of text transposed differs between that of $\mathfrak{P}^{45}$ on the one hand and $\mathfrak{P}^{66}$ and $\mathfrak{P}^{75}$ on the other. In $\mathfrak{P}^{66}$ and $\mathfrak{P}^{75}$, transpositions usually involve two words, occasionally three. But of the 37 transpositions of $\mathfrak{P}^{45}$, 20 involve more than three words. This is true of only three cases in each of the other papyri. The inference is plain: the scribe of $\mathfrak{P}^{45}$ bites off three to five words at a time; he copies phrases where $\mathfrak{P}^{66}$ usually copies syllables, and $\mathfrak{P}^{75}$ letters. A second inference is equally clear: the scribe of $\mathfrak{P}^{45}$ copies with great freedom and this freedom springs from his basic attitude as a scribe. From one point of view, $\mathfrak{P}^{66}$ is as free as $\mathfrak{P}^{45}$. He certainly creates more readings than $\mathfrak{P}^{45}$ does. But his freedom is failure to live up to his accepted task; whereas for $\mathfrak{P}^{45}$ it *is* his task. $\mathfrak{P}^{66}$ gives the impression of working in a controlled situation. If he catches a transposition while he is writing, he erases the out-of-order word and writes the correct-order-word over it. If the transposition is caught later, strokes between lines correct it. This never happens in $\mathfrak{P}^{45}$. He feels free to make the order of words what he wants to make it, and he is a careful workman. He does not fall into the slips and nonsense that $\mathfrak{P}^{66}$ does. Thus, though $\mathfrak{P}^{45}$ and $\mathfrak{P}^{66}$ are alike in treating their sources with freedom, their freedoms are very unalike. $\mathfrak{P}^{45}$ gladly is free of any obligation to reproduce *words* faithfully, but $\mathfrak{P}^{66}$ has accepted that obligation and regrets his failures to live up to it.

In $\mathfrak{P}^{75}$ the text that is produced can be explained in all its variants as the result of a single force, namely the disciplined scribe who writes with the intention of being careful and accurate. There is no evidence of revision of his work by anyone else, or in fact of any real revision, or check. Only one out of five of his singular readings (including nonsense readings) is corrected. The control had been drilled into the scribe before he started writing.

$\mathfrak{P}^{45}$ gives the impression of a scribe who writes without any intention of exactly reproducing his source. He writes with great freedom—harmonizing, smoothing out, substituting almost whimsically. Here again there is no evidence whatever of control by a second party (fewer than three singular readings per hundred are corrected), nor in fact of external controls of any kind.

$\mathfrak{P}^{66}$ seems to reflect a scribe working with the intention of making a good copy, falling into careless errors, particularly the error of dropping a letter, a syllable, a word, or even a phrase where it is doubled, but also under the control of some other person, or second standard, so that the corrections which are made are usually corrections to a reading read by a number of other witnesses. Nine out of ten of the nonsense readings are corrected, and two out of three of all his singular readings. In short, $\mathfrak{P}^{66}$ gives the impression of being the product of a scriptorium, i.e., a publishing house. It shows the supervision of a foreman, or of a scribe turned proofreader.

In summary, $\mathfrak{P}^{75}$ and $\mathfrak{P}^{66}$ represent a controlled tradition; $\mathfrak{P}^{45}$ represents an uncontrolled tradition. $\mathfrak{P}^{75}$ and $\mathfrak{P}^{45}$ are, according to their own standards, careful workmen. $\mathfrak{P}^{66}$ is careless and ineffective —although he is the only calligrapher of the three. He uses up his care, his concern, in the production of beautiful letters.

If $\mathfrak{P}^{45}$ represents an uncontrolled tradition and the others do not, there must be evidence of this in the pattern of sensible singular readings. That evidence will lie in the amount and range of editorial readings. I use this term advisedly. These three papyri are enough to show that scribes made changes in style, in clarity, in fitness of ideas, in smoothness, in vocabulary. They created readings which can properly be called "editorial." The role of the editor (the maker of a text-type) was to select rather than create readings and to gain consistency in the application of the ideals of good style, clarity, and the like.

EDITORIAL CHANGES: LOGICAL HARMONIZATION

If "Harmonizations to General Usage" be slightly extended to include logical harmonization to the general context, we have crossed into the realm of editorial changes. One type of these is usually identified as "doctrinal." But the so-called doctrinal changes seem to be only part of a more general class—a class in which the fitness of idea-content is appraised and improved. It is this fitness as much as a specific parallel that changes Jesus as the door of the sheep to the shepherd of the sheep, that changes "a" prophet to "the" prophet when it refers to Jesus.

EDITORIAL CHANGES: CONCISENESS IN $\mathfrak{P}^{45}$

As an editor the scribe of $\mathfrak{P}^{45}$ wielded a sharp axe. The most striking aspect of his style is its conciseness. The dispensable word is dispensed with. He omits adverbs, adjectives, nouns, participles, verbs, personal pronouns—without any compensating habit of addition. He frequently omits phrases and clauses. He prefers the simple to the compound word. In short, he favors brevity. He shortens the text in at least fifty places in *singular readings alone*. But he does *not* drop syllables or letters. His shortened text is readable.

Many of his omissions are striking—not to say startling. In 𝔓⁴⁵ the 5,000 do not sit down "by hundreds and by fifties," nor are we told how many loaves and fishes there were. In Mark 6:48 he does not bother to tell us that it was the fourth watch "of the night" since vs. 47 has already made it evening. In Acts 15:20 "unchastity" is absent from the list of prohibitions, and unfortunately the parallel in 15:29 is in a gap. The Ethiopian eunuch (Acts 8:36) does not say, "See, here is water!" since the water has already been mentioned. In Luke 10:21 there is no repetitive address to God, "Yea, Father." 𝔓⁴⁵ does not make Caiaphas High Priest "that year." In this papyrus, Jesus does not say, "I am the resurrection and the life"; he says more briefly, "I am the resurrection." If the subject of the verb can be understood, it is not expressed—whether it be the dumb demoniac, or Jesus. One word is made to serve for several. "His son" replaces "the Son of God" (John 11:4) and "to men" serves for "into the hands of men" (Mark 9:31).

As an editor 𝔓⁴⁵ is interested in clarity. In Mark 7:5, for example, he points out that the hands were "defiled" because they were "unwashed." At the tomb of Lazarus he adds the common form of the imperative "Come" to the command (John 11:43). In Acts 14:15 the over-concise Greek is clarified by the addition of a verb, "turn away from." By the judicious addition of a pronoun or a conjunction or the change in order or form, other passages are clarified (see John 11:2; Acts 9:39; Mark 7:7; 7:28; 7:33; Luke 13:32; Acts 16:33).

Should the removal of the difficulty from a difficult saying not be classified as clarification? In Luke 9:50, 𝔓⁴⁵ straightens out the hard saying that the man who is not against us is for us by making it read that he is neither for us nor against us.

That 𝔓⁴⁵ attempted stylistic improvements is unquestionable. The appropriate label for his improvements is not easily found.

Occasionally he makes the text "smoother" or "simpler." In Mark 9:28 he anticipates the Textus Receptus by relating a genitive absolute to a verb (which incidentally he supplies). His sentence is much smoother than the original (see Luke 10:37; 12:48). In Acts 10:11 the vision of the vessel let down from heaven is either simplified or made smoother by omitting the comparison to a sheet. In two passages he transposes a word or phrase an incredible distance, perhaps for better style: in Luke 10:40 the pronoun μου is advanced, and in John 10 the words "in the scripture" are moved ahead from vs. 35 to 34.

Style may be responsible for the dozen changes in verb forms. At least three times the tense is changed to the aorist. In another dozen passages words are replaced with synonyms—although ηλθεν for εγενετο in Acts 10:10 is not quite equivalent! Most of his changes are to the familiar and the common.

While certainty awaits further study, the use by $\mathfrak{P}^{45}$ of conjunctions, the article, prepositions, and negatives does not seem to be caused by a concern for style, although his frequent substitution of one conjunction for another *may* be a matter of style. In twenty-four passages, ten conjunctions are omitted, six are added, and eight are changed. The same ones are added, omitted, and interchanged. The article is added six times, but omitted nine others. As a whole $\mathfrak{P}^{45}$ seems to have been written by a typical scribe with some freedom to add or omit articles and other words. Both $\mathfrak{P}^{66}$ and $\mathfrak{P}^{75}$ exhibit similar changes in many ways. All three scribes omit articles more often than they add them. $\mathfrak{P}^{45}$ and $\mathfrak{P}^{75}$ omit more conjunctions than they add; $\mathfrak{P}^{66}$ does not. But $\mathfrak{P}^{66}$ and $\mathfrak{P}^{75}$ add οτι several times at the beginning of a quotation; and $\mathfrak{P}^{45}$ does not. Variations in the use of these words seem to be due to scribal license rather than to stylistic considerations.

The resemblance between these three in these matters may be due to their participation in the larger common error: the omission of short words. Dain notes this as one of the two errors common to all scribes. He found it especially in the linking words, the conjunctions, particles, prepositions, the verb "to be," and even negatives. But the evidence of these papyri in their singular readings points to license rather than to the habit of omission alone.

The editorial readings of $\mathfrak{P}^{45}$ include those aimed at concise expression, at clarity, and at a good style. The most distinctive of these is the intended omission of dispensable words. That this

striving for concise expression is intended and conscious is shown
by the absence of any large number of unintended omissions. In
the "leaps" from the same to the same 𝔓⁴⁵ with only 18 cases is
well below the others, 𝔓⁷⁵ with 36 and 𝔓⁶⁶ with 76.

Editorial Changes in 𝔓⁷⁵

𝔓⁷⁵ shares the concern of 𝔓⁴⁵ for clarity and for style, but lacks
the passion of 𝔓⁴⁵ for conciseness. In 14 passages there are clarifying
changes in 𝔓⁷⁵. In Luke 11:34 a second hand adds the word "eye"
before "evil." 𝔓⁷⁵ gives the name of the rich man in Luke 16:19.
In Luke 8:21, Jesus replies, logically enough, to the questioner
rather than the crowd. And once at least (Luke 8:32) the legion
of demons is referred to in the signular. In 𝔓⁷⁵ (Luke 11:32) Jesus
is a greater *person* than Jonah. Some of these are slight, superficially
logical harmonizations to context; e.g., the perfect tense in John
9:39 and the substitution of "he will be raised up" for "he will
recover," John 11:12 (cf. Luke 16:18; John 7:52; 8:55; 14:9).

𝔓⁷⁵ is probably striving for better style in changing verb forms,
which he does about as often as 𝔓⁴⁵ (though in a much greater
amount of text). Only three times does he substitute synonyms,
and one of these looks like harmonization to immediate context.
Twice he prefers the simple to the compound word. A half dozen
times he chooses brevity, possibly for style. The best example is
John 12:38 where instead of "the word which he said" the redundant
"which he said" is omitted. There are a couple of changes of case and
number. One of his habits is to omit personal pronouns; he drops
more than a dozen and adds one. This could be stylistic, but is
probably related to the occasional carelessness of 𝔓⁷⁵ in regard to
short words. In 𝔓⁷⁵ the scribe's impulse to improve style is for
the most part defeated by the obligation to make an exact copy.

"Editorial" Changes in 𝔓⁶⁶

Wildness in copying is the outstanding characteristic of 𝔓⁶⁶.
This makes it very difficult to decide whether particular readings
are due to editorializing on the part of the scribe or rather are
due to his general laxity and inefficiency. As I catalogued his
singular readings, I marked 43 as due to clarification, to smoothing
out the text, to simplification or to logical agreement with context.
Some of these exhibit a preference for the more familiar word or

idiom: επ αυτω for εν αυτω (John 12:16), και for τε (John 2:15),
"Jesus answered" becomes "Jesus answered and said" (John 18:37).
In John 3:3 αρχην became πρωτην because "first" is clearer here.[1]
𝔓66 corrects the broken syntax of John 8:40, "a man who I have
spoken the truth," to agree with RSV "a man who has spoken the
truth." In John 8:48 the tense of a verb is put back into the past to
fit the fact (cf. John 7:20). There are other "logical" changes of this
sort (cf. 9:4; 13:1).

There are rearrangements of the Greek text that are almost
certainly stylistic. Note the smoother feeling of πολλοι ουν των
ακουσαντων μαθητων of 𝔓66* contrasted with πολλοι ουν ακουσαντες
εκ των μαθητων αυτου(John 6:60) of 𝔓66corr and the others. There are
half a dozen similar if less successful rewritings.

In 𝔓66 some additions look stylistic. In John 5:29, "And those who
have done evil," which Boismard ascribed to carelessness, RSV
again agrees with the first hand of 𝔓66. In 7:40 εκ του οχλου ουν
becomes πολλοι εκ του οχλου οι. The very difficult passage in John
8:25 is cleared up by prefixing "I said to you."

In John 13:33 trouble lies in the unconnected και υμιν λεγω αρτι
at the end of the verse. 𝔓66 would end 13:33 with και υμιν λεγω;
he has a high point after λεγω. And he begins 13:34 with πλην αρτι
εντολην καινην. Manuscripts 1 and 565 on the other hand end vs. 33
with αρτι and begin 34 with πλην. These corruptions are alternative
ways of clearing up the difficulty.

Again it may be style, a feeling for simplicity, that leads 𝔓66*
to change "what the things were which he was saying to them" to
"what he was saying to them."[2] The significance of the agreement of
the Old Latin (except q) is diminished by the agreement of RSV.

Simplification probably explains the omission of τις in John 11:49
εις δε τις εξ αυτων where RSV again agrees. But more rigorous
editing (or erroneous harmonization) is needed to explain 15:4,
where "neither can you unless you abide in me" is reduced to "so
also (is) he who abides in me." I join Boismard in labeling as
"fantasy" the substitution in 5:28 of "desert" for "tombs."

I have already pointed out general agreement of 𝔓66 with the
other two in readings involving omission or alteration of conjunctions and the article. He favors ην instead of η for the third person
singular of the present subjunctive. One further detail, in his general

---

[1] RSV agrees with the first hand of 𝔓66.
[2] John 10:6.

omission of short words: he omits personal pronouns eighteen times, and adds them six times.

Enough of these items have been cited to make the point that 𝔓⁶⁶ editorializes as he does everything else—in a sloppy fashion. He is not guided in his changes by some clearly defined goal which is always kept in view. If he has an inclination toward omission, it is not "according to knowledge," but is whimsical and careless, often leading to nothing but nonsense.

Finally I present a list of suggestions drawn from the preceding study of transcriptional corruption. Some of these are no more than hypotheses for further study; some are firm conclusions.

   I. Singular Readings should not be included in any *apparatus criticus*. They belong to special studies.
  II. The singular readings of a particular manuscript should be studied not against Tischendorf or Nestle or the Textus Receptus, but rather against the consensus of the Text-type to which the manuscript belongs. The singulars of 𝔓⁷⁵ should be studied with reference to the Beta Text-type (Vaticanus and friends).
 III. Since corruption was universal, identical singular readings with only minor scattered support elsewhere should be assumed to be coincidental in these agreements—unless other external evidence establishes relationship.
  IV. The corruption of the text in 𝔓⁴⁵ sheds light on the process of corruption in an uncontrolled tradition. In that tradition a particular kind of freedom exists. It occurs where Greek sophistication is in short supply—in the backwoods where few knew Greek—and results in the making of an independent translation. In these areas appeal to a "standard" text was impossible, for the very idea did not exist.
   V. A translation to be good must be free. The translator is always tempted to extend that freedom unjustifiably. The result is inevitably agreement between any translation and a manuscript whose text was corrupted either intentionally or through carelessness. Boismard in a study of the readings of the first hand in 𝔓⁶⁶ suggests kinship between 𝔓⁶⁶* and various ancient versions. Since the makers of the RSV did not use 𝔓⁶⁶, I compared the *Singular Readings* of 𝔓⁶⁶ with RSV. In fifteen passages RSV agrees with 𝔓⁶⁶ singulars, and

in four others a parallelism is possible (cf. John 2:20; 5:29;
5:36; 8:40; 9:30; 9:33; 9:34; 9:37; 10:6; 11:27; 11:49;
12:2; 12:47; 13:1; 15:12; and as possibilities 1:27; 2:11;
5:22; 8:51). No one will suggest a genetic kinship here, but
if the agreement of $\mathfrak{P}^{66}$ were with an Old Latin ms. . . . ?

VI. The relationship of $\mathfrak{P}^{66}$ to established text-types should be
reconsidered with the nature and extent of $\mathfrak{P}^{66}$ corruptions
kept vividly in mind. $\mathfrak{P}^{66}$ might then look like a corruption
of the Beta Text-type rather than like a mixed text.

VII. A study of $\mathfrak{P}^{45}$ and Codex Bezae concentrating on the nature
of their corruptions might clarify the nature of the so-called
Western text-type. Kenyon's elimination of Bezae's major
variants from that comparison invalidates his conclusions,
for it is these very major variants that he depends upon
elsewhere to establish the existence of a Western text-type.

VIII. $\mathfrak{P}^{66}$ should not be cited as evidence for the omission of a short
word, except where its kinship with a group that omits the
word has been established.

IX. $\mathfrak{P}^{45}$ should not be cited as evidence for a transposition, except
where its kinship with a group that supports the transposition
has been established.

X. A study of the presence or absence of the article should
determine whether scribal usage had enough consistency to
justify the citation of the individual manuscript (even when
supported by others, unless those others are members of the
same established group).

XI. A study of general scribal practice in the omission of personal
pronouns might provide a guideline for the use of evidence in
this matter.

XII. Readings that are identifiable as harmonizations to immediate context should not be cited unless they characterize a
group.

XIII. The publication of a commentary on the singular readings of
these papyri and of other important manuscripts would be
most valuable.

XIV. Of writing many books there is no end, and much study is
a weariness of the flesh.

CHAPTER NINE

A CHRONOLOGY FOR THE LETTERS Ε, Η, Λ, Π, IN THE BYZANTINE MINUSCULE BOOK HAND [1]

The student of Greek palaeography faces no more difficult task than that of establishing the date of a document written in a calligraphic or book hand. This has long been recognized in the case of the Byzantine minuscule, the book hand of the late Middle Ages. Professor Maas says that in calligraphic books the "mixed minuscule" remains without noticeable variation from the eleventh to the fifteenth century.[2] This may be somewhat strongly stated, but it is not too much to say that it is almost impossible to place a manuscript within narrow limits between A.D. 1050 and 1350.

The conservatism of the Byzantine minuscule was strongest in biblical manuscripts. The use of the uncial script in lectionaries until the end of the tenth century is a well-known example of such conservatism. Here, more than in any other Byzantine area, questions involving date are hard to answar. It is largely for this reason that the greatest scholars have sometimes depended too much on date-colophons or local library tradition.

No name is more highly or more deservedly revered by students of New Testament manuscripts than that of Caspar René Gregory. Some errors that were noticed in his work may therefore be taken as a fair indication of the difficulty involved in assigning a date to a Byzantine codex of the New Testament. There is in Leningrad one folio of a Greek Gospel for which Gregory accepted the date A.D. 1247.[3] Yet he assigned the manuscript on Mount Sinai from which it was taken to the fourteenth century.[4] Gardthausen and von

---

[1] Originally published as "Some Criteria for Dating Byzantine New Testament Manuscripts," an Appendix in *The Four Gospels of Karahissar*, Vol. I, *History and Text*, by Ernest Cadman Colwell (Chicago, 1936), pp. 225-41.

[2] *Griechische Palaeographie*[3], pp. 78, 80-81, in Alfred Gercke and Eduard Norden, *Einleitung in der Altertumswissenschaft* (Leipzig, 1927).

[3] Leningrad, Pub. Libr., Gr. 308; see Gregory's *Textkritik des Neuen Testamentes*, III (Leipzig, 1909), 1197, under the number 2159.

[4] Sinai, St. Catherine's, ms. 169; see Gregory's *Textkritik*, I, 246, and III, 1134, under the number 1206. Gregory noted that the Leningrad leaf came from Sinai; thus, with the help of a photostat of Leningrad 308, I was able

Soden also referred it to the fourteenth century, but Professor Hatch has recently dated it in the twelfth century. For two Leningrad folios of Hebrews, Gregory accepted the dates 1090 and 1099. But the work of the same scribe in Jerusalem he assigned to the thirteenth or fourteenth century.[1] Papadopoulos-Kerameus and Professor Hatch agree with the later date. Differences of opinion in this area are not only natural but inevitable; yet all will agree that Gregory could not disagree with himself and be right both times.

Anyone who has attempted to establish the date of an undated Byzantine codex of the Gospels is not surprised at the frequency with which cataloguers say of a manuscript: "eleventh to thirteenth century." The expert is sometimes enabled by his experience and feeling for style to date manuscripts more exactly, but he is seldom able to document his judgment for the benefit of the layman. I shall never forget the awe with which in my younger years I watched an outstanding Byzantinist assign New Testament manuscripts to their appropriate decade at the rate of five a minute. But after all, all that taught me was that an expert could do that.

Two recent works help to make a more objective dating of Byzantine manuscripts possible. The first is a study of ornamentation in Byzantine manuscripts by Miss M. Alison Frantz.[2] Its wealth of illustration from dated ornamentation is as valuable to the student of palaeography as to the student of art. The second is the magnificent series of plates in which Professor and Mrs. Lake have published facsimiles of dated Greek minuscules down to A.D. 1200. This publication greatly increases the effectiveness of the orthodox method of dating (i.e., by comparison with dated manuscripts) in that it makes a much wider range of comparisons possible.

---

to identify it with Sinai 169 as reproduced by Professor Hatch in *The Greek Manuscripts of the New Testament at Mount Sinai* (Paris, 1932), Pl. 39.

[1] The Leningrad folios are Pub. Libr. Gr. 319, Gregory's No. 2163. They were written by the scribe who wrote the Apocalypse section of Jerusalem, Holy Cross 94. I made the identification with the help of photostats of the Leningrad leaves and Professor Hatch's reproduction of the Jerusalem Apocalypse in *The Greek Manuscripts of the New Testament in Jerusalem* (Paris, 1935), Pl. 45.

[2] M. Alison Frantz, "Byzantine Illuminated Ornament," *Art Bulletin*, XVI (1934), 43-76, with 25 plates. Another valuable contribution in the field of Byzantine art which is of value for dating manuscripts is Kurt Weitzmann's *Die Byzantinische Buchmalerei des IX. und X. Jahrhunderts* (Berlin, 1935).

But even the comparison of the undated manuscripts with dated manuscripts usually depends for its value on the specialist's judgment or feeling that resemblances exist. Even in the relatively simple question of whether or not two manuscripts were written by the same scribe, agreement is not easily obtained. All these difficulties suggest that something might be done to make a more objective dating of Byzantine codices possible. The author believes that he has made a start in that direction with the study of the frequency with which variant forms of the same letter occur.

Professor V. Gardthausen, in his invaluable work on Greek palaeography, pointed out long ago that the minuscule book hand first appears as a pure minuscule script, but that it is later invaded *seriatim* by most of the letters of the uncial alphabet. A seminar at the University of Chicago turned to the study of dated minuscules in an effort to date the first appearance of each uncial letter in the minuscule hand. At the end of three months it was agreed that the effort had failed—not so much in that the intrusion of the uncials could not be dated as that they could be dated too early. In other words, uncial forms of the letters studied appear in the minuscule script before the problem of dating becomes very difficult, i.e., before A.D. 1050. Our results merely confirmed one of the established beliefs of Byzantine palaeography: the minuscule script remained pure for a relatively brief period.

A year later, in scanning the statistics assembled by the seminar for the letter epsilon, I noticed that, although some uncial epsilons appeared at an early date, the minuscule epsilons consistently outnumbered the uncial forms until a century and a half after the first appearance of an uncial epsilon. This observation led to a study of the proportion of uncial to minuscule forms of epsilon in dated Byzantine manuscripts of the New Testament. The resources available in published facsimiles were supplemented by the purchase of photostats of sample pages of unpublished dated manuscripts. The study began with epsilon because the relative frequency of that letter's occurrence makes it possible to get some significant totals from a facsimile which gives but a small section of text. The letters eta, lambda, and pi were also studied; and the present chapter gives the totals of their occurrence in uncial and minuscule forms in more than one hundred dated Byzantine New Testament manuscripts. To make possible a brief presentation of these totals, it was found necessary to use abbreviations and symbols in referring to the published facsimiles. A list of these symbols and their reference follows:

Bick: Josef Bick, *Die Schreiber der Wiener griechischen Handschriften* (Vienna, 1920).

C-L: Pius Franchi de' Cavalieri and J. Lietzmann, *Specimina codicum graecorum Vaticanorum* (Bonn, 1910).

Curzon: *Catalogue of Materials for Writing ... in the Library of the Honourable Robert Curzon ...* (London, 1849).

G-M: C. Graux and A. Martin, *Facsimiles des manuscrits grecs d'Espagne* (Paris, 1890).

Hatch: W. H. P. Hatch, *The Greek Manuscripts of the New Testament at Mount Sinai, Facsimiles and Descriptions* (Paris, 1932); *The Greek Manuscripts of the New Testament in Jerusalem, Facsimiles and Descriptions* (Paris, 1935).

Lake: Kirsopp Lake and Silva Lake, *Dated Greek Minuscule Manuscripts to the year 1200 A.D.* ("Monumenta Palaeographica Vetera," 1st ser.) Fascs. I-V (Boston, 1934-36).

M-T: E. Maunde Thompson, *An Introduction to Greek and Latin Palaeography* (Oxford, 1912).[1]

Omont: Henri Omont, *Fac-similés des manuscrits grecs datés de la Bibliothèque Nationale du IXᵉ au XIVᵉ siècle* (Paris, 1891).

PalSoc: The Palaeographical Society, *Facsimiles of Manuscripts and Inscriptions*, edited by E. A. Bond, E. Maunde Thompson, and G. F. Warner, 1st and 2nd ser. (London, 1873-94).

NPalSoc: The New Palaeographical Society, *Facsimiles of Ancient Manuscripts...*, edited by E. Maunde Thompson, G. F. Warner, F. G. Kenyon, and J. P. Gilson, 1st and 2nd ser. (London, 1903-30).

Sabas: Sabas, *Specimina palaeographica codicum graecorum et slavonicorum bibliothecae Mosquensis synodalis saec. vi-xvii* (Moscow, 1863).

Sil: J. B. Silvestre, *Universal Palaeography*, translated and edited by Sir Frederic Madden (London, 1850).

Sitterly: C. F. Sitterly, *Praxis in Manuscripts of the Greek Testament* (New York, 1898).

Ts-S: Gregorius Tsereteli and Sergius Sobolevski, *Exempla codicum graecorum litteris minusculis scriptorum annorumque notis instructorum*: Vol. I, *Codices Mosquenses* (Moscow, 1911); Vol. II, *Codices Petropolitani* (Moscow, 1913).

V-P: G. Vitelli and C. Paoli, *Collezione fiorentina di facsimili paleografici greci e latini illustrati* (Florence, 1884-88).

W-V: W. Wattenbach and A. von Velsen, *Exempla codicum graecorum litteris minusculis scriptorum* (Leipzig, 1878).

Zom: Eugen Zomarides, "Eine neue griechische Handschrift aus Caesarea vom Jahre 1226 mit armenischer Beischrift," in C. Wessely's *Studien zur Paläographie und Papyruskunde*, Heft II (1902), pp. 21-24, with 1 plate.

---

[1] The plates that appear in Maunde Thompson's work duplicate the plates published by the palaeographical societies, but the greater accessibility of the smaller work justifies its inclusion here.

In the following list the evidence gathered from 111 New Testament manuscripts is presented in tabular form. In the columns under the letters, the number preceding the diagonal stroke is the total of uncial forms, and the number following the diagonal is the total of minuscule forms. Where there is no reference to a publication, the reference is to the folios studied in photostatic reproduction or—in the case of the Chicago manuscripts—to the manuscript itself.

The 111 New Testament manuscripts studied are grouped in date and content as follows: ninth century, 1; tenth century, 4; eleventh, 26; twelfth, 27; thirteenth, 24; fourteenth, 29; 71 Gospels; 14 Praxapostoloi (Acts and Epistles); 8 New Testaments (including fragments); 1 Paul; and 17 commentaries—6 of them with the commentary in the margin. The amount of text studied varies widely, and—as a result—the totals for some letters in some manuscripts are too small to be significant. The higher totals for the letter epsilon give greater validity to the generalizations based on its use than can be claimed for the other letters.

LIST OF EVIDENCE CONCERNING E, H, Λ, Π

	E	H	Λ	Π
Leningrad, Pub. Libr., Gr. 219, Gospels, A.D. 835, W-V, Pl. I; Ts-S, Pls. 1, 1a	0/218	0/93	0/44	0/45
Paris, Bib. Nat., Gr. 70, Gospels, A.D. 964? Sil, Pl. 78; Omont, Pl. 38 [1]	11/45	0/27	9/0	1/16
Athos, Vatop., 949, Gospels, A.D. 949? Lake, Pl. 153 [2]	0/21	1/12	4/2	2/13
Florence, Laur., Conv. Soppr. 191, Praxapostolos, A.D. 984, V-P, Pl. XXVI [3]	0/25	0/20	4/3	0/13
Athos, Laura, 19, Gospels, A.D. 992, Lake, Pl. 162	24/82	30/9	2/17	0/36

[1] The date is uncertain, for the date-colophon is written in a later, second hand.

[2] The colophon is a copy by a scribe who says he saw the original.

[3] This codex has comments in the margin. The text only was counted; there are a few uncial epsilons and pis in the margin, and in the marginalia lambda occurs 19/20.

	E	H	Λ	Π
London, Brit. Mus., Add. 39598, Praxapostolos, A.D. 1009, Curzon, p. 39, NPalSoc, 2d ser., Pl. 118 [1]	11/53	17/9	23/9	18/7
Madrid, Escorial, Y-III-5, Gospels, A.D. 1014, G-M, Pl. VIII, 26, 27	7/43	2/19	10/0	3/17
Athos, Laura, 138, Praxapostolos, A.D. 1015, Lake, Pl. 170 .	6/75	14/12	7/16	10/34
Milan, Ambrosian, B 56 sup, Gospels, A.D. 1022, PalSoc, 1st ser., Pl. 130; M-T, Pl. 62; Lake, Pl. 213	44/102	0/53	4/28	10/36
London, Brit. Mus., Add. 17470, Gospels, A.D. 1033, PalSoc, 1st ser., Pl. 202; Lake, Pl. 125. .	4/71	9/29	10/7	3/29
Rome, Vatican, Gr. 1650, N.T., A.D. 1037, C-L, Pl. 22	20/185	0/71	13/40	10/78
Patmos, St. John's, 76, Gospels, A.D. 1038, Lake, Pl. 38 . . .	2/35	6/11	5/2	0/16
Paris, Bib. Nat., Suppl. Gr. 911, Luke, A.D. 1043, Omont, Pl. 18; Lake, Pl. 265; and 2 fols. of this manuscript, Leningrad, Gr. 290 [2]	0/96	0/33	0/20	2/38
London, Brit. Mus., Add. 20003, Praxapostolos, A.D. 1044, NPalSoc, 1st ser., Pl. 179; Lake, Pl. 126 [3]	9/118	26/17	27/3	35/3
Paris, Bib. Nat., Gr. 223, Paul and mg. comm., A.D. 1045, Omont, Pl. 19; Lake, Pls. 267-69, text only	4/83	18/30	9/23	16/38
Athos, Laura, 6, Gospels, A.D. 1047, Lake, Pl. 179	14/23	23/0	10/0	1/15
Rome, Vatican, Gr. 2002, Gospels, A.D. 1052, fols. 27r, 53r, 63v, 117r	99/154	35/52	41/12	2/73
Leningrad, Pub. Libr., 643, Gospels, A.D. 1054, Ts-S, Vol. II, Pl. 14	7/150	11/35	3/19	11/40

[1] This is hardly a calligraphic hand, but very labored writing, called "Palestinian" by the Palaeographical Society editors.

[2] This a Greek-Arabic bilingual Gospel of Luke. It was formerly Jerusalem, Holy Sepulcher, MS 1.

[3] This manuscript is "written in rather rough minuscules." There is no ruling, and the year is written in a rather peculiar fashion. It can hardly be called calligraphic.

	E	H	Λ	Π
Paris, Bib. Nat., Cois. 28, Paul and mg. comm., A.D. 1056, Omont, Pl. 24; Lake, Pl. 280 [1]	63/205	96/34	49/21	1/105
Leningrad, Pub. Libr., 72, Gospels and mg. comm., A.D. 1061, Ts-S, Vol. II, Pl. 17 [2]	0/15	12/1	0/4	1/2
Sinai, St. Catherine's, 172, Gospels, A.D. 1067, Hatch, Vol. I, Pl. 3; and 1 fol. of this manuscript at Leningrad, Pub. Libr., Gr. 291	71/151	37/38	20/35	34/38
Vienna, Nat. Libr., Gr. Theol. 302, Praxapostolos and mg. comm., A.D. 1064-68, fols. 41r, 325r, text only counted . . .	9/116	20/65	41/5	29/4
Athos, Vatop., 919, Gospels, A.D. 1068, Lake, Pl. 184	6/74	21/8	4/17	1/25
Venice, Marc., 1170, Praxapostolos, A.D. 1069, Lake, Pl. 88, and fols. 198r, 250r, 276r, and last verso [3]	77/194	75/53	48/34	1/82
Moscow, University, MS 2, Praxapostolos, A.D. 1072, Ts-S, Vol. I, Pl. 20	18/80	18/36	9/28	3/40
Berlin, Preuss. Staatsbibliothek, MS 379 (Gr. Oct. 3), Matthew and John, A.D. 1077, Lake, Pl. 345	23/76	18/11	14/12	11/8
London, Brit. Mus., Harl. 5537, Praxapostolos, A.D. 1087, NPalSoc, 1st ser., Pl. 179b; Lake, Pl. 131	21/52	50/1	23/2	33/8
Vienna, Nat. Libr., Gr. Theol. 157, Paul and comm., A.D. 1088? fols. 89r, 145r, 171r, 227v [4]	166/225	126/28	81/2	12/139
Paris, Bib. Nat., Gr. 81, Gospels, A.D. 1092, Omont, Pl. 39; Lake, Pls. 306-7	0/149	80/1	33/0	4/36

[1] The text and scholia were tabulated separately; but as no difference in usage appeared, the totals have been combined.

[2] The script of text and margin differs greatly in style; therefore the totals of the text alone are given.

[3] Lake refers to this manuscript as an "apostolos."

[4] A question mark is put after the date, since the last verso shows no colophon.

	E	H	Λ	Π
Florence, Laur., IV 32, Praxa-postolos, A.D. 1092, fols. 52v, 53r, 139v, 140r, 128v	98/246	123/0	68/22	69/21
Athos, Laura, 61, Gospels, A.D. 1098, Lake, Pl. 189	29/41	13/7	6/3	2/0
Paris, Bib. Nat., Suppl. Gr. 1262, Praxapostolos, A.D. 1101, fols. 36-37r.	1/150	61/20	32/15	5/40
Berlin, Preuss. Staatsbibliothek, MS 357 (Gr. Qu. 55), Gospels, A.D. 1103? Lake, Pl. 347 [1] . .	5/29	20/1	9/0	4/12
London, Brit. Mus., Add. 28816, Praxapostolos and Apoc., A.D. 1111, PalSoc, 1st ser., Pl. 84; M-T, Pl. 67; Lake, Pl. 135 [2] .	1/70	34/4	27/4	24/3
Athos, Laura, 58, Praxapostolos, A.D. 1118, Lake Pls. 194-95 .	45/102	45/7	36/13	4/35
Sinai, St. Catherine's, 158, Gospels, A.D. 1123? Hatch, Vol. I, Pl. 23 [3]	10/46	5/7	11/8	10/7
Sinai, St. Catherines', 193, Gospels and comm., A.D. 1124, Hatch, Vol. I, Pl. 24 [4] . . .	4/101	29/40	30/2	15/37
Rome, Vatican, Urbin. Gr. 2, Gospels, A.D. 1128, M-T, Pl. 68; NPalSoc, 1st ser., Pl. 106 . .	19/41	10/12	9/7	7/12
Athos, Vatop., 960, Gospels, A.D. 1128? Lake, Pl. 196 [5]	1/22	1/15	7/0	10/6
Athos, Esphigmenou, 25, Gospels, A.D. 1129, Lake, Pl. 200.	25/19	16/2	7/0	1/17
Oxford, Christ Church, Wake MS 29, Gospels, A.D. 1130, Lake, Pls. 337-38:				
Fol. 76r	20/57	28/6	18/4	1/18
Fols. 48r, 125r, 162r [6] . . .	72/157	14/64	66/1	17/38

[1] Lake puts a question mark after the date, since there is no date-colophon as such but only the mutilated remains of dated references to the imperial family.

[2] Maunde Thompson's plate shows only the hypothesis of I John, while most of Lake's is taken up with the Euthalian preface to Paul.

[3] Hatch says that the date was added at a later date by Maximus hieromonachos.

[4] Figures on this codex are of doubtful value, as a strenuous effort has been made to distinguish the uncial script of the *keimenon* from the minuscule scholia.

[5] Date given in an ownership colophon by a second hand.

[6] The codex was written by more than one scribe. Folio 76r, in my judgment, is not by the scribe of the colophon, and the other three folios are. Their totals are therefore presented separately; note the variation in the eta

	E	H	Λ	Π
Athos, Dionysiou, 8, N.T., A.D. 1133, Lake, Pl. 197 [1]	27/55	28/0	39/0	32/0
Chicago, University of, 129, Gospels, A.D. 1133, fol. 7or [2] . .	20/66	24/6	29/3	14/10
Vienna, Nat. Libr., Theol. Gr. 79 and 80, N.T. and comm., A.D. 1139, fol. 11r of MS 79 [3] . .	106/306	134/44	140/0	153/24
Madrid, Escorial, X-IV-21, Gospels, A.D. 1140, G-M, Pl. XI, 39-41	32/16	12/3	1/4	0/0
Athens, Nat. Libr., 123, Gospels, A.D. 1145, Lake, Pls. 72-73 . .	13/138	23/47	41/1	1/57
Leningrad, Pub. Libr., 222, Gospels, A.D. 1145, Ts-S, Vol. II, Pl. 26 [4]	8/48	0/17	12/0	0/27
Rome, Vatican, Barb. Gr. 449, Gospels, A.D. 1153, Matt. 1:1; the end of John	10/11	6/1	6/0	0/2
London, Brit. Mus., Add. 5107, Gospels, A.D. 1159, Lake, Pl. 142	6/42	1/15	12/2	0/18
Paris, Bib. Nat., Suppl. Gr. 612, Gospels and comm., A.D. 1164, Lake, Pl. 320:				
Text	3/7	4/1	1/3	3/4
Commentary [5]	11/30	20/0	15/0	5/7
Paris, Bib. Nat., Gr. 83, Gospels, A.D. 1167, Omont, Pl. 48; Lake, Pls. 323-25	193/11	90/2	40/0	0/61
Paris, Bib. Nat., Gr. 90, Gospels, A.D. 1176, Omont, Pl. 49; Lake, Pl. 326.	166/16	61/1	34/3	10/54
London, Br. Mus., Add. 22736, Gospels, A.D. 1179, Lake, Pls. 144-145	79/42	28/12	21/0	3/18

column. Within the three folios the only variation noticed was that in fol. 48r, where the pi column reads 10/6.

[1] The manuscript has many abbreviations, and is written in a very unusual hand.

[2] This is a miniature manuscript with an irregular script which may be due to its minuteness.

[3] Hardly a book-hand, although scribe does his best to write in the calligraphic style. There are many abbreviations and no difference between the script of text and comment. Lake says, "This is obviously a private manuscript."

[4] A large uneven script.

[5] Only the first seven lines of the commentary were counted. The script of the text is large and stylized, that of the comment is small and highly abbreviated. The variation in the lambda column is probably due to the smallness of the total in the text.

	E	H	Λ	Π
Sinai, St. Catherine's, 180, Gospels, A.D. 1186, Hatch, Vol. I, Pl. 25	56/18	15/12	12/8	0/23
Vienna, Palat. Suppl. Gr. 102, Gospels, A.D. 1192, Bick, Pl. 11a	78/11	38/0	15/3	18/11
Vienna, Nat. Libr., Gr. Theol. 19, Gospels and comm., A.D. 1196, Bick, Pl. 12, and fols. 69v, 97v, 321v [1]	215/194	128/1	136/0	108/34
Rome, Vatican, Gr. 2290, Gospels, A.D. 1197, fols. 102r, 180r, 214r, 218r	206/52	102/10	82/1	11/62
Moscow, Synod. Libr., 16, Gospels, A.D. 1199, Sabas, Pl. 11; Ts-S, Vol. I, Pl. 24	98/91	52/4	29/5	6/36
Vienna, N.T. Dumba, Gospels, A.D. 1226, Zom.	2/78	22/0	15/9	4/18
Rome, Vatican, Gr. 648, Paul and comm., A.D. 1232, fol. 10r [2]	39/56	53/1	38/1	55/1
Sinai, St. Catherine's, 201, Gospels, A.D. 1244, Hatch, Vol. I, Pl. 48; part of this manuscript is at Leningrad, Pub. Libr., 396; Ts-S, Vol. II, Pl. 34 . .	40/90	37/24	25/7	19/18
Sinai, St. Catherine's, 164, Gospels, A.D. 1250, Hatch, Vol. I, Pl. 49 [3]	25/35	31/0	23/0	20/2
Paris, Bib. Nat., Gr. 117, Gospels, A.D. 1262, Omont, Pl. 56; and fols. 13v, 14r, 18v, 19r. .	183/70	117/10	70/2	64/14
Athos, Laura, A 35, Gospels, A.D. 1269, NPalSoc, 1st ser., Pl. 27	65/12	38/0	28/0	30/1
London, Brit. Mus., Add. 39597, Gospels, A.D. 1272, Curzon, p. 40; NPalSoc, 2d ser., Pl. 119	110/168	87/17	57/14	13/36
Moscow, Synod. Libr., 18, Gospels, A.D. 1275, Sabas, Pl. 12a; Ts-S, Vol. I, Pl. 25	33/81	19/10	21/9	1/28
Rome, Vatican, Gr. 644, Gospels and comm., A.D. 1280, fol. 212r [4]	99/108	65/3	64/0	30/45

[1] All of these folios are in the script of the colophon.

[2] Not a calligraphic hand; many abbreviations; no difference in script of text and commentary.

[3] A rather crude, wobbly hand.

[4] This is the work of the famous scribe Theodore Hagiopetrites. Four other manuscripts written by him are listed here: London, A.D. 1292,

	E	H	Λ	Π
Leningrad, Pub. Libr., 311, Gospels, A.D. 1281, Ts-S, Vol. II, Pl. 38	18/122	51/9	35/2	1/42
Rome, Vatican, Ottob. Gr. 381, N.T., A.D. 1282, C-L, Pl. 32	45/23	30/5	22/7	3/29
Serres, St. John Prodromos, Γ. 10, Gospels, A.D. 1282, M-T, Pl. 73; NPalSoc, 1st ser., Pl. 78	44/11	18/0	8/0	0/14
Vienna, Palat. Suppl. Gr. 107, Gospels, A.D. 1283, Bick, Pl. 14	3/41	15/4	6/2	3/15
Florence, Laur., Plut. XI.8, Gospels and comm., A.D. 1284, fol. 14r [1]	263/95	124/14	90/0	88/5
London, Brit. Mus., Burney 20, Gospels, A.D. 1285, fols. 88v, 91r, 91v, 92r, 143r	112/88	79/1	44/2	10/57
Sinai, St. Catherine's, 176, Gospels, A.D. 1286, Hatch, Vol. I, Pl. 50	35/10	13/1	15/0	14/2
Oxford, Bodl., Laud. Gr. 3, Gospels, A.D. 1286, fols. 23v-24r, ?v-?r, 132v-133r, last verso .	425/332	215/30	144/83	118/122
Rome, Vatican, Gr. 641, Gospels and comm., A.D. 1286, fol. 45r [2]	52/41	57/2	52/0	32/6
Ann Arbor, Univ. Mich., 80, Gospels, A.D. 1287, fols. 42r, 49r, 77r	311/102	153/0	101/38	129/17
Paris, Bib. Nat., Suppl. Gr. 1259, N.T., A.D. 1290, fols. 9-10r . .	106/150	132/6	55/3	86/4
Paris, Bib. Nat., Gr. 118, Gospels, A.D. 1291, Omont, Pl. 66 [3]	51/79	72/2	37/0	39/6
Rome, Vatican, Barb. Gr. 541, Gospels, A.D. 1292, C-L, Pl. 38	21/20	25/0	10/0	1/17
London, Brit. Mus., Burney 21, Gospels, A.D. 1292, Matt. 1:1 f. (end of John for E only) . . .	11/42	10/3	8/0	0/3
Williamstown, Chapin Library, New Testament, A.D. 1295, Matt. 1:1 f.; 19:3 f.	58/119	53/9	24/10	2/29
Venice, Mar., I.19, Gospels, A.D. 1301, fols. 27r, 114r	71/67	25/10	30/7	30/22

Williamstown, A.D. 1295; Venice, A.D. 1301; and Sinai, A.D. 1308. There is no difference in script in this codex between text and commentary.

[1] No difference in script between text and commentary.
[2] Not a calligraphic hand; very rapid, highly abbreviated.
[3] A small manuscript, written in a script that has no style.

	E	H	Λ	Π
Vatican, Gr. 1743, Apoc. and comm., A.D. 1301, fols. 5r, 81r, 107r, 112r [1]	147/61	132/18	55/4	31/47
Venice, Mar., I.20, Gospels, A.D. 1302, fols. 13r, 73r, 123r, 255r	185/59	94/1	69/4	41/37
Leningrad, Publ. Libr., 314, Gospels, A.D. 1303, Ts-S, Vol. II, Pl. 41	72/12	29/4	18/0	13/5
Chicago, University of, 135, Gospels, A.D. 1303, first verso and second recto of Luke	31/65	33/5	22/0	29/3
London, Brit. Mus., Add. 22506, Gospels, A.D. 1305, PalSoc, 1st ser., Pl. 205	35/19	21/0	5/4	1/16
Sinai, St. Catherine's, 277, Praxapostolos, A.D. 1308, Hatch, Vol. I, Pl. 57	34/37	31/4	13/1	10/19
London Brit. Mus., Add. 37002, Gospels, A.D. 1314, M-T, Pl. 74; NPalSoc, 1st ser., Pl. 52 .	73/30	42/0	20/0	2/24
Leningrad, Pub. Libr., 326, Gospels and mg. comm., A.D. 1317, both Leningrad folios counted, but in text only [2] .	114/48	61/1	45/0	28/29
Leningrad, Pub. Libr., 315, Gospels, A.D. 1318, Ts-S, Vol. II, Pl. 44 [3]	23/34	27/0	18/0	2/11
Milan, Ambros., E. 63 sup., Gospels, A.D. 1321, fols. 182v-183v	164/60	73/5	54/0	1/53
Milan, Ambros., F. 61 sup., Gospels, A.D. 1322, fols. 89v-90v .	126/14	40/1	34/0	44/5
London, Brit. Mus., Add. 11838, Gospels, A.D. 1326, NPalSoc, 1st ser., Pl. 130.	49/8	25/1	17/1	1/18
London, Brit. Mus., Add. 5117, Gospels, A.D. 1326, fols. 32v, 33r, 137v, 138r, 201v, 202r, 223v, 224r	355/236	127/78	171/24	93/99
Vienna, Palat. theol. gr., 221, Praxapostolos, A.D. 1330, Bick, Pl. 22	57/44	33/0	20/1	6/32

[1] Scribe has made an effort to distinguish script of text from that of comment, but his only success was with epsilon, and even there the difference was not great enough to change the general proportion of uncials to minuscules. A Leningrad praxapostolos of the same date is reproduced by Ts-S, Vol. II, Pl. 41, but the plate shows Euthalian preface and no text.

[2] This is part of Athos, Dionysiou 80.

[3] This is part of Athos, Dionysiou 30.

	E	H	Λ	Π
Rome, Vatican, Gr. 542, Apoc. and comm., A.D. 1331, fols. 43r, 113r, 163r [1]	128/141	102/2	51/38	2/95
Jerusalem, Patr., Saba 262, Gospels and comm., A.D. 1332, Hatch, Vol. II, Pl. 52 [2] . . .	64/73	63/3	49/6	9/42
Chicago, University of, 136, Gospels, A.D. 1332, first verso of Mark and Luke, first recto of John	4/121	52/0	22/3	3/33
Madrid, Escorial, X-IV-9, N.T., A.D. 1332, G-M, Pl. X, 38 . .	10/12	7/0	5/1	6/1
Leningrad, Pub. Libr., 235, Gospels and comm., A.D. 1337, fol. 15 [3]	330/146	229/13	133/2	77/83
London, Brit. Mus., Add. 5468, Gospels, A.D. 1337, fols. 34v, 204r [4]	120/38	62/0	54/1	2/44
Oxford, Bodl., Selden sup. 29, Gospels, A.D. 1338, fols. 126v, 127r, 216r	202/15	69/14	44/0	51/32
Sinai, St. Catherine's, 152, Gospels, A.D. 1346, Hatch, Vol. I, Pl. 58	35/0	10/12	11/0	12/1
Venice, Mar., I.22, Gospels, A.D. 1356, fols. 24r, 80r, 118r [5] . .	29/171	93/0	60/0	57/8
London, Brit. Mus., Add. 11837, N.T., A.D. 1357, fols. 56r, 347v, 464r, 464v	112/79	48/7	24/17	22/22
Paris, Bib. Nat., Gr. 47, New Testament and Apoc., A.D. 1364, fols. 3v, 4r	123/116	81/4	38/14	33/1
Madison, Drew University, MS 1, Paul, A.D. 1366, 1369, Sitterly, Pl. VI.	19/39	30/8	8/13	4/21
London, Brit. Mus., Burney 18,				

[1] The folios counted do not contain the Apocalypse, but they are in the hand and style of the last folio which contains the colophon to the Apocalypse. Their content reads like a commentary on the Fourth Gospel.

[2] Another page is reproduced in Ts-S, Vol. II, Pl. 47. This hand contains many sprawls and abbreviations. There is no difference between text and commentary.

[3] Another page is reproduced in Ts-S, Vol. II, Pl. 49. There is no difference between text and commentary.

[4] Gregory dates this codex in the year 1338, but the colophon seems to read September 26, which would make the year 1337.

[5] The scribe writes as though drawing each letter.

	E	H	Λ	Π
Gospels and Hebrews, A.D. 1366, NPalSoc, 1st ser., Pl. 180	8/35	21/5	8/3	2/18
Leningrad, Pub. Libr., 398, Gospels, A.D. 1382, Ts-S, Vol. II, Pl. 44	20/5	21/0	4/5	8/1

The important facts in regard to the letter epsilon can be briefly summarized. Before A.D. 1167, 48 manuscripts have more minuscule than uncial epsilons. In the same period, only 2 manuscripts have more uncials than minuscules, and both are written shortly before 1167; the first (A.D. 1129) has 25/19; the second (A.D. 1140) has 32/16. From 1167 to 1226, uncial epsilons outnumber minuscules without exception. From A.D. 1226 on, there is no regularity in usage—there are 30 manuscripts having uncial domination in epsilons and 23 having minuscule domination.

It should be noted that in this study "minuscule" is used of the 6-shaped letter, even when it appears as a high "hook." All other forms are called "uncial"—although, strictly speaking, "non-minuscule" would be a better term.

The value of this study of epsilon for purposes of dating an undated manuscript may be positively stated in two sentences. (1) A New Testament manuscript with uncial epsilons outnumbering minuscule epsilons was written after A.D. 1166 plus or minus. (2) A New Testament manuscript written in the period A.D. 1166 plus or minus to A.D. 1225 plus or minus will have more uncial epsilons than minuscules. The second of these rules is less certain than the first, since the number of manuscripts studied in this area was not large enough to secure perfect confidence. But the first rule can be relied on.

In the case of the letter eta, minuscule dominance alternates with uncial dominance through the eleventh century and the first half of the twelfth. The earliest occurrence of uncial dominance is A.D. 992, and the latest instance of minuscule dominance is A.D. 1159. From A.D. 1159 to the end of the fourteenth century, the uncial forms of the letter outnumber the minuscules. The only exception comes near the end of the period, in A.D. 1346; and the total here is small: 10/12.

The significance of this study of eta may be summarized in two rules: (1) A manuscript with minuscule etas dominant was written before A.D. 1159 plus or minus. (2) A manuscript written after A.D. 1159 will have uncial etas dominant.

In the case of the letter lambda, minuscule dominance alternates with uncial dominance in the tenth (?) and eleventh centuries down to A.D. 1075. From A.D. 1075 to the end of the fourteenth century, uncial lambdas outnumber the minuscule forms. There is no real exception to this, although one manuscript, dated A.D. 1140, had 1 uncial to 4 minuscules. But the total number here is too small to have much significance. At the end of the period, two manuscripts have minuscule dominance: A.D. 1369 and A.D. 1382.

Two generalizations may be based on this study of the letter lambda: (1) A manuscript with more minuscule than uncial lambdas was written before A.D. 1075 plus or minus. (2) A manuscript written after A.D. 1075 will have uncial lambdas dominant.

In the case of the letter pi, minuscule forms dominate down to the last third of the eleventh century. Two earlier *praxapostoloi*, dated A.D. 1009 and A.D. 1044, have uncials dominant; but they can hardly be called calligraphic manuscripts. The first has a labored script, while the second has no ruling and is written in a rough minuscule. It is an interesting fact that four of the next five manuscripts to have uncial dominance, dated A.D. 1064, 1087, 1092, and 1111, are also *praxapostoloi*. The fifth, dated A.D. 1077, contains Matthew and John. After the end of the eleventh century there is no regularity in the use of uncial or minuscule forms of pi.

The only generalization that can be made from this study of pi is that a manuscript in which uncial forms of pi dominate was written after A.D. 1066 plus or minus.

The limitation of this study to straight-text New Testament manuscripts was suggested by the well-known ultraconservatism of the biblical hand as against the non-biblical, and by the distinct palaeographic history of the lectionaries, as evidenced—for example—by their late use of the uncial script. To investigate the justice of our limitation a sampling was made of the use of epsilon in Old Testament, lectionary, and non-biblical manuscripts. Although this test has not yet been carried through an adequate number of codices the tentative results are very significant. So far the total of uncial and minuscule epsilons has been established for sample pages of 11 Old Testament manuscripts, 46 lectionary manuscripts, and 64 non-biblical manuscripts. These 121 manuscripts are all dated, and a larger proportion of them than was the case with the New Testament manuscripts comes from the tenth to the twelfth centuries; a very few come from the fourteenth.

The one significant result is that in each of these groups uncial dominance of the letter epsilon appears earlier than it does for the straight-text New Testament manuscripts. Uncial epsilons dominate in an Old Testament manuscript of A.D. 1075; in lectionaries dated A.D. 1047, 1066, 1078, and 1119; in non-biblical manuscripts dated A.D. 1005, 1040, 1064, 1079, 1103, 1112, and 1124; and 2 manuscripts have almost a 50-50 division: a non-biblical manuscript of 1065 and a lectionary of A.D. 1020. This list totals 14 manuscripts in which uncial forms of epsilon dominate, all written earlier than the earliest straight-text New Testament manuscripts in which the uncial forms predominate.

Although generalizations at this stage of the study cannot be final, the judgment may be risked that the use of the uncial form was regarded as an innovation and that the scribe who wrote biblical manuscripts was instructed to avoid it. This would explain its earlier intrusion into secular manuscripts, but it does not explain the relatively early appearance of the uncial form in lectionary codices, which were the most sacred possession of the church. Yet if the conservatism of the straight-text manuscripts was achieved by striving to reproduce the alphabet employed in earlier works of the same type, the difference within the sacred group can be understood. For the lectionary codex has no history, no period, in which it was written in a pure minuscule script. In the days of the pure minuscule, lectionaries were written in the earlier uncial style. When the change to minuscule came for these manuscripts, the contemporary minuscule hand was already a mixed minuscule. Thus the more rapid adoption of uncial forms by such books was a natural development. That the mixed minuscule is easier reading than the pure minuscule, and therefore better suited to a lesson book, may be a subjective judgment.

That the commentary manuscripts were not regarded as being on the same level as their straight-text brothers was also indicated in this study. Seventeen of these manuscripts were studied; and many of them had a style of their own—or, more probably, that of the contemporary business-hand or trained private-hand. They accept frequent use of abbreviations, flourishes, etc., much earlier than their non-commented brethren. In many cases a deliberate effort was made to differentiate the text from that of the comment. This made both scripts artificial. The special peculiarities of commentary manuscripts deserve further attention.

In conclusion a summary can be given of the results of this study of four letters in more than one hundred New Testament manuscripts. If a straight-text New Testament codex was written after A.D. 1150 plus or minus, it will have more uncial than minuscule forms of both eta and lambda. It may or may not have uncial forms dominating its use of epsilons, but any manuscript that does have more uncial than minuscule epsilons is later than A.D. 1166 plus or minus. A New Testament codex in which the uncial form of pi dominates the minuscule is later than A.D. 1066. If minuscules dominate in the etas, the manuscript is earlier than A.D. 1150. If minuscules dominate in the lambdas, the manuscript was written before A.D. 1075. A manuscript later than 1075 will have a majority of uncial lambdas. It seems probable that a manuscript written from A.D. 1150 to 1225 will have uncial epsilons dominating minuscules.

This sounds like enough rules to establish the date of all the manuscripts ever written, but it is not. Many of these statements are merely tests of dates that must be arrived at by other means. A few are still tentative and need to be tested by further evidence. Moreover, it must be admitted as a possibility that a scribe who is deliberately and strenuously archaizing can attain a style in the use of *some* letters that contradicts these rules, but a correct imitation of obsolete usage in regard to all the alphabet is hardly credible. While this possibility of variation remains, and criticism and further study are needed to broaden the base on which these results rest, they show that there is enough detailed evidence available for the scholar to produce a clear and usable set of tests that will date Byzantine manuscripts of the New Testament accurately and objectively.

CHAPTER TEN

METHOD IN VALIDATING BYZANTINE DATE-COLOPHONS: A STUDY OF ATHOS, LAURA B. 26 [1]

Fraudulent claims concerning the antiquity of a volume did not originate with the printing press. The printing press modified the form of the pretense: "A first edition," but only the form. Before the days of printing owners and dealers increased the value of a book by antedating it. The detection of the fraudulent date is made difficult by the common scribal practice of changing the style of writing when signing and/or dating his work. Sound method requires the comparison of every detail in a date-colophon with a large number of parallels.

Professor Kirsopp Lake's distinguished work in New Testament textual criticism includes an invaluable contribution to the study of Byzantine palaeography. In collaboration with Silva Lake he published photographic facsimiles of sample pages from dated Greek minuscule manuscripts down to A.D. 1200.[2] In that publication my attention was drawn to Laura MS B.26 (146), a Byzantine New Testament with Psalms and Odes, with a colophon giving the date A.D. 1084.

My attention was drawn to the manuscript in the attempt to date the Four Gospels of Karahissar (Leningrad Gr. 105). The Leningrad codex was judged to be the work of the scribe of the famous Rockefeller McCormick New Testament, but this script in its turn had already been identified as either identical with, or very similar to, the hand of Laura B.26. This caused trouble, for the study of the Four Gospels of Karahissar had assigned it to the thirteenth century. It was too much to suppose that a scribe could have written the Athos manuscript in the year 1084, and Leningrad 105 in the thirteenth century. To find which date was wrong, every element

---

[1] Originally published as "A Misdated New Testament Manuscript: Athos, Laura B.26 (146)," in *Quantulacumque: Studies Presented to Kirsopp Lake by Pupils, Colleagues, and Friends*, ed. by Robert P. Casey, Silva Lake, and Agnes K. Lake (London, 1937), pp. 183-88.

[2] *Monumenta palaeographica vetera*; First Series, *Dated Greek Minuscule Manuscripts to the Year 1200 A.D.* (Boston, 1934-1939).

involved in the dating of the two codices was carefully checked. This led to the study of the date colophon of Laura B.26.

Professor and Mrs. Lake published a photograph and a transcription of the colophon. Their doubt as to the exact date is indicated by a question mark after the date 1084. I quote their comment on the colophon in full. "The colophon is in a different script and probably a later hand than the manuscript. It may be a copy of an original on a missing leaf. The cycle of the sun is three years wrong and the indiction one year wrong for the date given." [1]

A photograph of this important colophon was obtained trough the courtesy of Mr. George R. Swain of Ann Arbor, Michigan, to whom we were referred by Professor Lake. In the following transcription, the line division of the original is retained.

Εγραφη επι της βασιλει(ας) του ευσεβεστατου κ(αι) φιλοχριστου κυ(ρου) α
λεξιου μ(ε)γ(α)λ(ου) δουκα σεμβαστου του κομνηνου επι ετ(ους) ς̄
φϙβ κυ(κλω) (ηλιου) θ̄ κυ(κλω) (σεληνης) ιη̄ ενδ(ικτιωνος) η̄ η αποκρεα
    ιανουαριω
λᾱ νομ(ικον) φασκ(α) μ(α)ρ(τιω) κε̄ χρ(ιστιανον) πασχ(α) μ(α)ρ(τιω)
    κη̄ η νηστεια τ(ων) αγ(ιων) αποστολ(ων)
ημερ(αι) λς̄

The items of date given here are nine in number: (1) in the reign of Alexius Comnenus, (2) in the year 6592, equals A.D. 1084, (3) sun cycle 9, (4) moon cycle 18, (5) indiction 8, (6) Sunday of abstinence from meat January 31, (7) "legal passover" March 25, (8) Christian passover (Easter) March 28, (9) fast of the holy apostles 36 days.

From the tables compiled by V. Gardthausen [2] and the almanacs of E. A. Fry,[3] we obtain the following information for the year A.D. 1084: sun cycle 12, moon cycle 18, indiction 7, Sunday of abstinence from meat February 4, Easter March 31, fast of the holy apostles 33 days. The only item in the list that corresponds with our colophon is the moon cycle, obviously a coincidence. But if we turn to the year 1445, we find that every one of these items corresponds with the data given in the colophon. This is the nearest year to A.D. 1084 in which sun cycle, moon cycle, and indiction have the numbers given in Laura B.26; and in this year the Easter data also agree. A University of Chicago tetraevangelion, ms. 136,

---

[1] *Ibid.*, Fasc. III, pp. 13-14 and Pl. 188.
[2] *Griechische Palaeographie*, II (Leipzig, 1913), pp. 487 ff.
[3] *Almanacks for Students of English History* (London, 1915), Table 10.

contains an Easter table which gives all of these data for the year
A.D. 1445.

This suggests at once that the colophon is a fraud, and further
evidence supports this opinion. For the sake of clarity, all the
evidence is presented in categorical form.

1. The items 3-9 in the colophon do not agree with the year given.

2. The items 3-9 agree with the date A.D. 1445.

3. Out of 141 date colophons written in the 11th century,[1] none
gives any Easter data of any sort.

4. The earliest use of Easter data in connection with a date-
colophon that is known to me is in the Vatican ms., Ottob. Gr. 381,
of A.D. 1282. Easter data occur also in Brit. Mus. Burney ms. 21,
written in A.D. 1292 by the famous scribe Theodore Hagiopetrites.
But there the Easter data are given in a separate section below the
main colophon, and it should be noted that the fast of the apostles
is not given. In Patmos ms. 192, there is no date colophon as such,
but the scribe of the marginal comments adds a wordy exordium
in which he gives the Easter dating in the years 1082 and 1109.
The fast of the apostles is not given, and νομικον πασχα is spelled
thus. Easter data are given also in a Paris ms., Bib. Nat. Gr. 1387,
to which they were added by a renovator of the manuscript in the
year A.D. 1388. These are the only instances of the use of Easter data
in date colophons observed in a survey of about 500 such colophons.

5. The form of the reference to Alexius Comnenus does not agree
with that found in date colophons from his reign. I have seen six
colophons explicitly dated in his reign, and in each case the formula

---

[1] These 141 colophons are found in the following works: H. Omont,
*Fac-similés des manuscrits grecs datés de la Bibliothèque Nationale du ixe au
xive siècle* (Paris, 1891); V. Gardthausen, *Catalogus codicum graecorum
Sinaiticorum* (Oxford, 1886); Kirsopp and Silva Lake, *Monumenta palaeographica vetera* . . . Fasc. I-V; C. Graux and A. Martin, *Facsimilés des manuscrits grecs d'Espagne* (Paris, 1890); The Palaeographical Society—*Facsimiles
of Manuscripts and Inscriptions*, edited by E. A. Bond, E. Maunde Thompson,
and G. F. Warner, 1st and 2nd Series (London, 1873-1894); The New
Palaeographical Society—*Facsimiles of Ancient Manuscripts, etc.*, edited
by E. Maunde Thompson, G. F. Warner, F. G. Kenyon, and J. P. Gilson,
1st and 2nd Series (London, 1903-1930); P. Franchi de' Cavalieri and J.
Lietzmann, *Specimina codicum graecorum Vaticanorum* (Bonn, 1910);
F. H. A. Scrivener, *Collation of About Twenty MSS of the Holy Gospels*
(Cambridge and London, 1853); *ibid.*, *An Exact Transcript of the Codex
Augiensis* (Cambridge and London, 1859). Since the total of 141 was estab-
lished, I have seen many more eleventh century colophons, but none with
Easter data.

is much simpler than that of Laura B.26. In three manuscripts—
Paris Bib. Nat. Suppl. Gr. 482, A.D. 1105, Leningrad Public Library
Gr. 100 (formerly Paris Bib. Nat. Coislin 212), A.D. 1111, and
Moscow Syn. Typ. Bib. 2479, A.D. 1116 [1]—the phrase is ἐπὶ βα(σι-
λέως, or —είας) Ἀλεξίου τοῦ Κομνηνοῦ. A London codex, Brit.
Mus., Harley ms. 5537, A.D. 1087, agrees with Patmos ms. 20,
A.D. 1081, and with Florence, Laur. Plut. IV. 32, A.D. 1092, in the
phrase βασιλεύοντος Ἀλεξίου τοῦ Κομνηνοῦ.

6. The 11th century date-colophons of any length (that is, those
that give several items) regularly give the month in which the manuscript was written. Out of 141 date-colophons from this century,[2]
116 give the month, 19 give year and indiction only, 4 give year only,
2 give year, indiction, and reign. Not one of the 141 gives a series of
date items without giving the month.[3] Yet the month is not given in
Laura B.26.

7. Our colophon has as its last item "The Fast of the Holy
Apostles." The ultimate source of all the Easter data here given is an
Easter table. But Easter tables did not contain this particular item
until later than the 11th century. This is plainly shown by Piper's
list [4] of nineteen Byzantine Easter tables which reach from A.D.
951 to 1432. The earliest one to contain the fast of the apostles is
dated A.D. 1286. It is not included in the Easter data given in
Ambrosiana MS. B.106 Sup. for the years 1003-1012 and 1224-1225,
nor in the colophon of the Vatican codex, Ottob. Gr. 381, dated
A.D. 1282; nor does it appear with the Easter data of Burney ms.
21 of A.D. 1292. But each of six tables written between 1354 and
1432 contains this item, as does the table in University of Chicago
ms. 136, which covers the years 1424-1469.

8. Our colophon spells the passover of the "legal passover"
φασκα. But Piper points out that it occurs in this form in only four
of his manuscripts, dated 1381, 1382, 1394, and 1432.[5] This form
occurs also in Ottob. Gr. 381, A.D. 1282, in Burney ms. 21, A.D. 1292,

---

[1] The last one has minor changes giving the exact year of the reign;
cf. Sabas, *Specimina palaeographica codicum graecorum et slavonicorum
bibliothecae Mosquensis synodalis saec. vi-xvii* (Moscow, 1863), supplement.

[2] See note 2, p. 143 above.

[3] There is a possible exception in Escorial ms. Ω-IV-32, which has a
dubious colophon in a second hand.

[4] F. Piper, *Karls des Grossen Kalendarium und Ostertafeln* (Berlin, 1858),
p. 134.

[5] *Ibid.*, pp. 135-36.

and in University of Chicago ms. 136, A.D. 1424; but not in Patmos 192, A.D. 1082. The difference between the 11th and the 13th centuries in this spelling is clearly seen in a Milan codex, Ambrosiana B.106 Sup. It has an Easter table with the data for each year in a circular frame. Kirsopp and Silva Lake (Pl. 212) reproduce the last 12 circles. Of these, the last 2 were originally blank; the 10 originals are dated 1003-1012. These all write πασχα. The last 2 circles were filled in for the years 1224-1225; they have φασκα.

9. The colophon in Laura B.26 is written in a different hand from that which wrote the manuscript. The form of the beta, such a spelling as σεμβαστοῦ, the fact that the writer of the colophon does not follow the ruled lines but meanders; e.g., in the third line, from a position on one line he moves up the page until the writing depends from the line above and then back to the original level; and the general appearance of the hand—all clearly show that the scribe of the manuscript did not write the colophon.[1]

10. A study of the proportion of uncial to minuscule forms of epsilon, eta, lambda, and pi in 111 dated Greek New Testament manuscripts established certain general observations of value for date. (1) Before 1166, these manuscripts use more minuscule than uncial forms of epsilon. In Laura B.26 uncial epsilons outnumber minuscules 112/16 on the first recto of Mark. (2) After 1150, these manuscripts always use more uncial than minuscule etas. Laura B.26 uses 47 uncial etas and no minuscules. (3) After A.D. 1075, these manuscripts use more uncial than minuscule lambdas. The Laura manuscript uses 32 uncial lambdas and no minuscules. In twenty-six New Testament manuscripts dated in the eleventh century the minuscules *always* outnumber the uncial forms of epsilon, but not in Laura B.26.[2]

11. We have examples of falsification of date of various Greek codices. For example, Brit. Mus. Burney ms. 20, written in A.D. 1285, (the very period in which Laura B.26 was written) had its date advanced three centuries to 985 by the erasure of one perpendicular stroke. The original date was ϛφϙγ (6793 = A.D. 1285); by this erasure it became ϛυϙγ (6493 = A.D. 985). Gardthausen gives several examples of Greek manuscripts which were falsely dated earlier than the year in which they were written.[3] It should be noted that

---

[1] Lake and Lake hold the same opinion, *loc. cit.*
[2] See Chapter IX (pp. 125-141 above).
[3] *Griechische Palaeographie*, II, 437 ff.

these false dates are almost always several centuries earlier than the actual writing of the manuscript.

Conclusions: These data show that what we have in Laura B.26 is a fraudulent colophon written by someone who wished to secure an early date for the codex. The suggestion that it may be a copy of the original colophon cannot be accepted.[1] A copyist would not have missed all the numbers, nor would he have failed to present an eleventh century formula. Had he been copying an authentic colophon, he would certainly have given the month. The appeal to errors in copying cannot explain the presence of festivals and spellings unknown in eleventh century sources. The maker of the colophon knew the dates of the reign of Alexius Comnenus, but he wrote his date in the style of the thirteenth to fifteenth century, not in the style of the eleventh century. Since he had no date-colophon to copy from, he supplemented his simple year date with a line from an Easter table. The line he chose was for the year 1445. This suggests that the colophon was written within about 50 years of that date, although this is by no means certain.[2] A careful study of iconography and script in Leningrad Gr. 105, which is very probably from the same hand as Laura B.26, located that codex in the second half of the thirteenth century.[3] Thus the colophon in Laura B.26, written about two centuries after the completion of the codex, is a fraud designed to antedate the manuscript several centuries.

---

[1] The suggestion that the colophon might be a copy was, to the best of my knowledge, first advanced by the late Professor Albert Friend of Princeton. See Edgar J. Goodspeed, *The Rockefeller McCormick New Testament*; Vol. I, *Introduction* (Chicago, 1933), p. 15.

[2] Few Easter tables cover more than 50 years. It is most probable that our colophonist would choose a line from the future end of his table.

[3] Ernest Cadman Colwell, *The Four Gospels of Karahissar*; Vol. I, *History and Text* (Chicago, 1936), pp. 95-120.

CHAPTER ELEVEN

HORT REDIVIVUS: A PLEA AND A PROGRAM [1]

Fenton John Anthony Hort needs to be brought back to life. He made a major contribution to the textual criticism of the New Testament in the nineteenth century.[2] He can make a major contribution today.[3]

In that day he presented a carefully reasoned account of textual criticism that was comprehensive in its discussion of method, in its reconstruction of the history of the manuscript tradition, and in its appraisal of Text-types. He did not try to be comprehensive in his discussion of the *materials* of textual criticism. He published no catalogue of manuscripts. He cited no manuscript evidence in a critical apparatus. But, having studied the evidence that others had accumulated, he applied to its interpretation the powers of a great intellect, and, with the help of his collaborator, produced the best edition of the Greek New Testament that we possess.

Much of the strength of his work derives from its comprehensiveness. He ignored no major facet of the manuscript tradition. Thus element after element of our later "discoveries" can be found frankly stated in his work. He recognized the early date and wide distribution of the "Western" text long before its champions did. He leaned more heavily upon patristic evidence than we do. He saw clearly that the "canonization" of the New Testament books did not result in accurate copying during the first three centuries. His work was comprehensive. The work of the last forty years has often been fragmented. Today we need a fresh comprehensive statement, and it must begin with Hort.

A careful restatement of Hort's work will go far toward correcting the extremist errors of the last forty years. These errors are a by-

---

[1] Originally published as "Hort Redivivus: A Plea and a Program," in *Transitions in Biblical Scholarship*, ed. J. Coert Rylaarsdam ("Essays in Divinity," vol. VI [Chicago, 1968]), pp. 131-156.

[2] Brook Foss Westcott and Fenton John Anthony Hort, *The New Testament in the Original Greek* (London and New York, 1881). The references in this chapter are to the second edition of Volume II (1896).

[3] Throughout this chapter the discussion of manuscript evidence is limited to manuscripts of the Gospels.

product of the *Sitz im Leben* of New Testament studies. Historismus is gone. Confidence in the ability of the historian to establish complete objective reality in the past has evaporated. This has led to a radical scepticism concerning the value of any historical study. Textual criticism is unimportant today because it is a minor subdivision of historical study. Our fathers classified it as a part of "Lower Criticism" and regarded it as essential. We classify it as a low form of criticism and regard it as dispensable. In an age in which physical science has redefined itself as probability, historical probability has lost its significance for theologians. This loss has been rationalized into desirability. Concentration upon systematic theology has eliminated interest in grammar and text. Existentialism without a past has helped to produce manuscript study without a history. Whether from these or from other causes, two deplorable conditions exist in the main stream of New Testament textual criticism in this generation.[1]

A study of monographs and manuals produced during the last forty years shows an amazing number that make no serious effort to reconstruct the history of the manuscript tradition. This can be said of Metzger's recently published manual.[2] Professor Robert Grant says plainly that the task is impossible. On second thought, I withdraw the adverb "plainly." What he says is: "The primary goal of New Testament textual study remains the recovery of what the New Testament writers wrote. We have already suggested that to achieve this goal is wellnigh impossible. Therefore we must be

---

[1] The exceptions that can be cited to anti-objectivity do not change the general picture. Their influence has been very limited. Quentin's "Rule of Iron" was rejected by the reviewers, and was abandoned in his own project when the New Testament was reached. It can be useful within a tightly-knit group of manuscripts, but not elsewhere. Vinton Dearing's objective method is not easily understood, and is still under appraisal. I owe the following comment to Irving Alan Sparks: "Dearing, however, though he seeks to erase any traces of personal judgment, does not find the basis of objectivity in historical data. His 'scientific' solution to textual problems divorces the *states of the text* (mental phenomena) from the manuscripts containing them. So just as historical probability has lost its significance for theologians, it has lost its usefulness for Dearing as well. Stemmatics for Dearing is a logical, not a historical, construct, and its objectivity rests on rational, not empirical, grounds. Thus Dearing is an 'exception' to the general picture of anti-objectivity only in a special sense; he too is under the spell of an age that has lost confidence in historical realities." Finally, the computer promises objectivity if we can decide subjectively what data it is to count. First efforts at its use have failed from lack of rigor in preliminary definition.

[2] Bruce M. Metzger, *The Text of the New Testament* (London, 1964).

content with what Reinhold Niebuhr and others have called, in other contexts, an 'impossible possibility.' " [1] Equally extreme is Clark's comment: "In general $\mathfrak{P}^{75}$ tends to support our current critical text, and yet the papyrus vividly portrays a fluid state of the text at about A.D. 200. Such a scribal freedom suggests that the gospel text was little more stable than the oral tradition, and that we may be pursuing the retreating mirage of the 'original text.' " [2] And, most recently, Kurt Aland is able to solve finally the problem of one Western Non-Interpolation after another without reconstructing the history of the manuscript tradition.[3] At the end of his article he does seem to sense a void, for he promises to reconstruct the history of the manuscript tradition in a subsequent article.

I use the phrase "reconstruct the history of the manuscript tradition" with the assumption that the purpose of the reconstruction is to aid in the restoration of the original wording of the text. Thus I deny that those have salvaged historical value who point out that every variant may tell us something about the history of the church. The current enthusiasm for manuscript variations as contributions to the history of theology has no solid foundation. Granted that a number of variant readings have been theologically motivated, would any serious student of the history of theology turn to these as a major source? Is it not true on the contrary that we can be sure of theological motivation for a variant reading only when the history of theology in that manuscript's time and place is already well known? [4] For example, in C. S. C. Williams's study of intentional variants, contrast the solidity of the Marcionite chapter with the uncertainty and tentativeness of the surrounding material. The much needed task of relating textual criticism to contemporary biblical theology and hermeneutics must be carried on at a deeper level than this.

What has been said above suggests that the direction needs to be

---

[1] Robert M. Grant, *A Historical Introduction to the New Testament* (New York and Evanston, 1963), p. 51.

[2] Kenneth W. Clark, "The Theological Relevance of Textual Variation in Current Criticism of the Greek New Testament," *Journal of Biblical Literature*, LXXXV, (1966), p. 15.

[3] Kurt Aland, "Neue neutestamentliche Papyri, II," *New Testament Studies*, XII (1965-66), 193-210.

[4] The *nomina sacra* in their development and variations are an exception. There the data from the manuscripts carry theological significance on their faces, and may provide fresh witnesses to theological developments.

reversed. Instead of talking about "The Theological Relevance of Textual Variation," we should discuss "The Relevance of Theology to the Establishment of the Text of the New Testament." But textual critics are not competent to discuss this. The technicians are too naïve theologically. For example, in the course of his argument that Luke 22:43-4 (the Bloody Sweat passage) is an interpolation, Aland says, "Who indeed would have omitted these verses if he had found them in the text before him?" Aside from the scribe of ms. 13 and corrector A of Sinaiticus, a review of Christian theology in the early centuries would make the answer easy. Thus C. S. C. Williams after a long discussion of possible theological motivation for omission of these verses decides that they were part of the original text.[1] Even Hort can be indicted here in the light of post-*Rechtgläubigkeit und Ketzerei* studies. Hort was never naïve. He did know early Christians who would have omitted this verse, but they were heretics! "Except," he says, "to heretical sects, which exercised no influence over the transmitted text, the language of vv. 43 f. would be no stumbling block in the first and second centuries. . . ." [2] This neat division between orthodoxy and heresy is no longer possible.

What the textual critic offers the theologian is the text as it existed in a specific time and place. But to do this he needs the help of the theologian, who is today, unfortunately, incapable of textual criticism.

Erich Fascher has had the boldness to attempt a fusion of hermeneutics and textual criticism.[3] His main thesis in regard to the history of the manuscript period is weakened by two limitations. (1) He asserts that Hort's theory should be changed in three ways— but two of the three are already in Hort: (*a*) The widespread antiquity of the Western Text, (*b*) the lack of homogeneity in the Western Text. It is obvious that he has not read Hort; but if so, he should not revise him.[4] (2) He deals primarily with isolated readings,

---

[1] C. S. C. Williams, *Alterations to the Text of the Synoptic Gospels and Acts* (Oxford, 1951), pp. 6-8. Note that the author understates the extent of lectionary evidence for the transposition, that he quotes without dissent Goguel's claim that the omission in Alexandrian witnesses would date from the time and under the influence of Athanasian orthodoxy, although the subsequent discovery of $\mathfrak{P}^{75}$ which omits the passage makes this doubtful.

[2] *Op. cit.*, "Notes on Select Readings," p. 66.

[3] Erich Fascher, *Textgeschichte als hermeneutisches Problem* (Halle, 1953).

[4] Kurt Aland confesses that "few of us [Germans] will presumably have

unrelated to the history of the manuscripts, and relates them to the history of Christian thought. The work is a valuable challenge to textual criticism, but it is not a supplement to it. The rejection of text-types destroys the bridge between the two disciplines.[1]

The second deplorable condition of our studies in the last forty years is the growing tendency to rely entirely on the internal evidence of readings, without serious consideration of documentary evidence.

The two great translation efforts of these years—RSV and NEB—each chose the Greek text to translate on the basis of the internal evidence of readings. F. C. Grant's chapter in the expository pamphlet on the RSV made this clear. The translators, he says, followed two rules: (1) Choose the reading that best fits the context; (2) choose the reading which explains the origin of the other readings.[2] Professor C. H. Dodd informed me that the British translators also used these two principles—Hort's Intrinsic Probability and Transcriptional Probability. One of the RSV translators while lecturing to the New Testament Club at the University of Chicago replied to a question concerning the Greek text he used by saying that it depended on where he was working: he used Souter at the office and Nestle at home. One of the British translators in admitting the unevenness of the textual quality of the NEB translation explained that the quality depended on the ability of the man who made the first draft-translation of a book.

Whether in early Christian times or today, translators have so often treated the text cavalierly that textual critics should be hardened to it. But much more serious is the prevalence of this same dependence on the internal evidence of readings in learned articles on textual criticism, and in the popularity of manual editions of the Greek New Testament. These latter with their limited citations of variants and witnesses actually reduce the user to reliance upon the

---

read their [Westcott and Hort's] Introduction . . . in spite of its primary importance" (cf. Aland, "The Significance of the Papyri for Progress in New Testament Research," *The Bible in Modern Scholarship*, ed. by J. P. Hyatt [Nashville and New York, 1965], p. 325).

[1] Eldon J. Epp gives a summary appraisal of Fascher and other workers in this vineyard in *The Theological Tendency of Codex Bezae Cantabrigiensis in Acts* ("Society for New Testament Studies, Monograph Series, 3"; Cambridge, 1966), pp. 19 ff.

[2] Frederick C. Grant, *Introduction to the Revised Standard Version of the New Testament*, ed. by L. A. Weigle (Chicago: International Council of Religious Education, American Standard Bible Committee, 1946).

internal evidence of readings. The documents which these rigorously abbreviated apparatuses cite cannot lead the user to dependence upon external evidence of documents. These editions use documents (to quote Housman) "as drunkards use lampposts—, not to light them on their way but to dissimulate their instability." [1]

The egregious example of the misleading nature of these narrowly restricted editions is the United Bible Societies' Greek New Testament. Yet this is the edition that Aland refers to as a "model"! His reference cannot be an inadvertence, since he has repeated it.[2] The printed announcement of this edition notes seven "Special Features" of which three relate to textual criticism: (1) "A new simplified critical apparatus with full citation of evidence both for and against variant readings"; (2) "Evidence from more than 500 manuscripts and early versions, and from 200 Church Fathers"; (3) "Committee evaluation showing degree of certainty for variant readings in the text."

Only as to the second of these is the reader clearly told the limitations of this model. The evidence of the 500 manuscripts and the 200 Church Fathers is largely drawn from second-hand sources. In no case does this edition give the complete evidence of any source.

But the reader will discover to his surprise that "Committee evaluation" in the majority of cases shows only a C grade or degree of certainty—not A, nor even B.

Most misleading, there is no statement that this "full citation of evidence both for and against variant readings" applies to an exceedingly small fraction of the variant readings that exist. In the Preface to the book itself (p. v) the statement as to restrictions is misleading: "(1) A critical apparatus restricted for the most part to variant readings significant for translators or necessary for the establishing of the text." But on p. vi there is a more accurate statement: "The sets of variants have generally been restricted to readings meaningful for translators; consequently there is an appreciable reduction in the number of variants in the apparatus (but there is fuller attestation for the variants selected)." The reduction in the number of variants is indeed "appreciable" if

---

[1] A. E. Housman, ed., *M. Manilii Astronomicon: Liber Primus*, 2nd ed. (Cambridge, 1937), p. liii.

[2] Most recently in *Studien zur Überlieferung des Neuen Testaments und seines Textes* (Berlin, 1967), p. 201.

compared with Nestle (25th ed.) and Kilpatrick's British and
Foreign Bible Society's edition (2nd ed.).

	UBS	KILPATRICK[2]	NESTLE[25]
Matt 11:1-8	1 variant	5 variants	6 variants
Mark 11:1-8	1 variant	4 variants	15 variants
Luke 11:1-8	6 variants	14 variants	13 variants
John 11:1-8	0 variants	4 variants	10 variants
In 32 verses	8 variants	27 variants	44 variants

Thus UBS has 1/5 as many variants as Nestle[25], and less than 1/3 as
many as Kilpatrick[2]. UBS often has no more than one to a page of
10-15 verses. This is a model only in the sense that a model is a lot
smaller than the real thing and also in the sense that a model cannot
do what the real thing does. Model ships may carry toy cargo on a
pond, but they cannot transport freight. A dependable apparatus
criticus would dwarf Nestle and Kilpatrick as they dwarf UBS.[1]

The scholars who profess to follow "the Eclectic Method"
frequently so define the term as to restrict evidence to the Internal
Evidence of Readings. By "eclectic" they mean in fact free choice
among readings.[2] This choice in many cases is made solely on the
basis of intrinsic probability. The editor chooses that reading which
commends itself to him as fitting the context, whether in style, or
idea, or contextual reference. Such an editor relegates the manuscripts to the role of supplier of readings. The weight of the manuscript
is ignored. Its place in the manuscript tradition is not considered.
Thus Kilpatrick argues that certain readings found only in one late
Vulgate manuscript should be given the most serious consideration
because they are good readings.

Sometimes, though more rarely, the argument is based on
transcriptional probability. Thus Kilpatrick has pointed out that
Atticism was rife in the second century and he claims that it affected

---

[1] For a thorough appraisal of the model, see the review by Irving Alan
Sparks in *Interpretation: A Journal of Bible and Theology*, XXII (1968),
92-96.

[2] This is not true of Vaganay's judicious use of this term. He favors
"eclecticism, that is, no shutting up of the different branches of the science
into water-tight compartments; verbal criticism, external and internal
criticism, all have their parts to play. . ." (Leon Vaganay, *An Introduction
to the Textual Criticism of the New Testament*, translated by B. V. Miller
[London, 1937], p. 91).

the wording of some manuscripts. Interestingly enough, he begins his argument with references to αποκριθεις ειπεν, admittedly barbarous Greek, and its variant εφη. He says, commenting on six passages in Mark, "Have the scribes changed the good Greek εφη to the barbarous αποκριθεις ειπεν or the other way about? If we may assume that their intention was to improve the evangelist's Greek rather than to degrade it, then αποκριθεις ειπεν will be original." [1] After Plutarch, he points out, Atticism became the norm; and he asks, "Did the scribes of this period try to bring the varied Greek of these books more into line with the prevailing fashion?" [2]

But in this matter we may *not* assume the intention of the scribes. Various intentions were possible to them. In four of these six passages, harmonization to Matthew and Luke may have been the intention. Or scribes may have had the intention of changing from the rare to the usual, from secular usage to gospel idiom. In the Westcott and Hort text the barbarous αποκριθεις ειπεν occurs 139 times in the four gospels (Mt. 48, Mk. 17, Lk. 42, Jn. 32), while good old εφη occurs only 35 times. These figures strongly suggest that in this matter the scribes were not Atticizing very well. Moreover, it is the Beta text-type that reads εφη in Kilpatrick's six passages, and the same text-type reads αποκριθεις ειπεν 139 times. Attention to Hort's theory would save us from some of the dangers of subjective judgment based on partial evidence. Duplacy has recently said, "Textual criticism is a historical discipline. As such, its primary duty is to take its sources seriously. . . . I will plead then," he says, "the cause of history, and above all in the name of history, the cause of the documents," [3] and with this Hortian judgment I am in full accord. We need Hort Redivivus.

We need him as a counter-influence to the two errors I have discussed: (1) the ignoring of the history of the manuscript tradition, and (2) overemphasis upon the internal evidence of readings. In Hort's work two principles (and only two) are regarded as so im-

---

[1] G. D. Kilpatrick, "Atticism and the Text of the Greek New Testament," in *Neutestamentliche Aufsätze* (Regensburg, 1963), p. 126. Gordon Fee presents an independent and significant criticism of this article in his dissertation ("The Significance of Papyrus Bodmer II and Papyrus Bodmer XIV-XV for Methodology in New Testament Textual Criticism," an unpublished dissertation at the University of Southern California, Los Angeles, 1966).

[2] *Ibid.*, p. 128.

[3] Jean Duplacy, "Histoire des manuscrits et histoire du texte du Nouveau Testament," *New Testament Studies*, XII (1965-66), 125.

portant that they are printed in capital letters in the text and in
italics in the table of contents. One is "ALL TRUSTWORTHY RESTORA-
TION OF CORRUPTED TEXTS IS FOUNDED ON THE STUDY OF THEIR
HISTORY," and the other, "KNOWLEDGE OF DOCUMENTS SHOULD
PRECEDE FINAL JUDGEMENT UPON READINGS."

In the second place, and it is a second place, we need Hort
Redivivus because additional manuscript evidence has become
available. Hort's theory and method need reconsideration in the
light of this new evidence. Hort himself said that the discovery of
new evidence forces the reconsideration of the old.[1]

But it is not the mass of recently acquired witnesses that makes
this important. Aland occasionally and mistakenly speaks as if the
gross number of witnesses, as such, has invalidated all that Hort
had done, and forces a new theory upon us.[2]

The discovery of additional manuscripts, including the early
papyri, has not demanded a drastic revision of Hort's two basic
principles. In saying this I differ sharply from Aland. His counting
of heads is ominously reminiscent of scholarly argument in the days
when the Textus Receptus was unassailable. The important question
is, "Where do these heads stand in a plausible reconstruction of the
history of the manuscript tradition?" Professor Aland, while
postponing attention to this question, has in his actual practice
followed Lachmann by a naïve acceptance of documents of early
date.

The clearest example of this lies in his deference to $\mathfrak{P}^{75}$. In
readings for Nestle[26], and explicitly in a recent article (as also in the
United Bible Societies' edition), he reverses Westcott and Hort on
the Western non-interpolations because $\mathfrak{P}^{75}$ disagrees with them in
agreeing with Codex Vaticanus. But there is nothing in that agreement that is novel to Hort's theory. Hort did not possess $\mathfrak{P}^{75}$, but
he imagined it. He insisted that there was a very early ancestor of
his Neutral text, that the common ancestor of Vaticanus and
Sinaiticus was a remote ancestor, not a close ancestor. $\mathfrak{P}^{75}$ validates
Hort's reconstruction of the history, *but $\mathfrak{P}^{75}$ does not add a new
argument* for or against that theory.

---

[1] *Op. cit.*, p. 14: "Evidence is valuable only so far as it can be securely
interpreted; and not the least advantage conferred by new documents is the
new help which they give toward the better interpretation of old documents,
and of documentary relations generally."

[2] *Op. cit.*, pp. 325-46.

The comparison to the champions of the Textus Receptus is not entirely fair, for Aland is clamoring about the numbers of *early* manuscripts; and in general early manuscripts *are* more important than late manuscripts. But the crucial question for early as for late witnesses is still, "WHERE DO THEY FIT INTO A PLAUSIBLE RECONSTRUCTION OF THE HISTORY OF THE MANUSCRIPT TRADITION?"

The other extensive early Gospel papyri fit into Hort's reconstruction of the history as well as $\mathfrak{P}^{75}$ does. Aland exclaims that $\mathfrak{P}^{45}$ shows that the $\mathfrak{P}^{75}$ text-type was but one of the types extant in the second century. But Hort made this same claim. If $\mathfrak{P}^{45}$ fits into what Hort called the Western Text, as it seems to do, we should remember Hort's insistence upon the early date of the Western Text.

The third extensive papyrus, $\mathfrak{P}^{66}$, is almost certainly a slightly corrupted copy of a basic $\mathfrak{P}^{75}$ type of text. But the early existence of a debased form of this text was insisted on by Hort. The exact nature of the early debasement may be shown by $\mathfrak{P}^{66}$ to be somewhat different in detail from Hort's concept, but the basic concept was there.

What forces the revision of Hort, or—at the least—serious consideration of his theories, is the appearance of significant new evidence. Four areas in which this new or better evidence is available are the following: (1) Extensive earlier papyri. $\mathfrak{P}^{45}$, $\mathfrak{P}^{46}$, $\mathfrak{P}^{47}$, $\mathfrak{P}^{66}$, and $\mathfrak{P}^{75}$ carry us back one or two centuries closer to the original. And what is equally important, they are documents containing a large amount of text. Thus they can be appraised as individual manuscripts (as the fragments cannot), and they can be located within the manuscript tradition. (2) The evidence of lectionary manuscripts is now at least half-way available. These documents, ignored by our ancestors, need to be placed in any comprehensive picture. (3) The evidence of increasing numbers of Fathers is available in scholarly, critical editions. (4) The evidence of the versions, notably of the Old Latin, is now available in works of great value. Increases in evidence of this sort indicate that if Hort is to be revived his work must be measured against significant new evidence. It is an understatement to say that this has not yet been done.

Can Hort be revived? Yes, if the focus is on method and history. In the face of a long generation of critical attack this may seem to be a bold statement. From Kirsopp Lake's evaluation of Hort: "His work was a failure, though a brilliant one," through Kilpatrick's choice of eclectic method, to Aland's declaration, "A gulf separates us from [Westcott and Hort], which can no longer be bridged," and "This much is certain, the presuppositions of Westcott-Hort are no longer valid," [1] the road is rough. But since I have myself participated in the demolition of one Hortian bastion,[2] my assertion that the task is possible will not be charged to sentimental romanticism. Soon after the appearance of my paper on Genealogical Method, I read as the Presidential Address to the Society of Biblical Literature a paper on "Biblical Criticism: Lower and Higher" in which the basic assumption is that Hort's theory was to be abandoned.[3] I think now that I was wrong, that Kilpatrick is wrong, and that Aland is wrong. Each of us, obsessed with some one glaring fault in Hort (Colwell, genealogical method; Kilpatrick, overemphasis on manuscripts; Aland, no Greek papyri) threw out the baby with the bath water.

Improvements on Hort in the statement of theory and the reconstruction of the history are possible. These are contained in the program which follows, but two examples are enough to make the case.

(1) Hort organized his entire argument to depose the Textus Receptus. While still a student at Cambridge, twenty-three years old, Hort clearly indicated in a letter the identity of the villain: "I had no idea till the last few weeks of the importance of texts, having read so little Greek Testament, and dragged on with the villainous *Textus Receptus* ... and Tischendorf I find a great acquisition, above all, because he gives the various readings at the bottom of his page, and his Prolegomena are invaluable. Think of that vile *Textus Receptus* leaning on late Mss.; it is a blessing there are such early ones. . ." (December 29 and 30, 1851).[4] Two years later (1853), he wrote "I have not seen anybody that I know except Westcott, whom, being with his wife at his father's at Moseley, close to Birmingham, a fortnight ago, I visited for a few hours. One result of our talk I may as well tell you. He and I are

---

[1] "The Significance of the Papyri for Progress in New Testament Research" in *The Bible in Modern Scholarship*, ed. by J. Philip Hyatt (Nashville, 1965), pp. 325-46; and "Neue neutestamentliche Papyri II," *New Testament Studies*, XII (1965-66), 209.

[2] "Genealogical Method: Its Achievements and its Limitations," *Journal of Biblical Literature*, LXVI (1947), 109-133. (= pp. 63-83 above).

[3] *Journal of Biblical Literature*, LXVII (1948), 3, footnote 3.

[4] Arthur Fenton Hort, *Life and Letters of Fenton John Anthony Hort*, I (London and New York, 1896), 211.

going to edit a Greek text of the N.T. some two or three years hence, if possible. Lachmann and Tischendorf will supply rich materials, but not nearly enough; and we hope to do a good deal with the Oriental versions. Our object is to supply clergymen generally, schools, etc., with a portable Gk. Test., which shall not be disfigured with Byzantine corruptions. But we *may* find the work too irksome." [1] This attack against the Textus Receptus is no longer necessary, and therefore improvements are possible. Hort's formal use of stemmatics served this purpose alone, and adds confusion to his work. Thus his arguments and his reconstruction start with the mass of recent manuscripts and work backwards. The chronology needs to be reversed.[2] We need to begin at the beginning. Better knowledge of patristic habits in quotation in the early centuries plus earlier documents enable us to write more accurate accounts of the early manuscript tradition.

(2) Hort's reconstruction of the history can be corrected by our increased knowledge from both ends of that history. Soden's contribution to the history of the manuscript tradition in the Byzantine period was significant.[3]

Yet in this revision we shall not surpass Hort merely by adding manuscript to manuscript. Unless we are as serious and thoughtful as he was, we labor in vain. Many a scholar, for example, uses the early fathers as some evangelists use the Scriptures—as proof texts. We need to apply the penetrating insight of such questions as Klijn's: "What is the relation between the kind of text found in these ancient writings [the Fathers] and the text of the N.T. in the available MSS? Is it possible to say that our MSS went through a period in which they were as freely handled as the text used by the authors of the earliest Christian writings? This impression we do not get." [4]

---

[1] Hort, *op. cit.*, p. 250. Professor I. A. Moir of New College, Edinburgh, brought these passages to my attention.

[2] See Chapter I (pp. 23 f. above).

[3] See, e.g., the summary statement in E. C. Colwell, *The Four Gospels of Karahissar*, Vol. I, *History and Text* (Chicago, 1936), xi-xii; David Voss, "Is von Soden's Kʳ a distinct Type of Text?" *Journal of Biblical Literature*, LVII (1938), 311-318; and Jacob Geerling's reconstruction of Family 13 and Family II in *Studies and Documents*, Vols. XIX-XXIII. The unpublished work of Wisse and McReynolds makes possible a comprehensive review of von Soden's classifications in the Gospels.

[4] A. F. J. Klijn, "A Survey of the Researches into the Western Text of the Gospels and Acts," *Novum Testamentum*, III (1959), 165.

THE PROGRAM

The program of textual studies requires that the critic take five steps. I, Begin with readings; II, Characterize individual scribes and manuscripts; III, Group the manuscripts; IV, Construct a historical framework; V, Make a final judgment on readings.

I. BEGIN WITH READINGS

The readings of individual manuscripts are the objective data with which ultimately the critic must deal. He should be familiar with a very large number of these, including readings that never find their way into an apparatus criticus. This familiarity can be obtained either by making or reading complete collations of a number of documents. These documents should include early papyri, the great uncials, and commonplace Byzantines—among the Greeks. But these documents should also include Old Latin and Vulgate manuscripts, Old Syriac and Peshitta, Coptic manuscripts, and Greek and Latin Fathers at least from the early centuries. But at this stage the study of readings is not final, for knowledge of documents should precede final judgment upon readings.[1]

The knowledge derived from a study of these readings will lead to an understanding of scribal habits and practices without which the history of the manuscript tradition cannot be written. We need a series of compendia of corruptions from the Greek manuscripts, from the individual versions, from the Fathers—comparable to the work of L. Havet on the Latin manuscripts of the classics. *But the knowledge gained from one of these compendia cannot be transferred to another, nor can the knowledge gained from one period be generalized for another, nor can the treatment of one part of the New Testament be generalized for the entire canon.*[2]

---

[1] Hort, *op. cit.*, p. 31.

[2] C. R. Gregory's volume of *Prolegomena* to Tischendorf's 8th Edition lists corruptions drawn from the fourth through the sixth century, pp. 57 f. Van Groningen has produced the most comprehensive and sound list of the causes of variation in Greek manuscripts, but it is derived primarily from the manuscripts of the Classics and therefore does not eliminate the need for a list derived primarily from New Testament manuscripts. Yet the range of his knowledge and the soundness of his judgment make his study invaluable for New Testament studies (Bernard Abraham van Groningen, *Traité d'histoire et de critique des textes grecs* [Amsterdam, 1963]).

II. Characterize Individual Scribes and Manuscripts

At least for important witnesses (and ideally for all that are used) the peculiarities of the individual scribe need to be known. No one has said this better than Hort: "It . . . becomes necessary in the case of important MSS to observe and discriminate the classes of clerical errors by which their proper texts are severally disguised; for an authority representing a sound tradition can be used with increased confidence when its own obvious slips have been classed under definite heads, so that those of its readings which cannot be referred to any of these heads must be reasonably supposed to have belonged to the text of its exemplar." [1] Identifying the scribe as distinct from his source is not easy. Vinton Dearing has pointed out that we are in fact prone to minimize the difficulties and assume that we are looking over the scribe's shoulder when we are in reality looking at his source.[2] Yet the scribe's contribution *can* be identified—notably in singular readings, especially in nonsense readings, or in readings that have won universal rejection not only from other scribes but from all editors as well.[3]

The goals of this study at this stage are to know the manuscript insofar as it is the product of the scribe who copied it. The scribe's fingerprints upon the codex are the object of search. (1) What units of text did he copy (single letters, or syllables and short words, or single complete words, or phrases and clauses)? (2) What was his pattern of errors? (3) Was he a careful or a careless workman? (4) If careful, was his care limited to exact copying or did it include care for a better expression of the content of his exemplar? That is, to what extent was he an editor as well as a scribe?

The identification of the scribe's habits in these special readings enables the student of a particular manuscript to discard variants that otherwise would be regarded as part of the genetic strain of that

---

[1] *Op. cit.*, p. 36.

[2] In a personal letter to the author.

[3] See Chapter VIII (pp. 106-124 above). In retrospect, I feel more confident of my own identification of the scribal habits of $\mathfrak{P}^{66}$ and $\mathfrak{P}^{75}$ than I do of those of $\mathfrak{P}^{45}$. In $\mathfrak{P}^{45}$ few of the "singular readings" meet the two additional requirements stated above. Study in this area has been advanced by two scholars: Gordon D. Fee, "The Corrections of Papyrus Bodmer II and Early Textual Transmission," *Novum Testamentum*, VII (1965), 247 ff., and Errol F. Rhodes, "The Corrections of Papyrus Bodmer II," *New Testament Studies*, XIV (1967-68), 271-281. The latter study provides a thoroughgoing classification of errors with citation of manuscript support.

manuscript. Textual criticism must return to the position taken by Tischendorf in regard to singular readings: "A reading altogether peculiar to one or another ancient document is suspicious." This primary position of Tischendorf's, which Tischendorf failed to follow with respect to Sinaiticus and Hort failed to follow with respect to Vaticanus, merits the most rigorous observance. For example, the fact that the scribe of $\mathfrak{P}^{66}$ copied syllable by syllable, added to the further fact that he often produced nonsense by dropping a short syllable, removes all weight from his omission of the article or of a short preposition. Thus the characterization of the scribe aids in the characterization of the manuscript.

To insist that these are two characterizations is to make a subtle distinction. But its subtlety does not detract from its value. Each manuscript that establishes a landmark in the history of the manuscript tradition should have its fingerprints taken, and its value assessed. The second stage in the program is knowledge of individual documents.

III. Group the Manuscripts

The third stage is to establish the group relationships of manuscripts, and to evaluate the groups. As I have argued elsewhere,[1] these relationships are of three kinds, and the resulting groups need to be clearly differentiated from each other.

The *family* is a group of manuscripts so closely related to each other (often from closeness in time and place of origin) that a stemma can be reconstructed and the archetype, or its text, reconstructed. Examples are Family 1, and Family II. Note that the use of stemmatics flourished in classical studies of a controlled text, and that the enduring familes of New Testament manuscripts also come from the period of a controlled text.

The *tribe* is a group of families with looser relationships between families than within families, yet a group whose interrelationships are relatively close, relative—that is—to the looser relationships of the members of a text-type. The tribe is thus defined by its position between the family and the text-type. It is larger than the one, smaller than the other; more closely related than one, less than the other. The great value of this category is that it prevents the confusing identification of these groups with either or both family

---

[1] See Chapter I (pp. 1-25 above).

and text-type. The classic example of confusion in the terms applied is the Caesarean Group, called Family Θ by Streeter and a text-type by others. It now seems clear that it is neither.

The *text-type* is the largest identifiable group of manuscripts. It has a longer life span than most families or tribes. Thus it will have some members that may be weaker than the members of either of these smaller groups. Examples of text-types are Kenyon's Beta (Hort's Neutral), and Kenyon's Alpha (Hort's Syrian).

Two steps are essential for establishing the existence of any of these groups of manuscripts, and a third step is helpful but not essential. This third step (which comes first in the actual process of identification) directs attention to passages in which the attestation divides three or more ways. A study of these multiple readings often provides a clue to group relationships. This is a time-saving device, and is in no way essential to the establishment of group relationships.

Because of my use of this device (or because of the enthusiasm of some of my students for its use), I have been credited with championing something called the Multiple Method. I should like to seize this opportunity for acting modestly (an opportunity that comes but rarely to the scholar) and leave any claim that there is a Multiple Method to the championing of others.

The essential steps for establishing the existence of a group of manuscripts are (1) demonstrating that the members of the group share the support of a list of readings not found in other groups, and (2) demonstrating that the members of the group support one another in approximately 70 per cent of all cases where variation occurs between Greek manuscripts. This demonstration is possible for families, tribes, and text-types. Thus it follows that the sporadic readings of a particular type do not demonstrate the existence of the type in a particular time or place.

One word of caution is needed concerning the grouping of manuscripts: in this task we are not concerned with good readings or bad readings, with original readings or corrupt readings, but only with shared readings. Klijn makes this point clear.[1] We concern ourselves with quality of readings at other stages of the program, but not here.

Hort admitted that mixture dealt a fatal blow to the use of genealogical method, but he insisted that the history of the manu-

---

[1] *Op. cit.*, pp. 167-171.

script period could be written in spite of mixture. And he was right.

IV. Construct A Historical Framework

The task of textual criticism is to establish the form of the text in time and place. This is historical study. Thus the fourth stage in the program is the writing of the history of the manuscript period. Hort's dictum is *"All trustworthy restoration of corrupted texts is founded on a study of their history, that is, of the relations of descent or affinity which connect the several documents."* [1] This history can be written in spite of mixture, but only if stemmatics is abandoned. This abandonment must include the pattern of constructive thought appropriate to stemmatics. Most of our manuals present charts that assume that the method of building a family-tree is appropriate to the reconstruction of the total history of the manuscript period. These charts (e.g., the charts illustrating the difference between Streeter's theory of local texts and Hort's theory) need to be thrown away.

Where groups are clearly defined by the methods stated above, mixture itself can be clearly defined. My own study of Leningrad ms. 105, a good candidate for the title of "Most Mixed MS.," [2] showed that where groups had been established, the amount and nature of mixture between groups can be established. But family, trees cannot be built! And groups have not been clearly established in the first two centuries. What can be done is to write a historical account of the process of mixture that produced the documents.

When we approach the larger task of writing the history of the entire manuscript period, we must start with a new characterization of the process. *The story of the manuscript tradition of the New Testament is the story of progression from a relatively uncontrolled tradition to a rigorously controlled tradition.* The important questions in the writing of this history are, Where were controls applied? Why? By whom?

The progression when uncontrolled was characterized by scribal changes—when controlled it was characterized by editorial selection. Each of these includes improvements as well as corruptions; but in general scribal change meant corruption, and editorial

---

[1] *Op. cit.*, p. 40.
[2] Colwell, *The Four Gospels. . .*, pp. 216-222.

selection with its consequent controls meant improvement over the preceding anarchy and meant also the blocking of major corruption.

Certain presuppositions underlie this thesis. Close agreement between manuscripts is possible only where there was some control. Wide divergence between manuscripts indicates lack of control. The basic presupposition behind these two is the assertion that scribes do not automatically, as scribes, copy accurately. The early papyri demonstrate this. Even when the scribe was a skilled calligrapher, accuracy in copying could be beyond his ability. In the early centuries of the New Testament period accurate copying was not a common concept. There were scribes capable of making accurate copies when adequately motivated—as for example when copying for a library. But that the New Testament required this kind of treatment was not a common idea. $\mathfrak{P}^{66}$ has almost two hundred nonsense readings. $\mathfrak{P}^{69}$ (also from the third century) omits carelessly, mangling a sentence (at Luke 22:41, 45).

Nor were translators more capable of accuracy when they worked without control. The makers of the "Old" versions—both Latin and Syriac—make J. B. Phillips look like a careful workman. The manuscript copies of these early translations continue the tradition of an uncontrolled text. One page of a critical edition of the Old Latin makes this plain to the dullest eye.

The progression from no concept of control for accuracy to some control is clearly visible in the quotations of the New Testament by the Fathers in the early centuries. In the earliest block, quotation is so free that it makes the demonstration of knowledge of a particular book difficult. Moreover, it is highly significant that the first expression of scholarly concern for an accurate text was concern for the text of the Old Testament. The same Origen who produced the Hexapla quotes the New Testament now from one strain of the tradition, now from another. At the beginning, the Old Testament was the Christian Scripture; and that beginning lasted longer than we think. It influenced concepts and attitudes at least into the third century. Granted that the Fathers were worse than the scribes, the scribes still enjoyed a remarkable freedom from control.

The chances are high that the first controls were introduced by scholarly Christians. The controls produced more good than bad. They sought "ancient" and "good" copies. From these they produced reasonably accurate copies. These first efforts must have been sporadic. Without the keen concern and vigorous support of an organized Church they could not establish the authority of a standard text, henceforth to be carefully controlled.

That concern and support became apparent in the fourth century. The Alpha text-type was most probably born then, and the Beta text-type—as text-type—is probably no older.[1] Jerome's Vulgate adorns that century; it is the classical example of concern for a controlled, a standard text. The Syriac tradition was standardized about the same time.

But when did the Delta text-type (the "Western Text") arise? While scholars still speak of its earlier existence and of its almost universal distribution, they no longer speak of it as a text-type. If the term text-type derives its meaning from the Alpha and Beta text-types, Delta is not a text-type. It lacks that homogeneity which gives the others the name text-type. Yet the amount of agreement it possesses calls for explanation.

Most students of its content identify it as an uncontrolled text, a popular text rather than a scholar's text. Where is it found? In the earliest translations into Latin and Syriac;[2] in some of the early Fathers; and bilingual manuscripts. Is it impossible to turn Streeter's theory around and modify it to say that the Western text is the local text of the early centuries? The truly provincial texts were those first missionary copies carried to illiterate groups or into the backwoods where Greek was not used as a language. From these copies came the careless early versions. From them, some church leaders quoted. Some of them appeared in a would-be learned, bilingual dress. They are pre-recension texts in their origin. They are corrupted texts due to the uncontrolled nature of their propagation. That the Latin "Westerns" have one batch of readings, and the Syrian "Westerns" another, supports the assumption of their provincial origin or their provincial development.

Any attempt to write a comprehensive history of the manuscript period requires a decision between provincial origin and provincial development. I tentatively choose the latter—provincial development from a common origin of the Western groups. That origin deserves to be called the Early Koine,[3] the popular missionary text

---

[1] The Early Koine may have been subjected to a very partial revision toward Beta before the fourth century.

[2] Not in Coptic, whose Sahidic version usually agrees with the Beta text-type.

[3] (1) The general nature of the text in the earliest period (to A.D. 300) has long been recognized as "wild," "uncontrolled," "unedited." (2) manuscripts

of the Christian movement. In sharp contrast to the medieval Koine (the Alpha Text-type), it was not an edition prepared by sophisticated scholars. It was, rather, the lay-preacher's Gospel. Again in contrast to the medieval Koine, its copying was not controlled. It was controlled as some preachers and evangelists control their selection and use of Scripture.

The course of its development has been accurately described by Streeter in his theory of Local Texts. It became differentiated in Syria, in Latin Africa, in Armenia. Streeter's expansion of the so-called "Caesarean Text" to include practically all of Soden's Western (i.e. Iota) groups was fundamentally sound, but erroneous in one superficial item and one serious item.

His superficial error was that the text he was describing did not come from Caesarea; but the exact location of its origin is of little importance. He was describing the gradual expansion, corruption, and differentiation of the Early Koine.

His most serious error was not his claim for more unity and homogeneity than this group of witnesses contains. His fatal error was his treatment of the Beta Text-type as a comparable local text. This it is not. Both Alpha and Beta are editions carefully made and fairly well controlled in copying, with a pattern of subsequent corruption quite different from that of the Koine in the early period.

But in this same early period scholars were converted to Christianity. The Paschal Sermon of Melito of Sardis shows us that before the last quarter of the second century men who were masters of rhetoric had entered the Church. From the same period $\mathfrak{P}^{75}$, containing large sections of Luke and John, is best explained as an attempt at scholarly, accurate production of a copy of the Gospels.

---

from this period and manuscripts which preserve the text of this period have an unusually large number of singular or subsingular readings, most of which are corruptions. (3) Manuscripts from this period do not cluster into closely-related groups. (4) The ancient editors who brought order out of this chaos did so by *selecting* readings from these earlier manuscripts. They probably began their work by selecting a "good" earlier manuscript. (5) The agreements among the earliest witnesses are in part due to a shared ancestry, in part to coincidence in corruption. (6) The earliest versions add to the corruption of "primitive" free-handling of the text the natural corruption of the translator—which often ran on the same tracks. (7) Therefore, agreements between the earliest versions and the earliest Greek witnesses without substantial Greek support are to be suspected of being agreement in corruption.

The format of its page obviously comes out of the book trade, not out of the needs of the mission movement. In length of lines (25 letters) and number of lines to the column (42) it is very close to the pattern of the great fourth century vellum codices, Vaticanus and Sinaiticus (18 and 15 letters respectively to the line; 42 and 48 lines to the column). The point is that $\mathfrak{P}^{75}$ looks like a column from a book-roll. Contrast $\mathfrak{P}^{45}$ with about 48 to 50 letters to a line. It looks like a page, even though it is a page with 39 lines. $\mathfrak{P}^{66}$ also looks like a page, not like a column—with 24 letters to a line but an average of only 19 lines to a page.

When to this formal resemblance to published books the content-relationship is added, $\mathfrak{P}^{75}$ is seen to be one of those "ancient and good copies" which educated Christians sought out in the fourth century as the basis for better editions.[1] It has the closest relation to Codex Vaticanus. This first effort at a good copy almost certainly sprang from scholarly concerns rather than ecclesiastical. And one comment on the editorial work of scribes and editors needs to be made now—capable scribes and editors often left the text closer to the original than they found it.

From what has been said, it follows that the dividing line in the history of the text is the achievement of control. This means editions with sanctions. In the period prior to this achievement, manuscripts with the same ancestry differ widely. After this achievement, manuscripts with the same ancestry differ so little that they become almost identical.

For example, from the pre-control period compare 34 verses (John 9:1-34) of $\mathfrak{P}^{66}$ and $\mathfrak{P}^{75}$. They are basically the same genetic strain, yet they differ from each other 39 times in this short block of text—more than one to a verse. From the control period, take two manuscripts: the Isaac Gospels and 2322. They belong to Soden's K^r group—the last of the great Byzantine recensions of the Alpha text-type. In 31 verses of Mark 11 they never differ. Moreover, if ten K^r manuscripts are compared throughout the Gospel of Mark, "six of the ten agree [in 180 variants from Stephanus]. Every manuscript has at least 80 per cent of these variants, and seven . . . have over 90 per cent. . . . And only four of the ten

---

[1] G. D. Fee, *op. cit.*, has shown as intimate a relationship between $\mathfrak{P}^{75}$ and B as exists within Family 1.

manuscripts have more than fifteen variants outside of this list of 180" in the entire Gospel of Mark.[1]

Examples of this sort can be multiplied many times. They show clearly that one crucial guideline in writing the history of the text is the presence or absence of control in the copying of the text. This will prevent the listing of scribal habits across the centuries as though they were always the same.

In the writing of the history of the text another tabu must be observed. Do not write the history of the New Testament *en bloc*. There is a history of the individual gospel. There is a history of the gospels—but the Gospel of Mark seems to have a special history. There is a history of the Letters of Paul, another of Acts, another of Revelation.

In a recent publication Walter Thiele has pointed out [2] that the text of Augustine in different parts of the Bible presents contrasting elements: Non-Western in the Gospels, a little more Western in Paul, much more Western in Acts, and Western in the Catholics. Kirsopp Lake's choice of Mark as *the* Gospel to study was based on the peculiar history of that Gospel in the manuscript period.

Thus the historian will be forced to reconsider the meaning of mixture in the early period as contrasted with the later. In those first centuries block-mixture, as in the Washington Gospels, is common; and it almost certainly derives from the varying histories of the available exemplars, which rarely overlapped in content. A second cause of what we have called "mixture" is that coincidence in corruption which is possible to all uncontrolled, or poorly-controlled, texts.[3] But when manuscripts were numerous and concern for the best text existed, real mixture resulted from the correction of one type or family by another.

V. FINAL JUDGMENT ON READINGS

As the last stage, judgment has to be made on variant readings in the light of the previous stages plus the internal evidence of readings. In the study of internal evidence of readings Hort needs

---

[1] Voss, *op. cit.*, p. 317.

[2] *Die lateinischen Texte des I. Petrusbriefes* (*Vetus Latina: Aus der Geschichte der lateinischen Bible,* 5) (Freiburg, 1965).

[3] As I have argued elsewhere, the stemmatic, genealogical pattern of thinking keeps us from seeing the large role played by coincidental agreement.

no improvement. His canons for the appraisal of readings have won continued and widespread approval. Intrinsic probability (fitness to context) and Transcriptional probability (choosing the reading that can explain the origin of the others) are an effective and inclusive summary of all detailed canons of criticism. But Hort was more fully aware of their limitations than many contemporary scholars are.

He warns us that the assumptions involved in Intrinsic Evidence of Readings are not to be implicitly trusted: ". . . it is needful to remember," he says, "that authors are not always grammatical, or clear, or consistent, or felicitous; so that not seldom an ordinary reader finds it easy to replace a feeble or half-appropriate word or phrase by an effective substitute; and thus the best words to express an author's meaning need not in all cases be those which he actually employed." [1]

He reminds us that "the basis on which Transcriptional Probability rests consists of generalisations as to the causes of corruption incident to the process of transcription." [2] These generalizations come from a study "of those readings which can with moral certainty be assumed to have been introduced by scribes." [3] And, with the exception of careless blunders, all readings, including these, have a kind of excellence: a quality that derives from the author or a quality that appealed to a scribe as an improvement. Serious contrast of these two excellences is imperative.

Where Intrinsic Probability coincides with Transcriptional Probability the student secures a high degree of certainty. "But," Hort reminds us, "a vast proportion of variations do not fulfil these conditions." [4]

Therefore we need to revive another part of Hort's final procedure as editor. It is briefly stated in a section often overlooked (entitled "History of this edition"): "No rule of precedence has been adopted; but documentary attestation has been in most cases allowed to confer the place of honour against internal evidence, range of attestation being further taken into account as between one well attested reading and another." [5]

---

[1] *Op. cit.*, p. 21.
[2] *Ibid.*, p. 23.
[3] *Ibid.*, p. 24. The collection of data in this area has only begun.
[4] *Ibid.*, p. 29.
[5] *Ibid.*, p. 17.

Much of the value of reviving Hort lies in this emphasis. As Professor Sidney Mead once said of the historian's work, "He doesn't claim certainty, but he asks that the witnesses be allowed to bring their evidence to court, and that the evidence will be taken seriously." If Hort is revived, it will be.

INDEX OF NAMES

NEW TESTAMENT TOOLS AND STUDIES

EDITED BY

BRUCE M. METZGER, PH.D., D.D., L.H.D.